A Tyranny Against Itself

A TYRANNY
AGAINST ITSELF

Intimate Partner Violence on the Margins of Bogotá

John I. B. Bhadra-Heintz

PENN

UNIVERSITY OF PENNSYLVANIA PRESS

PHILADELPHIA

Published by
University of Pennsylvania Press
Philadelphia, Pennsylvania 19104-4112
www.upenn.edu/pennpress

Printed in the United States of America on acid-free paper
10 9 8 7 6 5 4 3 2 1

A Cataloging-in-Publication record is available from the
Library of Congress
Hardcover ISBN: 978-0-8122-5343-6
Paperback ISBN: 978-0-8122-2494-8
eBook ISBN: 978-0-8122-9806-2

To Nia—
For teaching me to ask the more beautiful questions,
and offering me the strength to answer
them with greater care.

CONTENTS

INTRODUCTION

There was a dead dog in the road. Well, really in the median, but there it was, only a few hours ago, lying motionless in the middle of the main boulevard that cuts through Usme. Dead, just dead, its front paws bound up in a greasy green cloth, laid unceremoniously among the rest of the refuse that was ready to be taken away. To be fair, it was about the most exciting thing that I had ever seen along that stretch of road. Beside the bustle of shops, old men sitting down to "tintos," or your occasional stranger hocking a stolen phone, not much else seemed to happen. I tell myself that chances are it was nothing more than someone's dead pet, one that had met its inevitable end, or a street dog that had died and been moved to that concrete island in the middle of the avenue. But then I realize that right across the street is the Comisaría de Familia, open for business. Inside its doors are any number of women, children, and men coming to seek attention for some form of family violence, or give account of their roles in it. Could it just be coincidence or was it collateral damage instead? Was this dead animal another casualty caught up in an intimate war, a bizarre instrument of intimidation against someone who might, or had, come to place a complaint against their partner? It all seems a bit far-fetched, but for some reason the possibility keeps nagging at me, irritating like a grain of sand stuck in an unreachable recess of my mind. As our overfilled bus wheezes and struggles past that spot on the hill, I just can't seem to shake it. Now that dead dog is gone, and I still have no idea why.

I walk off the bus and several steps later I'm back in front of the public library, waiting for Diego. Making his way up the hill from the opposite direction, I spot him, still with that same bounce in his step that is inimitably his own, a boyish energy that belies his forty-odd years and when he sees me a smile stretches tentatively across his face, eager and anxious. As we have done the past two weeks, we go inside, check in with the security guard, and make our way back to an abandoned space, a meeting hall actually, one that is vacated and conspicuously large for our small gathering. Voices echo oddly off the walls of this oversized room. Today Diego even lets me get out my recorder before he starts to talk. This is more the man that I had imagined, not the easy, outgoing one that I had grown to know but a person more restrained, measured in his words, one who one month ago had walked into the Comisaría de Familia to defend himself before strangers. He had been there to answer to an order of protection that had been taken out against him by his partner, Luisa, the culmination of a year of escalating violence that he had previously managed to keep locked away within their home. This time, however, after a year together and with Luisa almost five months pregnant, in their last fight Diego had nearly suffocated her to death. This had proven to be Luisa's moment of "no aguantar más," and with the help of the Comisaría she had left Usme altogether, going from the outer rim of the city and into its very core, finding refuge there in the city's center in an undisclosed shelter, hidden in plain sight among the perpetual motion that makes up Bogotá.

Our previous meetings had notably eschewed all of this, focusing instead on the broader arcs of Diego's life, from his childhood outside of Bogotá to his long string of menial and manual jobs. Today though we had agreed to talk about his relationship, for him to bring Luisa into the picture and explore how he had come to make sense of his own violence, what the aftermath had meant to him, and where he wished it would all go. We could no longer avoid speaking about it, and his hesitance alone tells me that it is time. So today we sit down again, face-to-face, sizing each other up anew, acutely aware of the uncertain space that has filled back in between us. Then, to my surprise, with very little prompting Diego slides back into his familiar role of the storyteller, carrying on almost ad nauseam about how he and Luisa first met, what his hopes and desires had been when they moved back to Bogotá, how his life had changed by knowing her, his frustrations, his anger, his attempts to cope, and in the negative spaces that he leaves, he even starts to sketch out the shadow of his shame. He speaks like a person deprived of conversation. Whatever his initial reservations had been, he is still eager to be heard, if not exactly to be seen, and sitting there chair to chair, straining to hear him over the hum of a floor buffer turning over outside the room, I slowly begin to realize that I have been approaching him all wrong. Rather than talk to me about control, as I had been trying in so many different ways to ask him, today Diego can speak only about dependence, the many ways in which he himself relied upon Luisa. But despite having carried on for almost two hours now, he still cannot bring himself to actually say it; for all of his talk he can't allow himself to properly form that word.

* * *

Coming to understand partner violence, or any violence for that matter, is in my experience no straightforward task. How does one dig into this intimate form of tyranny and emerge with not just a deeper appreciation of it but a means of actually engaging with those who are involved? Where does one even begin? At least initially, the mere acknowledgment that it is a form of tyranny is probably a decent place to start. It focuses our attention onto this violence's more chronic, routinized forms, and it strains the misconception that it is merely the sum of a series of aggressive acts.[1] When seen as a tyranny, partner violence reveals itself to be more fundamentally a question of control, but moving beyond this basic insight will require a different set of tools. In order to begin to perceive the complex dynamics that animate and perpetuate this violence, we have to come prepared with a few more questions of our own. Here there are three, and they form the core of this book: how is it possible to commit this violence over an extended period of time, how is that violence made to be permissible, and ultimately what is at stake for the people who are involved? These three questions are, of course, inseparable. Each one asked on its own is rendered essentially meaningless. Asked together, though, what they amount to is an attempt to see these relationships in their totality, and through them we might come to more clearly see the threads that cut across these seemingly bounded affairs. Through them, we open up apertures into the operations of power and violence more broadly.

   In thinking of partner violence in terms of tyranny, we also invite ourselves to think of it not just as an exercise of power, but more specifically as an exercise in "sovereign" power brought down to scale.[2] This framing helps us to connect it more accurately to broader regimes of social control, to see their analogic and material connections and locate some of their contradictions along the way. In the earlier parts of this book, this idea of sovereignty will be explored in more traditional terms, that of coercive control and its monopolization of violence, its states of exception, and its contouring of social space. A more complete understanding of partner violence, however, requires eventually going beyond these limits, and later on these scaffolds will give way to a more expansive and generative approach. To these ends, the chapter "Stakes" will explore how perpetrators of partner violence are as dependent on the very people that they abuse as the other way around, and the chapter "Contradictions and Consciousness" will explore how the search for sovereignty shapes the emergence of consciousness for perpetrators and victims alike. Taken together, what they demonstrate is that in order to understand these seemingly intimate affairs we must first be able to see far beyond them; in order to meaningfully engage them, we must be able to trace the many tensions that constitute them as well.

This orientation to constitutive tension is essential and it offers us an appreciation that violence is not just structural; it is also not just intersectional as well. Violence, unlike mass, does not just press down like a gravitational force along the hierarchies that we ourselves have constructed, multiplying its effects at their areas of overlap. Violence is itself created through the straining at its joints; it emerges through our everyday efforts to repair, rearrange, and either secure or escape from the many nexuses in which we live. While concepts such as "structural violence" and "intersectionality" have proven to be exceedingly helpful in tracing the contours of power and locating many of its effects, they have done little to illuminate why violence is committed in the first place.[3] In order to understand the perpetration of violence, and in this case the perpetration of partner violence, we must instead bring into view the tensions out of which it emerges. We must search out the confluences of social process that produce it and in them find the critical contradictions, the creative tensions, not the dialectic but what we might even call the "tengentics," the specific means by which systems of institutionalized power are made to be violent to those who are caught up in them.[4] Only by doing so, only by finding the unstable nexuses from which this violence is committed can we begin to see the vulnerabilities in these broader systems, and only then can we start to imagine how to leverage these weak points in the interest of their inward collapse. As such they are apertures for critical engagement, with violence on a systemic level to be sure, but more urgently with the people who actually make those systems up. They are a direct line to those who have taken these tensions and, from them, come to commit violence of even the most intimate kind.

Into Violence

And so in this way this book explores the experiences of partner violence—from the perpetrators to the survivors, those who respond and those who observe—but what are their stories about? Surely they are in part about partner violence, but equally so they are about deep ambivalences and their creative contradictions, about not just being caught up in the webs that we ourselves have spun but about being pulled apart by them, and the daily, often violent work that gets done to try to bring them back together.[5] They are about not just the challenges made to authority but also how through acts of violence authority challenges itself. Most of all, they are about the suffering that is endured throughout this process, and the many consequences it entails. Admittedly, what I am able to present here is weighted toward understanding the perpetrators of this violence: their histories, their worldviews, their doubts and desires, their positions, their priorities, and what is at stake for them through it all. But these are not "sympathy for the devil" stories.[6] Sympathy, like pity, is a response handed down only from a position of assumed power, and its purpose is typically to apologize or excuse. It has no purpose here. People, empathy, and a critical agonism, however, do. Here the purpose is to enter into the heart of intimate violence with the urgency to understand, to embrace the complex personhoods of those who in the moment might be victimizer or victim, because only by seeing people as shot through by contradictions can we possibly envision ways to work ourselves out of these systems of routinized, daily terror.[7] It is therefore not my purpose to present an anatomy of partner violence either. Dissection of anything may help us to see it better, but it also leaves the subject dead, and violence is absolutely nothing if not very much alive.[8] We simply cannot deign to understand it if we do not treat it as such, to look for the picture in motion, the push and pull, and not the cold, still image.

Ultimately though this must all come in service of something, lest we fall into an indefensible "voyeuristic pornography of violence" and I can only hope that this makes a contribution to the vast universe of work that is being done to address this form of abuse.[9] The most important work done on partner violence is undoubtedly that which deals directly with those who shoulder the greatest burden of suffering, the victims of it, by seeking to either level the topographies of power or find alternatives to our current arrangements of gendered affairs. It is only in service to this awesome work that I can humbly proceed. By opening up the experiences of its perpetrators, it is my hope that we can continue our search for ways to ping the bubble of partner violence, to even disassemble from within the very systems and social logics that drive its continuation, and to find alternatives that are in fact better for all of those involved. After all, as Martha Ackelsberg has said, "The exercise of power in any institutionalized form—whether economic, political, religious, or sexual—brutalizes both the wielder of power and the one over whom it is exercised."[10] Better, in other words, need not be a zero-sum game.

There is always also a *there* to stories and, even though partner violence is committed everywhere around the world, each experience of it happens in a particular place. Understanding that somewhere and its history first of all gives us some sort of access to the phenomenology of inhabiting a particular place and time, how life is in practice intricately woven into broader systems of relational power.[11] It opens up unexpected doors to understanding how motifs of power that are played out along other dimensions of social relations are also manifested in the intimate violence of partner abuse. By retracing the threads that transect these various planes, rather than recapitulate a "Russian doll" imagination of our social worlds, we are rewarded instead with a far more fruitfully complex understanding of how violence happens. Doing so begins to reveal the multidimensional fractal of violence— the common processes that create self-similarity across scales and their infinite frontiers—illustrating to us how structures of social relations and their justifications mutually reinforce each other throughout society, as well as the contradictions that they create along the way.[12] If the social sciences are to maintain their relevance in the world, we must not only be able to trace out the contours of power and violence in our societies but also be able to find critical vulnerabilities to them as well. This should absolutely be our purpose here, and in the case of partner violence, however intimate in scale it may seem, it is only with this broader perspective that we have any chance to truly glimpse what these points of engagement might be.

In this vein, the stories told here take place in Usme, the fifth district of Bogotá, Colombia. La Zona Quinta.[13] Extending away from the limits of the city, it is the capital city's southern reaching cone, a rapidly expanding, low-income, semi-urban, semi-rural peripheral contact zone of just under a half million residents.[14] Straddling the margins of the city, Usme is also one of the districts of Bogotá with the highest levels of partner violence. In one recent community-based survey of the twenty districts that make up the capital, Usme had the second highest rate of partner abuse with over 80 percent of women in a relationship reporting that their partner displayed some significant level of partner-controlling behavior.[15] Not surprisingly, in my experience this issue found resonance not only in numbers but also in the sentiments of community leaders, from the organizers of youth foundations to the Catholic clergy, even public library administrators. But Usme is more than just a place where partner violence happens. Usme is an all too frequently silenced history, a shadow biography of sorts to the capital and, by extension, to Colombia itself. It is a place that is both complex and *complicado*, but most of all it is a place that I quickly came to love, populated by people for whom I continue to have immense respect.[16]

It is where I spent sixteen months over the span of over two years, a half-Colombian/half-gringo semi-stranger, an undisputed outsider who was nevertheless welcomed graciously into so many homes and workspaces. And while much of my time in Usme was specifically dedicated to speaking to and following around perpetrators of partner violence, survivors of it, and professionals in the Comisarías de Familia, among others, it is only by being there that one begins to perceive the broader worlds in which those lives are lived. It is only by inhabiting that place that one begins to appreciate the enormity, and the conflicted beauty, that is Usme. To me, Usme will always be the *páramo*, an endless patchwork of motley green interrupted by its quarries, strips of broken earth that burn cold like amber in the crisp air of the *altiplano* (high plains) morning. When I close my eyes to think of Usme still, my mind will always see both the sacred ground that rises up against the urbanizing tide and hear worldly rap lyrics that rise up against indifference. At the end of the day, Usme is bringing home the bread at dusk and *madrugando* again for the four-in-the-morning bus back to the city. It is a place that I miss dearly whenever I am away, and a place that will require its own dedicated attention in order to be properly seen.[17]

The Power of Analogy

The very first time that I arrived in Usme, it was at the generous invitation of a professor from the National University of Colombia. Over the previous years, he and a group of citizens from the district had been working to develop environmental justice programs aimed at the preservation of popular control over the land on which Usme is built. Each project represented an effort against the continued degradation of the Páramo de Sumapaz. A high-altitude moorland, the páramo is not only the largest of its kind in the world but also the source of fresh water for the rest of the city and the lungs that breathe against its stifling smog. For a time, the discovery of an ancient Muiscan cemetery had stemmed the tide of advancing construction projects, but even that could not forever delay their inevitable march southward. Perched right up at the borderlands between the two, the meeting of the group that morning had been called to discuss the recent round of rejections for city-funded grants. Projects to build paths for hiking, resources to help bring community members together to organize around their land: each one had been turned down by the city's government. In a small living room overlooking the hills, we clutched steaming cups of heavily sweetened tinto close to ourselves, warding off the residual chill coming in from the overcast day. Despite the cold though, and the even more dismal news, the conversation remained lively. Sitting in between reams of files and stacks of assorted books, everyone there began to hash out the next steps that they might take together. The frustration was palpable, but not to be so easily discouraged each person contributed to the brainstorm in their own time: what could they change, what could they resubmit, what other agencies might they interest? One man in particular though, Alberto, was particularly upset, each word fuming a bit more than his last. Eventually, at a pause in the conversation, he said something that I will never forget. Even before I had told him why I was working in Usme, of my interest in issues of partner violence and its broader social connections, he looked at me directly and said, "The government says 'popular' and 'with the people' but in reality they don't really care. It's like a parent who hugs and kisses his children in public, and then when they are home hits them over the head."

When I heard Alberto say this, I did not realize at the time that what he was saying, and how he was saying it, would be a constant theme that I would encounter in Usme. Analogic reasoning, seeing the repetition of patterns throughout society, was simply common sense, a daily practice of engaging and understanding the world.[18] In making this statement I do not believe that Alberto was proposing some causal theory of violence in the family, but his recasting of the common "state-as-family" metaphor to the "state-as-abusive-family" is striking nonetheless. When later in that meeting I did ask the group what they saw as the major issues currently facing their communities, Alberto was quick to add youth violence and gangs. When he stipulated that this problem fundamentally derived from parents' failure to control their children, I was left to wonder what his own analogy might mean if he reversed its direction. If proper parenting meant strict control, then what might good governance be?

The people I know in Usme have taught me much about the value of analogic reasoning and its potential to enrich our connection of the broader social historical context to the intimate present. Rather than seeking meaning only in the direct chains of causality, analogic reasoning opens up other avenues for making sense of the world. Of importance are not just the strengths of relation along a unidirectional continuum of time but also the repetition of themes across scales and dimensions of social relations. The greater the repetition of a particular motif, the more valuable it is in organizing our appreciation of the world and our engagement with it. This is, after all, the basic purpose of any program of research, just as it is what we do on a daily basis as we try to take shape of the shifting phantasmagoria of the lives that we lead.[19] Even within the rigorous disciplines of the empiric sciences, such a notion has finally taken root, spreading through any field that takes seriously the frameworks of complex systems or emergent complexity.[20] From the brain to society to whole ecologies, our great fractal existence continues to defy our complete understanding, but at our disposal is the tool of analogy to at least call to our consciousness the self-similarities that exist across it.

All of this is no less true in the case of partner violence, and to fully appreciate it we must draw the connections that tie these intimate acts to their broader social worlds. Drawing common understandings of it, basic repetitive patterns that connect across these planes of social relations, recognizes this basic truth, and I would certainly not be the first to do so. When women-led mobilizations in Chile called for "democracy in the country and in the home," this was not just reflective of an abstract recognition that authoritarianism has many manifestations, it was also a direct response against prior efforts by the Pinochet regime to locate the authority of the central government in a highly normative vision of the nuclear family.[21] In a more mundane instance, on the very first day that I did fieldwork in a Comisaría de Familia in Usme, I witnessed this conversation between the intake psychologist and a woman who was there to make a *denuncia*:

PSYCHOLOGIST: Was he ever verbally abusive? Calling you names?
DENUNCIA SEEKER: Name-calling and insults? Oh, absolutely, that was my daily bread.
PSYCHOLOGIST: Was he controlling in other ways?
DENUNCIA SEEKER: Oh, yes, he was like the governor. He controlled everything.

Concentrating and controlling resources, actively devaluing the "other," along with dispossession and paternalistic ideologies: these are motifs that a deeper dive in to the history of Usme will also make clear. But does this mean that people abuse their partners simply because other histories of power relations have "taught them" those logics? Of course not, because people are far more than just cultural dopes.[22] There are, however, nontrivial similarities in both justification and form between these collective histories and the smaller-scale workings of partner violence. As such, these broader histories are not just contextual cues that illuminate the everyday insults that residents of Usme endure, sources of anger and shame that weave their way into intimate conflicts. They are also the bedrocks of the central social logics that I repeatedly encountered when listening to perpetrators and survivors alike, and they are themes that will continually emerge throughout the course of this book.

Onward

Such an interconnected view is the only viable approach to understanding this intimate violence in Usme, a place whose collective history is defined by a variety of interwoven dynamics of violence and whose residents disproportionately represent one of the longest ongoing conflicts on the globe. I believe the operative word for building such an understanding here is "interpositionality," and anthropology is unusually suited to this task.[23] While others have argued that the job of anthropologists in the modern world is to operate at the furthest margins of our dominant social orders, and to then look back and critique the societies from whence they came, it is only in the process of actually working back from those margins that most of the vulnerabilities to those systems start to appear.[24] Finding them requires assembling the experiences of the many people who have already come into conflict and, out of their existing contestations, have come to see the limits, as well as the internal instabilities, of those otherwise established regimes.

The people who populate the pages that follow are therefore not intended to be representatives of all of the experiences of partner violence in a community like Usme, but they have been carefully chosen because they are illustrative of the most salient issues that emerged throughout the course of this work. During its early months, that work was mostly consulting city archives to gain a deeper understanding of the history of Usme, followed closely by several months of interviews and observation within the Comisarías de Familia. Within Usme there are two Comisarías, and it was only by being invited in to see the process of consulting them—from the first encounter with the receptionist to the lawyer who decided orders of protection to the social workers who followed those cases for up to two years—that I was able to build early frameworks for understanding the intricacies of partner violence in this setting. Though this study would go on to include many more interviews with service professionals and community leaders in Usme, it was the staff of the Comisarías who remained some of my closest partners through the duration of this work.

It was also through the Comisarías de Familia that I began to approach perpetrators of partner violence, and ultimately it was only through the Comisarías that I was able to identify the men who were willing to speak with me at length.[25] That they volunteered to meet and talk about their lives, having been recruited through the Comisarías de Familia, is itself a reminder that they cannot be taken as a representative sample of abusive men in Usme. That they wished to speak at all with a stranger about their lives, under no obligation, with an openness to reveal themselves and encounter their own histories, was beyond that of many of their peers. Nevertheless, investigations about this violence must start somewhere, and this sample is what formed the core of this work. It is also for this reason, this initial encounter through the Comisarías, that all of our first meetings happened on some kind of neutral grounds—most often a public library—and why our first couple of interviews focused not on the more immediate circumstances that had brought us together, but on the longer histories of their lives.[26] This way, when we later returned to the violence that they had more recently committed, having first made that detour through the broader arcs of their lives we could come back to talking about that violence with a better understanding of each other's intentions. This, of course, never completely obviated the hint of a forensic gaze from our conversations, but even still, the kinds of proof and posturing that were so typical of the audiences held within the Comisarías were largely absent from our interactions. When we eventually abandoned the interviews altogether in the interest of meeting on the streets and in their homes, we did away with these dynamics almost altogether.

What set apart these interactions—our interviews in the libraries and our time together in the community as opposed to their audiences in the Comisarías—was most obviously the setting itself, but it was also the purpose of those encounters and the amount of time that we had to share. As will be explored in much more detail in Chapter 6, "Response," the audiences held in the Comisarías are very much intended to answer the "what" (did partner violence happen) and the "whereto" (what is to be done about it). Motives, circumstances, and worldviews often have little relevance there other than in shaping, to a limited extent, the kinds of legal tools that will be brought to bear in preventing further abuse. And it happens on a schedule. By contrast, our time in the community was only modestly structured, if at all, and in the time that we had, under the promise of confidentiality, we were usually able to more openly explore how their lives had brought them to this point. For survivors of violence this often came through not just in the stories that they told but in their stringing of them together: the way that they daisy-chained events to fill the silence frequently told more than the content of any one tale. For perpetrators, our starting with life history interviews had the unanticipated advantage of building a space in which those men could start to reassemble some of the pieces of themselves and make connections that they had previously not seen. Even when many of the men I worked with would lead off with the kinds of well-practiced justifications that they had built up over time, ones they often tried to interject in their Comisaría audiences, over time our retracing the stripes of their lives provided ways to obliquely rethink them and build a space in which men could reflect more openly on the violence that they had come to commit. This was, of course, not intended to be a therapeutic process per se, but a process of encountering each other critically and empathically along the way.[27]

For fear that the power dynamics with their partners would obviate any meaningful consent for participation, I never directly recruited the partners of the perpetrators that I knew. That said, by being invited into the domestic space of one man in particular, Diego, I was able to begin to build a relationship with his partner, Luisa, a dynamic that I will explore in much greater detail in Chapter 4, "Stakes." Generally speaking, engaging with survivors of violence was a far more organic process and was only rarely mediated through the Comisarías de Familia. In several cases it was women whom I had come to know through other avenues who would eventually confide that they had been subjected to such violence and suggested that we set aside a time and space to talk about it in greater detail. In contrast to interviews with perpetrators, these became opportunities for survivors to share the wisdoms that they had won from living through it, our time spent together in the community a chance for them to outline how they had come to break out of the boundaries of their homes. What emerged from all of this was a multitude of windows into partner violence in Usme, ones that mostly centered on the perpetrators themselves but found grounding and counterbalance from survivors, professional responders, community organizers, and the deeper histories of the contexts through which each of them lived.

Overview

Across these many experiences, as will be explored throughout the entirety of this book, two underlying schema consistently emerged. The first is the sense of becoming trapped in some way and pushing back against those enclosures. It was one of the very few common threads that seemed to weave itself through all of the experiences of the people that I knew. Acknowledging it means that to understand partner violence is not just to ask what are the webs in which people have suspended themselves, it is to ask how they have become ensnared within them, constrained by them, injured through the process of their violent repair. For survivors of abuse this entrapment was the most self-evident, intimate construction of isolation buttressed by multiple failures of social support.[28] They were not alone in experiencing this though; those who committed that very abuse felt it as well. Caught in the cycles of their own behavior, recapitulating their own marginalization in how they justified their violence, the perpetrators that I knew consistently demonstrated that just to exercise power over another is not to be liberated yourself in any way. Even those who responded to the crises of these violent relationships, the staff of the Comisarías de Familia, were not immune to this. Endowed with incremental increases in legal power, the very tools that gave them the authority, and the means, to intervene also became constraining in their own right, limiting their ability to do their work in ways that they still hoped to achieve.

In addition to this sense of entrapment, cutting across these experiences was the underlying element of driving tension, as already briefly discussed. These stories of partner violence, regardless of the angle from which they are told, are largely constituted by contradiction, but rather than be paralyzing, these paradoxes, these tensions are generative in the most severe ways. Throughout the chapters that follow, these tensions will be given a number of different names: interpositional independence, surrogate power, the dependence inherent to control. What unites them all is that these tensions are not just characteristic of the lives and relationships examined, on whatever scale that may be, but these tensions are what give life to them. Understanding them more fully, seeing how they penetrate across and bridge scales of social relations, connecting them in unlikely ways, requires a broader appreciation of the contexts in which this intimate violence is performed. It is also through the processes by which these tensions are engaged that the boundaries of social life are created: how the "self" comes to mind, how spaces like the "home" are constructed, even how national frontiers are negotiated.[29] As these limits of the experienced world come to appear to be increasingly inevitable and natural features they not only become habit, but can become restricting and injurious even to those who lead the work of creating them.

It is in this respect then that the first chapter deals with the history of Usme, outlining the major arcs of power and violence that have given the district its contemporary form. Tracing these faithfully requires attention to one issue in particular, co-production: not only has Usme been formed through the history of the nation of Colombia, but through those many centuries of encounter the nation has just as equally been formed by Usme. Beyond this, the objectives of this chapter are both modest and ambitious. Modest, because the questions guiding it are limited: what are the relevant spatial inscriptions of power and how have they been formed; from whence do centrally organizing logics of hierarchy, like "paternalism," come? It is ambitious because these historical narrations are ultimately of no use to us unless they can be connected meaningfully to the present, a "today" that incidentally never takes place exclusively in the "now." It is on this general note that the chapter ends and gives way to the rest of the book, indexing only some of the possible connections between partner violence in Usme today and its historical legacies that are never really in the past. Is it the militarization of everyday life and masculinity; is it the creation of unsafe urban spaces and the alienating effects that they have? How have dislocations in the form of urban migration left some people more vulnerable to partner violence, and how have those same migrations also played into the perpetration of it? If simplicity is the inevitability of description, complexity and the beginnings of answers to these questions can only come from a more detailed engagement with people's lives.

So while such broad points of departure—conceptually with regard to the topic of violence and historically with regard to Usme—allow us the space to sketch these rough outlines of connection, it is still necessary to eventually ask a more specific set of questions in order to guide a lucid understanding of the actual acts of partner violence. In this regard, there are by my account three central questions that we must pose. These questions, when asked together, allow us to momentarily tease apart and examine the composite threads of the fabric of this abuse, without irreparably causing damage to our understanding of it: How it is possible for someone to continue to abuse their partner over a prolonged period of time? How is that violence made to be ethically permissible? And what is at stake for the perpetrators of abuse? These questions—discussed in the "Possible," "Permissible," and "Stakes" chapters—form the overall structure of the core of this book and are the fundamental basis of insight into the kind of chronic, controlling partner violence that is of particular interest here.

One of the most common questions when it comes to partner violence is why do the survivors of it not leave those relationships, either earlier than they do or even at all? The mere possibility of maintaining a violently coercive relationship over months, years, or a lifetime is no trivial matter, and understanding how victims are isolated into such situations is a critical first step to appreciating the dynamics of abuse. That is the focus of Chapter 2, which is based on the stories of two women: Luz, who was able to avoid violence by an intimate partner altogether, and Carolina, who had survived the extremes of it by two different men. What both of their stories illustrate is that survival is, of course, an intricately active endeavor, and both of their respective forms of resistance highlight different cracks in this intimate form of domination. For Luz this meant charting her life through a reliance on multiple sources of support—referred to here as interpositional independence—whereas for Carolina it came through her responses to the unintended consequences of rape and reproductive coercion. What emerges from their experiences are the first insights to how chronic, coercive partner violence is indeed fundamentally a question of sovereignty on the intimate scales, and an exploration about how power over another can only be sought through the construction of particular social spaces.

Chapter 3, "Permissible," shifts from the survivors of abuse to the perpetrators of it, focusing on the ideologies that they drew on in order to legitimize the violence that they committed, at the very least seeking to rationalize it to themselves. The chapter begins by describing my first encounter with one particular man, Diego, and then proceeds to trace the connections between the justifications that he invoked and those of the other perpetrators with whom I worked. Based on these engagements, ideas of paternalistic authority and their violent states of exception, rather than machismo per se, are followed out from intimate relationships in Usme to the history of U.S.-Latin American relations over the preceding centuries. Illustrating these connections serves dual purposes. First, it argues against any notion of an exotic or easily "otherized" cultural pathology as a means of understanding partner violence in Usme. Second, it also means that abusive men like Diego, by committing their violence, actually come to align themselves with the very ideologies that have upheld their own forms of social marginalization. In addition, this chapter introduces the idea of "surrogate power" as a means of understanding this uniquely paradoxical social position, its broader implications for understanding both sovereignty and hegemony, as well as what it could mean for engaging directly with perpetrators of partner violence.

Just because chronic, coercive partner violence can be made both possible and, to a certain extent, permissible still does not mean that anyone would actually do it. There still has to be some kind of impulse for someone to commit this violence against their partner. Chapter 4 explores in depth then what was at stake for Diego throughout the violence that he committed, built on over a year's worth of follow-up with him that took us out from the Comisaría de Familia and into his community, his places of work, and, eventually, into his home. Through a more detailed account of his own life history, engagement with his current partner, Luisa, and the legal process in which he found himself, the singular framing of abusive relationships around the notion of control is challenged. Instead, the multiple, profound forms of dependence that Diego felt toward the very partners that he had abused are examined, along with their social origins and the forms of shame that became entangled with them. In doing so, one of the central contradictions of violent intimate relationships is exposed, and consideration of this contradiction between control and dependence begins to reveal how the very effort to hide those forms of dependence can itself drive a great deal of the violence that is committed. Of all the men with whom I worked, I was undoubtedly the closest with Diego, and it was in large part through exploring this particular contradiction that much of our relationship was mediated. As such, how the exploration of this tension between control and dependence provides one possible avenue for sustained, direct engagement with perpetrators of abuse is also considered.

It is from these chapters—exploring the history of Usme and beginning to answer the three core questions that comprise this book—that the theme of generative tension emerges. From interpositional independence to unintended consequences, surrogate power, and the contradiction between control and dependence, the first part of Chapter 5 serves as a reprise and clarification of some of these developing ideas, bringing them into direct conversation with one another through the common denominator of tengentics. Doing so serves the purpose of beginning to consider how together they form complex nexuses of engagement for the seemingly intractable issue of partner violence. This potential for engagement and change is then followed in the second half of the chapter through an exploration of the experiences of another perpetrator of violence. Jairo, unlike Diego, experienced a much more durable change in his relationship during the year after his partner took out an order of protection against him, and the unique conditions in which this change was fostered are examined.

The final chapter, "Response," carries forward the issue of engaging partner violence, focusing on the primary social institution officially charged with responding to it in Bogotá, the Comisarías de Familia. It is simply impossible to understand the response to partner violence in Usme, and how perpetrators are held accountable to any extent, without understanding the work that is done through this state agency. Based on longitudinal engagements with its staff in Usme, this chapter retraces the history of this particular social institution, the manner in which its contemporary functions are carried out, and begins to explore some of the unrealized aspirations that its own staff had for what the Comisarías could someday become. Focus is given to how the Comisarías de Familia represent a new kind of public intrusion into the previously private affairs of partner violence, representing the confrontation of competing sovereign systems, as well as the ways by which the very legal tools that invest Comisaría staff with authority have also come to constrain the work that many there wish to achieve. Building from an ongoing dialogue regarding novel ways of addressing partner violence in the community, this chapter explores the desires of Comisaría staff to include alternative forms of justice in their work and the possible means of realizing these aspirations.

These desires index broader possibilities for rethinking how we address partner violence as a society, and we can hardly afford to disregard them. In them, we find the constant striving for some sort of exteriority, some means of breaking out of the confines in which we so frequently find ourselves, the search for a less violent means of remaking our social worlds. All of those whom I came to know in Usme—from survivors to perpetrators to Comisaría staff—wanted lessons to be learned from their own experiences, and I strive not to disappoint them here. It is my sincere hope that what follows can contribute to broader projects of transformation, personal or collective, efforts to make real a world in which we move beyond our current means of affliction. Onward, *vamanos*.

Figure 1. The prison, La Picota, located just north of Usme along Avenida Caracas, separating the northern entrance of the district from the rest of the city. Taken April 2015 by the author.

Figure 2. The quarry that is located near the Portal Usme station of the Transmilenio bus system, near the northern entrance of the district along Avenida Caracas. Taken April 2015 by the author.

Figure 3. Outside of the public library branch in Usme: in front of it is a public amphitheater. Taken April 2015 by the author.

Figure 4. Usme, from south of the plaza of Usme Centro. Taken June 2015 by the author.

CHAPTER 1

La Zona Quinta

Perdóname si los ofendo
Vivimos en un país en la cual
Hay pocos buenos recuerdos
Bañados en sangre
Partidos inmortales
Explotación de petróleo
Ya si miento, lloro, flora
Y trata de mujeres
El descubrimiento de color, se ha repetido
Tengo raíces indígenas
Malicia indígena
Represento también
Los ríos, pueblos, y las veredas, ellos
Han sido olvidados, también obligados
A dejar sus cultivos
Después protestas para campesinos, todos ofendidos
Después oprimidos, por qué? (por qué?)
Por protestar en este momento, le recita
Calles calientes, rap quinta inicial
—Quinta Inicial, from a freestyle rap performance

No puedes comprar mi vida
Mi tierra no se vende.

—Calle 13, "Latinoamerica"

"Welcome to Usmekistan." So reads one graffiti tag on the public library in Usme. Next to it another person has written, "Usmekistan is consciousness." In posting these messages, these clandestine pundits have taken a popularly demeaning term for Usme's social and geographic marginalization, "Usmekistan," and turned it on its head. Usme may be marginalized, but out of that marginalization consciousness has emerged. But consciousness of what? For one, Usme's history is more than just marginalization. Though it is indeed that, it is also a peculiar mélange of both exclusion *and* exploitation, and a process of constructing an intimate "other" to the capital city. If nothing else this "othering" is part of that awareness, and down the road from the library another mural reads, "Don't make *our* lives a part of *your* war."[1] If only the discrepancies were so clear. Who is the "us," who is the "them," and where the front lines of social warfare can be found are hardly self-evident. In the pluralistic, and continuously pluralizing, district of Usme, a zone of not just contact but of production as well, the lines are continuously moving about a land that itself cannot stay fixed. This is, more than anything else to me, what is La Zona Quinta, Bogotá's fifth district. If it is a place of consciousness, then it is so because it has been a place of encounter, a space of meetings through which new collectivities and social fissures have continuously emerged. To understand the longer history of Usme is to make evident the modes of power that have shaped this district, the city to which it now pertains, and even beyond to the rest of the country and its neighbors.

Since the founding of Bogotá as a colonial city of Colombia, Usme has lived as a shadow: close at hand, always present, silent. Unlike shadows, however, the history of Usme is one of a fabricated silence and one where the "shadow" has also formed its host, not just passively followed behind it.[2] In line with what scholars of colonialism more broadly have argued, modern Colombia was as much constructed by Usme as the other way around.[3] Contrary to the still-common myths of urban-rural separation, Usme is not a region "left behind" in the modernizing "progress" of Bogotá but rather has always been a driving force behind it.[4] As for the silence to its role, if most of the dominant histories have forgotten it, at least many of the residents of Usme have not. In a project done by the office of the mayor of Bogotá to commemorate the bicentennial of the country, groups of community leaders from each of the city's twenty districts were asked to reflect on the past, present, and desired futures of their communities. Here is what one representative from Usme had to say:

We lost much during the Independence of our country's Republic. In this territory, more than any other, we lost, because part of the terrains destined for indigenous groups were ceded in these feats for independence, in all these fights ceded to the interior. Ceded to whom? To the big landowners, generals, colonels of this country, and the people were left in deficiency. For this reason Usme has been mistreated and this is how we proceed. I think that this is part of what should be given in this contribution to the Bicentennial: to say that we have nothing to celebrate.[5]

In such a dire diagnosis this kind of consciousness comes into full display. The overlapping forms of power that this person references—militarized, ethnically charged, and intensely gendered political economies and forms of governance—are not just part and parcel of Usme's history. Instead, they are what put this "peripheral" district at the center of so many intersecting ones. They are what begin to outline the motifs of violent control that reverberate all the way up and down from the level of partner violence to geopolitical struggles over the preceding centuries. Particularly relevant here, and throughout many of the chapters that follow, are paternalistic claims to authority and their equally gendered contestations; domination as the seemingly contradictory confluence of both control and dependence, marginalization and exploitation; and the intricate fracturing of social relations that is accomplished through these tasks. To trace these threads out in their greater geographic breadth and historical depth is a task that I can only begin to accomplish here, but, as they are further elaborated throughout the chapters that follow, their purpose remains the same. It is not only to lay out the wider angle view of the landscape in which intimate acts of partner violence happen, though that is itself important, but also to provide the perspective necessary to see where there are continuities with these broader histories, where there are tensions, how violence might emerge from their multiple fraught connections, and what we might ultimately be able to do about it.[6] We attend to them because only by first being able to see across these scales of human experience might we better prepare ourselves to listen for the echoes of the operations of power that reverberate across them. In their dissonance, we might just find new possibilities for realizing a less violent world. To be able to engage with intimate acts of violence, we must first survey the complex fabrics into which they are woven.

It is for these reasons and more, not just some rote exercise of historiography, that the history of Usme must be given here its own dedicated attention. Organized around eras of social subversion in Colombia and punctuated by critical moments—such as the end of La Violencia and the adoption of the new constitution of 1991—this is but a primer on the story of Usme's shadow role in the building of modern Colombia, its relevance to processes of power that transcend even beyond those borders, and a very first glimpse into how they might resonate down into even the most intimate affairs.[7] Tracing these threads requires starting points, however, and there are no better anchors from which to begin than the material reminders that make up this district. Indexing the layered histories from which La Zona Quinta has emerged, these are the details that give flavor and shape to everyday life in Usme, the details that are all too easily taken for granted when going there. To truly enter into Usme is to learn how to see them: in order to understand Usme, you first have to know how to find it. *Ahí vamos.*[8]

Into Usme: Ascent

Riding southbound through the core of the city, I see tall office buildings quickly give way to the crowded streets of the red light district in Barrio Santa Fe and the unswept roads of the Bronx. Parque Tercer Milenio to the left lays as an open expanse over what was not long ago one of the most crowded markets in the city, "El Cartucho," now obliterated in a project to combat urban blight.[9] The numbered street signs start to be labeled "South" as groups of "lechonerías" (restaurants selling a typical rice dish from the Department of Tolima) line the street.[10] San Cristobal, Rafael Uribe Uribe, Ciudad Bolívar, Tunjuelito. One by one the districts of Bogotá pass by and just as the city opens up for a moment and breathes, Usme begins. Guarding this peculiar gateway is the federal prison ("La Picota"), an army artillery base, a quarry, a cement plant, a brick-making factory. Each tells its own story and each separates Usme from, and yet connects it to, the rest of the city.

Numb from sitting so long, I hurry off the Transmilenio at the terminal station, hoping I can still catch the direct bus to Usme Centro, also sometimes known as "Usme Pueblo," the central plaza that serves as the unofficial transition point from city to countryside. Making my way through the turnstiles I dart around the columns and to my relief find three small lines of people arranged as if about to board a phantom "alimentador," but my relief is

clearly not shared by those already waiting. In a few short minutes I see two
almost empty buses going to the nearby neighborhood of Marichuela depart
the station, a sight to which I have become all too well accustomed. While I
am inwardly pessimistic that I have missed the last bus, those around me seem
to be increasingly outwardly agitated. One man yells down the bus line, waves
a hand, and then, as if in programmed unison, the back line of people steps
out over the curb and into the road. Though barely five people strong, they
have successfully blocked the span of the road, and their stances, yelling, and
whistling seem to say that they don't plan to go anywhere unless it's on the bus
that they were promised. As if reluctantly cajoled out of a slumber, one bus
labeled "in transit" starts to slowly creep forward. Soon it's upon the blockade
and the tension I feel at the nape of my neck tells me that it's not slowing down
fast enough. Hardly five feet away from the last man in its path, the driver
seems more concerned with flipping his hand at his antagonist than coming to
a stop for him. Thankfully, he does slow down just in time and the man
side-steps the oncoming bus, but I swear he drags his arm as if to shoulder-
bump the passing driver.

  I step up onto the bus to hear the shouts between some of the passengers
and the bus's operator. "Hijueputa!," "carajo!," and other assorted obscenities
momentarily fill the air. The shouting dies down almost immediately though,
and for the rest of the ride everyone seems happy enough to stew in quiet. All
the while I can only think of sitting in a living room a year ago, in Usme
Centro, hearing my companions voice their dissatisfaction over the limited
number of rides coming out to where they lived. I feel that what I've seen today
is an everyday reminder of that simmering anger, of living at the margin of the
margin, an anger that even a late bus can incite when it is taken to be another
sign of indifference. As ephemeral the rupture, as relatively inconsequential as
the little blockade might have seemed, its deeper sentiments still spoil the air.
With our windows shut tight against the ever-present cold, we ride onward,
suffocating on the lingering malcontent.

  As we ascend further, the sun rises up over the ridge to the east and begins
to break up the morning fog.[11] Around us, shop owners welcome their first
customers off of the wide and dusty paths that make up the sidewalk in the
neighborhoods that pass us by. Barranquillita, Santa Librada, Marichuela.
Behind me, a woman erupts in a fit of sharp, barking coughs, and as I zip my
rain jacket the rest of the way up, pulling it against my neck, I mutter a faint
"salud" back to her. My thoughts about community health draw my eye once
again to the landfill of Doña Juana, the only repository for all of Bogotá, which

rises out of the ground beyond the Tunjuelito River below. This fungating, massive eyesore only continues to spread, immortalized, continuing to grow despite having long outlived its original date of planned obsolescence. Filling up more than its fair share of the valley between the barrios and their surrounding hills now, its open top makes it look like some bizarre snow-capped mountain, one whose slick features set it noticeably apart from the jagged surfaces of its surrounding hills.

I turn away as we continue to jostle up over the hills and play slalom with the potholes, directing my gaze instead out the other bank of windows. Through them I see straight and narrow lines that subdivide the verdant tapestry we are all now enveloped in, hedges that break up the land into smaller plots to labor, fences that take families and turn them into neighbors. Beyond these fields are distant so-called invasions—communities whose only crime is to be the most recently arrived—as well as the exposed clay of some of Usme's quarries, the ones that threaten to steal away the ground on which all these lives are made. The further away toward the mountains that they go, the less I can tell which is which, and I quietly smile to myself at the irony. As if beckoned by my thoughts, we cross into another neighborhood and now outside my window are stacks of bricks assembled in the lots of the "ladrille-ros," as well as the rows of cantinas and homes that separate them. If these construction material enterprises constitute much of Usme's new economy, the sheep roaming around their front yards remind me that this was not always the case. Agriculture is still alive and well.

These ruminations are abruptly interrupted though by a sight that I still cannot believe. As I look back out at the now-empty valley, hanging just above the Tunjuelito, projecting out from the remaining haze of the morning is a rainbow that I am actually looking down upon. Apparently the sun has not risen high enough yet to clear out the last moisture from this deep ravine. With the river, the ravine, the forests, the cliffs, the tartan patchwork of small plots of arable land, and now this unlikely vista beneath me, before I step off of the bus I am left with one final thought: for all its hardship, for all the rancor, Usme is, simply put, stunning.

* * *

Even this briefest of tours down the road and into Usme begins to lay bare the complicated and ever-evolving relationships that have made up this district, each landmark a signifier that points us to the lived histories that constitute it. Take, for example, the long row of lechonerías Tolimenses, those that are found extending southward along the Avenida Caracas in Bogotá. From the cumulative effects of Colombia's political conflict, by the year 2012 the total number of internally displaced persons (IDPs) in Colombia had reached 3.9 million, an estimated 70 percent of whom are women, and had further increased to 4.7 million by the middle of 2013.[12] This figure means that at the time Colombia not only had the highest number of officially designated IDPs out of any country in the world but also had more IDPs than any other single *region*.[13] In a country whose total population is just under 50 million, this represents a staggering number of people, and the majority of those who have found themselves dispossessed of their homes have later found themselves in one of the country's major cities. In Bogotá, a full quarter of IDPs who have settled there come from Tolima, a strategic department that lays along the corridor between Bogotá and Cali, a place where much of the conflict has been fought.[14] Though people from Tolima can be found throughout the city, they have settled predominantly in the southern districts, such as Ciudad Bolívar, San Cristobal, and Usme. The legions of lechonerías that have risen up in their wake are but a relatively benign reminder of this violent past, as the restaurants are catering to a nostalgia for a land left behind. Less benign though are the other daily reminders in Usme of this history of violence, ones that often burst unexpectedly into the rhythms of everyday life: limbs lost to land-mine amputations; the pleading stories projected over the noise of the Transmilenio buses; rumors whispered about those who have been "disappeared," either from the rural areas of the country or right out of the city itself.

In a country where over three-fourths of the population now lives in cities though, those who have been internally displaced hardly make up the only new arrivals to Usme. As Colombian scholars such as Andrés Salcedo have carefully documented, even the outlines of "forced" migration are anything but clear, and in reality most migrants have been motivated by some continuum of interests that can include physical insecurity in the countryside, economic opportunities in the cities, and reunification with previously dislocated family networks.[15] Whatever their reasons for arrival, this continuous, rapid influx of people has made Usme both a vibrant social space as well as a place of continued contestation. Within its borders, through the experiences that its residents carry with them into it, one might manage to see the entire history of Colombia and because of them, despite its marginal location, Usme sits at the very center of its many histories of power. As others have much more expansively argued, this is hardly unique to Usme; indeed, it represents a dynamic common to many impoverished, peripheral zones of Latin American cities. On the one hand, such communities are magnetic for public debate because they contrast with more normative visions of cityscapes and they represent proximity to issues such as poverty, race, and other forms of violence, making them symbolically central to radical critiques. On the other hand, people in these areas survive largely because residents of them are so adept at making them function, usually by tying themselves into broader schemes of power and profit.[16] In other words, living on the "margins" of the city is a deeply contradictory affair: there is exclusion in multiple forms from social and political life, but a simultaneous inclusion into other systems of power as well.

While Usme might not be entirely unique in this regard then, there is still something viscerally evocative about how marginalization in Usme is displayed, every single day, and the sights that flank its northern entrance are hardly innocent reminders. Put together with other routine performances, such as stop-and-frisk or document checks in the terminal station of the Transmilenio, or even less frequent rides out from that station to Usme's more distant reaches, each element helps to build a perversely rich experience of exclusion.[17] La Picota, "the Pillory," one of the city's largest prisons, opens up right onto the main avenue leading into Usme, and every Saturday and Sunday the families and friends of its residents line up to make the most of their limited visitation hours. Along with the military base, these sites reinforce not only a geographic marginality but also a social one in what is often labeled by outsiders as a *zona roja* (red zone). In this case "red" implies not just a routine insecurity but also the left-leaning politics of the region, a not-so-subtle reference to some of the Marxist guerrilla groups that were formed not far from Usme's borders, and it confers an especially transgressive, dangerous reputation on the area. The term is one that I heard often, from the first time that I stepped off of a bus in Usme Centro and an outreach worker from the city's public health department told me to "keep open the eyes on the back of my head," whenever I told people where in the city I lived. Notably, it is a term that I have never heard a resident of Usme use with any real sincerity. In addition to the military base and the prison there is the landfill Doña Juana, a dump that fills the valley between Usme and Ciudad Bolívar and has for a long time served as the only trash repository for all of Bogotá. In a material sense, Doña Juana is seen as a direct threat to the environmental integrity of the area, and with good reason too

after an explosion in 1997 caused a major spill of its contents into the Tunjuelito River.[18] On a more symbolic order though, it is also often seen, along
with La Picota, as an affront to the dignity of Usme's residents, proof that
they are seen as the *desechables*, the "throw-aways" of the city.[19]

If the prison, military base, and landfill are material signifiers of marginality, then the cement plants, brick factories, quarries, and arable land,
not to mention the updated public transportation of the Transmilenio system, all signal important ties that connect the district to the rest of the city
in vital ways. Moreover, they begin to tell the ways in which Bogotá has not
only exercised political control over Usme but also depended heavily on
Usme throughout the preceding centuries of their coevolution as well. In
one sense, given that Usme is still a predominantly rural area, its relationship to the rest of the city has historically been one of agricultural production, as the supply of foodstuffs from Usme has literally fed the growth of
Bogotá.[20] This was especially true for the hundreds of years before it was
officially incorporated into the city, when Usme was a changing mixture of
Muisca settlements and colonizing haciendas, growing staple crops like potatoes and beans or raising livestock for sale. Today's quarries, most of
which operated illegally until recently, have begun to compete for this terrain, threatening to steal out from underneath the feet of residents the very
land on which more traditional livelihoods have been made.[21] If Usme previously supplied the food that fed the residents of the rest of the city, today it
also provides the raw materials that feed the insatiable construction industries that continue to build it. From the quarries to the brick makers to the
cement plants, these industries are essential to the massive construction enterprises that dominate the Bogotá economy, one that continually grows in
order to try to meet the ever-present influx of new people.

These industries are not just abstract entities in Usme though: they were
the basis of the livelihoods for many of the people I knew. It is in these very
industries that many of the men that I met had made their living, and even
some, like Nicolás, had done so from a very young age. Born and raised in
Usme, Nicolás had left his own violent home at the age of nine, fleeing a tyrant
of a stepfather and camping in the hills for years with other friends his age,
drinking and experimenting with drugs at night, working in the quarries
for less than minimum wage during the day. Looking back he had no regrets
about it, about trading the blows of his stepfather for the verbal assaults of
his new bosses, or trading the physical insecurity within his home for the
material insecurity of his newly precarious life. To trade the rage of this

stepfather for the grinding labor of excavating the earth was to substitute one form of violence for another, sure, but according to him at least at night his friends and his *basuco* could help him forget. I myself would come to know Nicolás many years later, after he had already come down from living in the hills, had moved back into his childhood home, had cowered his stepfather into quiescence, had begun dating someone and inflicting on her a violence similar to what he had experienced growing up, had received an order of protection from his partner and seen her leave his life. Amid all of these changes, and the crisis of reflection that they brought with them, there was one relative constant for Nicolás: his work. Always finding some kind of employment in the extractive industries that make up Usme's economy, even while he found his own home in a perpetual state of dissolution, he was at least able to earn an income by building up the houses of others.

In the broader case of Usme, its residents have provided not only the raw materials for this construction but also the labor force to put them to use, the food to feed those who occupy those homes, the security guards to watch over their doors, and the domestic workers to clean up inside. If it was not in the quarries then it was in these other economies that many of the people with whom I worked—perpetrators and victims of partner violence alike—made their living. One way or another, most people made their way by sustaining the lives of others. And it is in part through economies like these, and all of their forms of exploitation, that residents of Usme not only made their living but also fought against their marginalization as well, staking their relevance by making themselves known. It is indeed through their very labors that Usminians have always been indispensable producers on which broader economies have been maintained.[22] Together they have not only sustained individual livelihoods but also helped to build the largest city in Colombia. In doing so they contributed to more than just economic axes of power. As some Colombian scholars have argued, beside just serving as the home of the country's federal government, it is the very scale of Bogotá that has helped to maintain its social centrality in an otherwise deeply divided land.[23] By building that city into what it is today, whether intentionally or not, residents of Usme have both worked themselves into local and global economies and also even placed themselves at the very core of Colombia's nation-building project. No small feat for an honest day's work.

Already, this tangle of conflicting histories, these contestations that have come to bear on making Usme what it is today, begins to hint at how Usme is represented by a dense nexus of social relations, of intersecting systems. It also begins to show how marginalization and exploitation, exclusion and inclusion, are not mutually exclusive terms; they can instead be mutually reinforcing processes bound up in broader projects of power. Even just keeping a wide-eyed view on the bus ride down into Usme can tell us as much. Eventually though we do have to get off and walk around, and in order to begin to understand how partner violence actually arises within this complex milieu, that is exactly what we must do. If the intimate acts of partner violence are inseparable from the contexts in which they are committed, we must be able to make meaningful connections between them. This first pass into Usme only begins to put some of these processes side by side; it does not even begin to put them meaningfully together. To juxtapose various forms of violence is not to make facile implications about the causation of one by the other, but to begin to build a vocabulary with which to engage the phenomenology of it, how one comes to happen in any particular place. In order to begin to tie those threads together, however, requires an even deeper dive: first into the history of a place that at this point has only been cursorily described, and later into the experiences of the people who have made up these conflicts through the trajectories of their lives. The rest of this chapter will serve to perform the former, and the rest of the book is an extended exploration into the latter. From in between them, we may more readily see the broader dynamics of partner violence. From this very brief intro into Usme, we can now more fruitfully proceed.

The Uses of Usme: Bogotá's Intimate Colony

Before there were social encounters there were geological ones, and it only seems appropriate that the area that is today called Usme sits at the transition point between the highland moors of Sumapaz and the high plains of the altiplano mesa. This juncture and its surrounding areas first became populated in the early Holocene era, though the groups that would later be known as "Muisca" would not arrive until three to seven thousand years ago. With their arrival came the introduction of the Chibcha language—"Muisca" being a derivative of "Moxca," meaning "people" in Chibcha; "Usme" being a derivative of one of their political leaders, "Usminia"—as well as a transition from hunting and gathering to agricultural production, and that created new social arrangements organized hierarchically under chieftainships. These legacies and their contemporary construal can still be seen today: plants that were domesticated during this period remain as staples in the diets of Bogotanos, a rediscovered ancient burial ground delayed for a time the advancement of new construction in Usme, in the department of Boyacá a lunar and solar calendar stands testament to the centrality that agriculture had in both commercial and religious life, and even a salt mine from the Muiscan era can still be visited in the now-converted "Salt Cathedral."[24] To see the hierarchies of the time, one need only follow the gold, in this case all the way to the Bank of the Republic's Gold Museum in the center of Bogotá, a place where the golden ornamentation worn by Muiscan *caciques* has been collected and displayed. Today these works of art stand testament to not only the concentration of power and wealth that developed within Muisca groups, as well as the technological evolutions achieved during those periods, but also the later relationships that ultimately led to their removal and relocation into what is today a national museum.

These relationships of dispossession and exploitation were, of course, realized through the colonial encounter, or, as Orlando Fals Borda called it, the "colonial subversion," a period of time in which the place that later became Usme was a major site of contestation.[25] For one, when Gonzalo Jiménez de Quesada first arrived in Muiscan territory, what his conquistadors and he encountered was not a unified Muiscan society. While tied together through a common language and shared histories, as a unified political organization "Muisca" did not precede the Spanish conquest. Like so many other collective identities, "Muisca" did not precede the colonial encounter but emerged directly through it.[26] What existed at the turn of the sixteenth century was instead a vast population divided into loyalties between four confederations, historical divisions that the category of "Muisca" today tends to obscure, and the conquistadors attempted to exploit the tensions between these sovereigns. Ultimately, through the all-too-familiar means of the killing of chieftains and the importation of foreign diseases, the Muisca did not prevail, and over the following centuries a progressive overwriting of their social orders ensued. Of particular relevance here were the transitions from a tributary system of agricultural production to the political economy of the *latifundia* hacienda system, as well as the supplanting of the hierarchies created within the Muisca groups with more decidedly Catholic ones instead.

The conversion to the new political economy happened in both fast and slow ways. Initially came the first wave of dispossession and redistribution of land into *encomiendas*, tracts of land parceled out to the various

conquistadors that arrived first to the Andean region. By the conclusion of
the sixteenth century, those tracts had already been enclosed into the vast
haciendas under which indigenous peoples were subordinated to work, and
whatever remained was either used for mining or turned into indigenous
reservations. The slower invasion of land happened over the course of centuries and was primarily carried out by poorer Spanish descendants, those who
progressively migrated to Usme, mixed with Muisca peoples, and, through de
facto tenancy of land, chipped away at what little remained of the reservations. This individualization of collective land later allowed the larger land-
holders to buy up new parcels and expand their territories, the result of which
was the decline of the reservations in the eighteenth century and their near
total obsolescence by the middle of the next. Now basically the sole model of
economic organization in Usme, the otherwise landless—Muisca, mestizo,
poor Spanish—had little choice other than to sell their labor for wages and
rent small pieces of land for their own subsistence crops, a nominally mixed-
economy method of production that clearly signaled the early separations in
ownership of capital. Beside producing new configurations of social relations, the hacienda owners (*hacendados*) also stood at the helm of producing
much of the food required to feed what was at first the growing colony and
later the independent nation, in particular its eventual capital city just to the
north. The hacendados did so, unsurprisingly, under exacting demands and
excruciatingly unequal relationships that allowed them to set the prices of
commodities, charge fees for renters to have their own animals, and even
require that half of what workers grew for themselves, in addition to what
they cultivated through their waged labor, be relinquished to them, the
owners of the land. So extreme became this stratification of power that it
became self-limiting in production, as Alfred Hettner, a German traveler to
the region at the end of the nineteenth century, noted:

> Most of the area that makes up the mountains around Bogotá al-
> ready has an owner. . . . It is with the masters and landowners where
> lies the greater part of the responsibility for the social situation . . .
> because instead of lifting those under their command, today many
> still remained determined not to let it thrive in order to continue
> exploiting it for their own benefit. There are cases in which the owner
> is opposed to a tenant buying another head of cattle or cultivating
> over a broader surface of land. Small landowners, instead, are pre-
> vented from engaging in the production of exportable goods.[27]

With these stratifications of power came new problems. The institution-alized hierarchies that emerged through the evolution of the hacienda system in Usme could not just exist nakedly as such: it had to be justified in some way. In colonial Usme, as it was for most of Latin America, much of this justification found its home within the church, and what Fals Borda makes clear in his epochal reconstruction of Colombian history is that what he called the colonial subversion was most of all a *Catholic* subversion. At its core was the objective of the colonization of consciousness as well as the creation of a society organized around those principles.[28] The conquest, he argues, was profoundly shaped by the piety of Queen Isabella of Castille, who saw the opportunity for colonial rule as a mystic reward for those who had taken religion out of the monasteries and into the battlefield. It was a chance to create a new world order at all levels, a Christian one, from state apparatuses to popularly held beliefs. From this came the central components of what Fals Borda argues are the two most important ideas to emerge during this period: first, a rigid division of labor propagated across generations as a morally justified way of life, and second, urban concentrations as the mode of civilized life. Taken together, these formed what he calls "caste urbanism," and what it amounted to was a very particular *Pax Hispanica* in which submission was the intended moral order. Even in a very physical sense these ideas were enacted through the reorganization of social space with towns now built on a gridiron with a central plaza, and in every plaza the construction of a church, with Usme representing no exception to this rule.

None of this is to suggest that hierarchy was a new concept to the area, as it had existed as well within Muiscan groups prior to the arrival of the Spanish. But whereas sovereignty under Muisca chieftains had been mediated by agreement and a complex system of gift exchanges, under the new order it was to be sustained instead by naturalized presumptions of superiority. It is even worth noting that the very term "hierarchy" has origins within the Catholic Church, originally referring to a social stratification based on a presumed proximity to God, and these were the pretenses that were to pro-actively justify the organization of the Catholic colonial order. Beyond the political, class, and ethnic lines of distinction produced from this philosophy were also the crucially gendered dimensions that this sanctified hegemony took as well. Given the doctrine of a "father" above and the institutionalized privileging of men within the Church itself—priests themselves being referred to as "fathers"—it takes little imagination to see how Catholicism

played a role in establishing gendered regimes of power throughout this period and beyond. From the "padres" of the Catholic church to the "patrons"
of the haciendas, even before the official inauguration of the "patria" of the
Colombian state, power along nearly all dimensions had taken decidedly
gendered forms. Hardly relegated to the colonial past, these systems continued through the nation's independence, at which time Colombia was inaugurated as a *masculine* nation, a political collective organized under the
social contract of a self-fashioned paternalistic state.[29]

Taken together, these two issues of political economic restructuring and
the religious ideologies that justified it convey much of the significance of
colonization and how a new, perversely generative, social order was arranged. Most of all it helps to understand who came to manage it. Even if
what later became known as Usme was not at the very geographic center
of what would later become the Colombian state, it was never far from it,
and from the very early stages of defining Colombia, Usme was a centrally
important space in which those broader social arrangements were negotiated. And so even if Usme itself has never really been the seat of sovereign
power in Colombia, these early beginnings show that it has always been a
proximate, even if largely obscured, crucible in the construction of that
cause.

Gaitán, a New Urbanism, and Annexation

If the productive role and colonial urban/rural construction of a place like
Usme can be understood in this way, then understanding how it later came
to be further maligned and marginalized as a zona roja requires picking up
some threads that developed throughout the nineteenth century and reached
their culmination somewhere near the middle of the twentieth. This period
between 1850 and 1930 was a critical time of economic expansion and nation
building for the Colombian state, the era in which key patterns of centralization and exclusion were forged, and what emerged from them was an intensely fragmented state organized heavily around regional governments.[30]
Unlike the federalism of countries like the United States, these concentrations of governance were tied directly to the largest cities themselves, to the
point where mayors of the major metropoles like Bogotá, Cali, and Medellín
still today enjoy some of the greatest authority in the country and often go
on to run in, and win, the presidential election. Beyond geography, by the

1930s Colombia had already also experienced at least three-quarters of a century under the split between the Conservative and Liberal parties, an ongoing manifestation of an incomplete social subversion of the colonial Conservative order.[31] Solidified in the bloodshed of the War of a Thousand Days (1899–1902), this political divide continued to fester throughout the so-called Conservative Peace, coming undone only by the upheaval brought on by the onset in 1929 of the Great Depression.

In trying to explain why these partisan and geographic fault lines of power have been so persistent, many have suggested that the inherently difficult terrain of Colombia has made the domination by any one group exceedingly difficult, but more recently some have begun to call that into question. Rather than seeing this history as the limited realization of a state whose pretensions are to become an all-powerful entity, the common denominator across these eras of Colombian history may instead be an incoherent state that reinforces the imagination of an urban-rural divide, while seeking to maintain power in the former and allowing other actors to regulate the latter.[32] In the colonial era this was accomplished by giving the urban-dwelling hacendados the authority to govern and shape their rural domains as they saw fit, as happened in Usme, whereas during the period from 1850 to 1930 this meant the liberal expansion of rural industries outside of the regulation of the state.[33] Throughout the political conflict of the second half of the twentieth century this evolved into allowing paramilitaries to police the resource-rich areas of the country, reaffirming a system whereby cities were to be managed more exclusively by the state, and rural areas were left to be the subject of "governance by other means."[34] In other words, in Colombia there has long been a system of core-periphery relations with regional capitals as their anchors, a system of contradictory relationships in which productive regions have been tied to areas of accumulation at the same time that their political involvement has remained limited at best. It is a cultivated dynamic whose sum is a more complicated form of domination and control, a mutual dependence based on an incomplete exclusion, and for as long as it has existed Usme has straddled the divide.

Only by appreciating this particular kind of governance, and the central roles that cities have played in Colombian history, is it possible to understand why the 1930s to 1940s was such a crucial era, and why the annexation of Usme in 1954 was so significant to staking national sovereignty in its aftermath. Perhaps the best way to retrace this important era is through the role of one person at the center of it, Jorge Eliécer Gaitán, who was a rising politician, champion of women's advancement in society, and eventual martyr of the Left.[35] Still invoked in graffiti tags around Bogotá, during rallies in the Plaza Bolívar, and by many of those whom I knew in Usme, it is difficult to overestimate the lasting influence that Gaitán has had on Colombia's politics and the organization of its capital city.[36] Originally involved with the socialist movement and mobilization on the country's "periphery"—such as the banana workers' strike, as made famous in Gabriel García Márquez's *One Hundred Years of Solitude*—during the 1930s Gaitán made two critical changes in his tactics to transform Colombia. First, he would come back to Bogotá and eventually serve as the mayor of the city before his fateful presidential run. Second, he would join the Liberal Party and seek to reform it from the inside out, rather than run counter to it through socialist organizations.[37] In the run-up to the presidential election in which he was assassinated, Gaitán was already known as "the people's candidate" and had mobilized voters from the rural areas around Bogotá in a manner never seen before. Along with the northern regions of Boyacá, this included the socialist bastion of Usme/Sumapaz, despite the historic divisions between the Liberal Party and socialist movements earlier in the twentieth century.[38] Following his murder and the riots in Bogotá (the *Bogotazo*), La Violencia commenced and the urban uprising spread out across the country, out of the cities to again incite Liberals and Conservatives to kill one another on massive scales.[39] During the early days of this conflict, Sumapaz—which at the time included Usme—was one of the principal locations to which leftist militants retreated before extending their actions to other regions such as the plains (*llanos*), Tolima, Antioquia, and Santander.[40] In one way then, at this juncture of Colombian history, Usme, this southern finger of Bogotá, was a crucial contact zone of the political conflict. As the use of terms like "zona roja" make clear, in a war that was always supposed to be fought in the countryside, Usme/Sumapaz represented a transgressive region that brought the violence too close to the sanctity of the capital city. At a vulnerable time for the country, it interrupted the imagination of the urban/rural divide, one that had been up to this point carefully cultivated, events like the Bogotazo notwithstanding.[41]

Given this history of the relationship between Usme and the rest of Bogotá up until this point, it may seem counterintuitive that in 1954 Usme was officially incorporated into the city. All the same, barely after the resolution of La Violencia, Usme was annexed along with five other surrounding municipalities (Decree 3463). For over fifty years the populations of these districts, Usme in particular, had swollen as a result of rural dispossession and urban migration, and with these changes anxieties in the capital had continued to grow regarding their expansion and proper planning, accompanied then by a series of laws that were intended to progressively expand Bogotá's dominion over them over time. Their eventual annexation then was neither an isolated event nor an inevitable outcome of their growth: it was a long evolution punctuated by rapid change, an opportunity quickly seized on in the aftermath of a crisis and mobilized to new ends. In seizing these districts, a newly designated Distrito Especial (Special District) of the capital city was made, and the name itself provides much of the clue as to why Usme was included. Still reeling from the shock of the massive scale and widely disseminated nature of the killing in La Violencia, there was an urgency in the interest of national sovereignty and the maintenance of a tentative peace in which the nation's capital would become somehow unique from the other cities that stood at the centers of their respective regions. Increasing the size, legal power, and formal designation under the new title of Distrito Especial afforded Bogotá precisely this status, and annexation was a primary means of accomplishing it. In the process, the move ushered in not only a new designation for the capital city but also a new era for Colombia as one of a truly *modern* state.[42]

Curiously, if not surprisingly, following the annexation Usme received comparatively little attention in the planning of the city. Whereas the historical record shows that the other five newly added districts were the subjects of intense planning, Usme remained noticeably absent from any such designs. While economically Usme continued to be a critical resource for the growth of Bogotá, even under its official incorporation it still remained subject to the same exclusion-exploitation dynamics that had defined its relationship to Bogotá and the rest of the country over the preceding centuries. Renewed interest in the district would not really occur until another vital moment in Colombia's history, around the time of the drafting and adoption of the 1991 constitution.

The 1991 Constitution of Rights
and Participation in the "New" Nation

In the intervening period between these moments, La Violencia and the 1991 Constitution of Rights, there was a protracted process of power redistribution that was advanced on multiple fronts. Even in the most basic sense in Usme, this happened with regard to changing land tenure and began in the middle of the twentieth century with the gradual collapse of the hacienda system. During this time, lands that had once been dispossessed from indigenous groups and *campesinos* were in turn ceded to new immigrants to the district. That the hacienda system even existed up until this point sets Usme apart from some of the other areas in the immediate surrounding area of Bogotá, in particular the department of Cundinamarca in which the hacienda system for coffee cultivation had already collapsed during the onset of the Great Depression.[43] Compared to these other areas, Usme was characterized by the cultivation of potatoes, beans, and other crops that were less directly tied to global markets, and therefore it did not experience this transition of land redistribution until later in the century. When it did, it was because of the continued pressures of urban migration and the development of two competing economies in the district: the existing agricultural cultivation and the creation of the more capital-intensive mining industries. The migration itself not only continued the rural dispossession that had led up to the annexation of Usme in the first place but also was exacerbated by the simmering political conflict that followed La Violencia and accelerated internal displacement. As the urban frontier descended from the north and headed down toward Usme, the haciendas that had previously existed in this area were progressively taken over by those who would go on to work in these new industries and live in rented properties. Elsewhere, farther south in the still rural areas of Usme, other migrants helped to achieve the necessary critical mass to pressure and eventually dispossess the large landowning *latifundistas* in favor of a system of agricultural production organized around the smaller *minifundista* holdings.[44]

In this latter half of the century, forced displacement was not the only means by which the political conflict shaped the development of Usme and its broader perception. When the leftist militant groups that had established themselves after La Violencia survived, so too did the "zona roja" reputation. By the time that 1991 and the drafting of Colombia's new national constitution came around, Colombia as a whole was reaching a climax in its political violence. Innumerable militant groups, between the leftist guerrillas, the paramilitary "autodefensas," drug cartels, and the national military, were now all involved in a conflict characterized by increasingly complex fault lines and zones of engagement. In a conflict that had been previously seen as rural, the operations of cartels in Medellín and Cali and the actions of urban guerrillas like the M-19 in Bogotá had begun to disrupt the neat urban-rural geography of imagination, and this cultivated new fears of urban intrusion. A sort of existential crisis characterized this moment in time, just as a National Constitutional Assembly was convening to imagine what a new Colombia would look like. With the war seeming to escalate endlessly, either at the doorstep of the capital or already inside of it, a better idea of what Usme meant to the rest of the country can perhaps be gleaned from the excerpts of some articles printed in the media at the time:

"Leadership and Solidarity"[45]
"It is a fact: the guerrilla has arrived in Bogotá. A criminal phenomenon that not long ago we thought was remote, peripheral, or residual now knocks furiously on the doors of the city. . . . Acts as terrible as those in Usme, which have happened to hundreds of others and almost daily in the national territory should shudder and move public opinion for a long time."

"Cundinamarca: 30 Municipalities Have a Guerrilla Presence"[46]
"Its strategic position, the proximity of the metropolis and its topography continue turning Cundinamarca into one of the corridors of guerrillas, paramilitaries and drug traffickers. . . . Reports indicate that part of that strategy has been driven by the FARC in Usme, Subachoque, Choachí, Pasca, and Guayabetal where they intend to establish militias."

"The Guerrilla Has Crossed the Line: The Killing in Usme Shows the Level of Brutality That the Guerrilla Coordination Has Come To"[47]

"The Fifth Zone [Usme]: A Quarry of Problems"[48]

"Putting the Brakes on the Invasions"[49]

"The Twentieth Century Has Not Yet Arrived to Usme"[50]

"The JAL of Usme: A Model for Organization"[51]
"What can an ex-guerrillero dedicated now to graphic arts, an office equipment repair technician, a decorator, an employee, two vendors, the leader of a cooperative, and architect, and a peasant have in

common? Superficially, nothing. But putting them together is one of the graces of the invention called the Local Administrative Board [JAL]. The other grace is to get them to agree and organize a development plan for an area like Usme."

"A New History for Bogotá"[52]
"The hour has arrived for the administrative decentralization of the Bogotá. At the beginning of this July, Local Administrative Boards [JALs] will be installed in the twenty districts that make up the Capital District."

Put together, this brief collection of headlines and excerpts begins to build a picture of a complicated yet predominantly negative perception of Usme. The first three refer to various acts of violence that guerrilla groups had begun to commit closer to the city, along its southeastern corridor, and together they demonstrate a double meaning to the phrase "crossed the line." In one sense the line crossed was a moral one. The attacks described in the article "The Guerrilla Has Crossed the Line" related a case where the Fuerzas Armadas Revolucionarias de Colombia (FARC) members had killed a resident of Usme and then planted explosives the next day to blow up the caravan of officials who came out to investigate the incident. While another journalist recognized that these kinds of acts and worse had been happening around the country, there was still a sense that the cold calculation of the attack had somehow crossed yet another threshold. Perhaps more significantly, the line crossed by these attacks was a geographic one. These recent acts shocked the urban conscience in Bogotá to see the threat of militarized violence in the city as coming not only from self-fashioned urban groups like the cartels or M-19 but also from groups with a profoundly rural self-identification like the FARC. By operating in Usme, the FARC was crossing a geopolitical threshold that had been very deliberately constructed over a long period of time, and through annexation in 1954 it had even been coupled to national sovereignty through the creation of the Distrito Especial. That these FARC attacks crossed into districts like Usme was an affront to that very project, at a time when a new constitution was being drafted in that same city, no less.

When Usme was not being portrayed as an active threat to the security of social and political life, then the next few articles show it being cast as a collection of problems, even a "quarry of problems," that required attention.

From the threat of "land invasions" to the absence of social services or basic infrastructure like potable water, the underlying message remained the same: Usme is the rural and backward "other" that, despite its proximity to the rest of Bogotá, had still been somehow left behind somewhere in the nineteenth century. Even when the authors of these articles were a bit more generous and acknowledged the historic role that Usme had played in feeding the rest of the city, the implicit comparison to a modern and progressive urban core remained the same. By casting Usme as not the city's breadbasket but rather its quarry of problems, Usme was maintained as the infantilized, despondent neighbor in desperate need of Bogotá's rescuing. In reestablishing this dynamic, be it through militarized imposition or the support of social programming, the patronizing overtones that had always defined Usme's relationship with Bogotá were soundly reaffirmed. It was mostly in this way then, that at the time of the drafting of the new constitution, Usme and the rest of Bogotá, indeed in many ways the rest of the country, were mutually constructed in each other's image. If Bogotá represented the seat of a sovereign nation, then Usme was its frontier zone with the dangerous and rural guerrilla. If Bogotá was the modernizing and progressive center of the country, then Usme was its "backward" and problem-ridden neighbor, even if the truth was that Usme was already a part of the city itself.

Despite the predominantly condescending gaze given to Usme though, there were some notable exceptions, and ones that themselves motioned to broader aspirations in the redistributive politics of the time.[53] This was the case with the Local Administrative Boards (JALs) and how they had been employed in Usme as a tool for greater local control over the allocation of resources. As the last two articles illustrate, this use of the JAL in Usme not only was a model for the development of other similar councils, something that was actually included in the new constitution itself but also reflected the broader impetus to decentralizing power that also characterized this period. This was, if anything, the major philosophical ideal behind the political restructuring of the early 1990s and, ever the microcosm, the developments in Usme up until this point illustrate these ambivalent tendencies. On the one hand, there were the redistribution of land and the invocation of the JAL; on the other, the growth of capital-intensive transnational industry and militarized intervention. In this conflicted period of political change then, one is left to ask, what did the constitution of 1991 really represent?

In many ways it is impossible to separate the constitution of 1991, alternatively known as the Constitution of Rights, from other concurrent or soon-to-follow changes in Colombia. These included the structural adjustment programs that were being imposed by entities such as the World Bank, as well as the multitude of changes to social services such as the health care system (Ley 100) or the subsequent institution of new services like the Comisarías de Familia (Ley 294). The new constitution itself was born out of an adoption of international rights discourses, led by political mobilizations in the late 1980s that sought to increase citizen participation in politics as well as break the institutionalized corruption that had accrued over a century of bureaucratic clientelism. In it, values like the preservation of a "dignified life" for all citizens were declared and new legal tools like the *tutela* were instituted to ensure that citizens' rights would not be denied; these tools continue to be used today, especially with regard to the health care system.[54] Perhaps in a basic philosophical sense, the economic structural adjustments that were also implemented during this period followed from a similar impetus of decentralizing power away from the central state.[55] Rather than borrowing from a human rights discourse, however, they drew their inspiration from a neoliberal one that was being implemented in countries around all of Latin America. Instead of drawing their force from popular mobilization, their pressure came from transnational institutions such as the World Bank and International Monetary Fund, to whom Colombia and most of the rest of Latin America had defaulted on loans following the "lost decade" of the 1980s. The history of this transition and its effects on socioeconomic well-being in Colombia and Latin America have been well documented, paralleling the experiences elsewhere in the world of persistent or growing inequality along economic dimensions of social life.[56]

From this "lost decade" and the subsequent neoliberal turn, another less likely series of transformations emerged: these were new and more complex collective mobilizations, particularly along gendered and ethnic lines. As scholars of social movements and popular protest in Latin America, Colombia included, have noted, the neoliberal turn also had the effect of "thickening" civil society and leading to the organization of more diverse sets of actors in making claims on the state.[57] Out of the constitution of 1991 emerged not only a new set of laws but also a new kind of *constitutionalism* and organization of subaltern groups. In Colombia this was especially important for the mobilization of indigenous groups, but this process of decentralizing power was also carried out along profoundly gendered dynamics as well, themselves the result of feminist movements that had long been developing in the region.[58] Those preceding feminist movements in Latin America had been heavily influenced by the histories of militarized political repression, especially in countries such as Chile and Argentina, and many of the mobilizations grew out of previous social actions where women leveraged their more traditional roles as mothers, sisters, and wives to make claims on authoritarian regimes. These became the bases of regionalized movements that progressed to make more direct and subversive claims about gender norms themselves, as well as admix with other resistance movements in creative ways.

One major turning point for this transition came in July 1981 when the first *encuentro* of the Feminist Conference of Latin America and the Caribbean convened in Bogotá, a series of hemispheric conferences that continues to this day. By establishing at this first conference November 25th of each year as the International Day for the Elimination of Violence Against Women, the marker for addressing gender relations themselves and gender-based violence was effectively set.[59] The forms of violence under scrutiny were no longer restricted to those of repressive state regimes but rather the daily abuses of women. Over the course of the ensuing decade these mobilizations would continue to mature and in the 1990s also lead to legally institutionalized reforms such as the establishment of agencies like the Comisarías de Familia (to address partner violence) and the Secretaría de la Mujer (for programming new economic opportunities and other forms of support). And so even while the 1991 constitution famously reaffirmed the family as "the fundamental nucleus of society," such proclamations, and the political imaginings that they represented, cannot be so easily taken for granted.[60]

At the same time that these feminist movements were growing in scale and scope, Latin America was also collectively going through its "lost decade" economically, and the triumphant attitude of capitalist countries elsewhere around the world was not experienced in the same way in the region. One synthesis that emerged out of this juncture was the weaving of a new form of Marxist-feminism that did not only preference the former.[61] In this particular Latin American revision, this became a synthesis where feminist issues were no longer thought of as distractions to the "real" economic causes of suffering and inequality. Instead it was argued that feminist concerns could play instrumental, indeed indispensable roles in the subversion of power along many of its various dimensions, and that such resistances must necessarily be intersectional in their approaches.[62] The enduring influences of this can still be seen today in Colombia, echoed in everyday expressions such as graffitied slogans in Bogotá like *"sin mujer no hay revolución"* as well as the following media coverage during the 2014 International Day for the Elimination of Violence Against Women: "The invitation is also that men participate in these mobilizations, to unite forces and understand that this fight is not just for women but also a joint effort. For Laura Blandón, to go out in the street 'is an issue that concerns us as the people and as the popular classes in resistance. To denounce that we are exploited, marginalized, and impoverished.' In addition, it is necessary to understand that, 'the fight of women is the fight of the popular class, without the liberation of women there cannot be liberation of all the people.'"[63]

Rather than placing class struggle *before* the struggle for gender equality, these comments reflect a view that had been thoroughly elaborated throughout this preceding period: that these struggles are intricately interwoven and mutually reinforcing, that class conflict cannot be resolved without addressing women's liberation as well. In them, this person reminds us that the achievements of these movements have not been limited to just the passage of various legal statutes. Instead, they live on in enduring shifts in belief about what power should mean and what resistance can look like on many different scales.

Taking all of these dimensions of reform together, the period of the 1990s was a complex era, where some of the previously constructed ideologies were questioned and the role of spaces such as Usme came under vigorous reconsideration.[64] Since the era of the colonial subversion, Colombia as a modern nation had been recursively built around an idea of Colombia as a *masculine* nation, buttressed by a long history of legitimizing logics such as paternalistic benevolence and moments of violent intervention, a topic to which I will return in greater detail in the following chapters. Perhaps of all the dimensions by which these concentrations of power were questioned then, the contestation over gendered relations brought this basis of Colombian society into clearest view and illuminated the broader scope of what was at stake in moving toward more decentralized systems of power. Over this period of time, however, there occurred not only ideological shifts but also an ongoing political conflict that continued to shake Colombia to its core. How the legacies of these contemporaneous processes have carried together into the present day, and what they mean for living in La Zona Quinta, not to mention how they might help us to understand the everyday realities of partner violence in such a setting, remains a topic yet to be explored.

The Fragmentation and Militarization of Everyday Life

Jairo is late. It isn't the lateness that worries me though: it's the nagging suspicion that I have picked the wrong corner. Pacing around, trying not to look lost, I eye some arepas heating over a grill. Finding men to work with had so far been difficult; people willing to open up about the abuse that they had committed were even rarer than I had thought. In that regard Jairo had been an exception, and having already gone through a number of interviews with him I am eager to finally meet with him out in the community, somewhere outside the walls of the libraries where we had previously met. To have this day be a lost opportunity would make for a very bad omen, and a missed connection here would be a major blow.

Just so, I spy him slowly making his way up past the stalls, bumping into vendors and passersby, greeting each one as if he had stumbled onto a long-lost friend. In my anxiety I had almost forgotten how gregarious he is. It turns out that in the end he wasn't so much late as he was detained. "You like arepas?" he calls out to me. Clearly he spotted my wandering eye. "Eat one every day," I smile back his way. "Well, you haven't lived until you've had arepas de choclo, John, finding the good ones though, that's the tricky part. One time when I was on deployment outside of Pereira . . . ," he trails off. With the understanding that maybe these particular corn cakes aren't worth our trouble, we set off, making our way further down Caracas before turning to hike up Avenida Boyacá. Even having lived in Bogotá for a while now, I'm reminded again of the altitude.

A former army medic, Jairo had just recently come to live in the city. Following his military service he had returned to Meta province just long enough to train as a nurse, and for the ten years or so afterward he had worked on an endless rotation of infrastructure projects out in the Colombian countryside. Somewhere along the way he had met his current partner here in Bogotá and, a bit unexpectedly, they had had two children. With both of them now in primary school, after years of being gone for long stretches of time he and his partner decided that he needed to come back and live with them, full time, in Usme. Set up in the barrio of Santa Librada, part of the northern and more urban part of the district, the last year had been a trying one to say the least, one that was characterized by escalating conflict and, eventually, outright physical abuse. Jairo and I had come to meet sometime after the order of protection, and after sitting face-to-face for so many sessions we were both eager to get out and explore around his community. He never invited me into his home though, and whether or not this was because of his irrepressible urge to go out and explore, or if it was the result of a barrier that we never overcame, I still do not know.

Making our way up the hill toward the Cerros, between gasps of breath that I try to casually hide, I ask him about his upcoming job as an outreach nurse. "It's exciting, John, it's like nothing that I've gotten a chance to do before, working with homeless patients, and the leader of our group is the director of the whole program, someone high up there. Buddy-buddy with the mayor from what I've heard, apparently they go way back, maybe even back to when he was in M-19 but who really knows." I try to sneak in a follow-up question but before I can Jairo has already moved on. "Look over there, John, you see that guy hanging out by the bridge? You have to look out for people like that. They'll have one person on each side of the bridge and when you're in the middle of it they'll collapse in on you. That's how they don't let you escape, that's how they get people, you can't 'dar papaya' like that. Always be on the lookout."

I see what he means, or at least I think I do. At the entrance of a pedestrian overpass for the four-lane road is a man on a phone, standing disinterestedly at the foot of the staircase. On the other end there's nobody, or at least no one obviously loitering around, but suspended twenty feet over a busy avenue on a two-meter-wide path I can certainly see his point. Having already myself gone through the Bogotá rite of passage that is getting mugged, I find myself surprisingly open to taking his advice. "It's only getting worse, you know," he adds, "what they're doing with demobilization is great and all but the influx of 'desmovilizados' is only making places like this worse. I mean, I don't blame them, you live your whole life as a guerrillero, that's all you know, then the government gives you an apartment in the city with no one you know around you and what would you do? I feel bad for them but at the same time . . . ," he trails off again.

Turning northward, back toward Santa Librada, we make our way down a residential street as Jairo goes on to point out the sites of various recent crimes. Larceny, fights, even a murder a few months back: every corner seems to be marked by the stain of some kind of recent altercation. "Did you know that one of those robberies they caught on camera?" he asks. I hadn't. For that matter I hadn't heard of the thievery to begin with. I'm starting to realize that my ear is not nearly as close to the ground of street crime as maybe it should be. "Yeah, there was a guy with a surveillance camera over his door that happened to catch them on his feed. I don't remember if the quality was good enough for them to blow it up and actually identify the people, but I've been thinking for a while about getting a set of my own for our house. I just need to do a little research. There are a lot of pricey ones out there but I think if I look into it enough I can get a good set for a reasonable price, maybe even some with night vision. I might know a guy who can help. What to do with the recordings though I haven't figured out yet, maybe just having some cameras will be enough of a deterrent even if they don't actually work, just have a light that stays on and some signs posted up. I'm telling you, after dark around here you have to be careful, I make sure my kids aren't ever out after dinner."

We walk on, and over the next hour or so we wind our way through his neighborhood, making our way past streams and up staircase sidewalks that I hardly knew existed. Talking more about the everyday dangers of his barrio and how he navigates them, I never manage to steer us back to his upcoming job, his children's schooling, or how he and his partner are now getting on. I'm finally starting to see how nearly all-consuming security, a subject we never really addressed before, is for him, as his upcoming occupation will have him navigating the streets of Usme's neighboring districts. Not to be fully deterred by it, he is still more than happy, compelled even, to go on and get out there, his gusto for striking out in new directions impossible to miss. Still, those preoccupations are always right there, a central part of navigating those new experiences and protecting his family back home. No matter how hard I try he won't let it go.

* * *

Remaking Colombia in the aftermath of over a half century of open and clandestine warfare requires not only the rightful restitution of rural lands but also the establishment of meaningful rights to the city. It requires looking for the many ways by which the legacy of this multipolar civil war has become embroiled in the much longer histories through which Usme has been formed. And so before ceding way to the stories and experiences of the survivors and perpetrators of partner violence, there is one final aspect of everyday life in Usme that warrants its own attention: the ways in which Colombia's political conflict have more presently come to shape it. Some of

them have already been alluded to, but while the specific details of the political conflict have not been the focus here, there is no way to deny that
Usme has been profoundly altered by its broader effects. When over five
million people have been internally displaced in Colombia, when over three-
fourths of Colombian citizens live in cities, and when Usme has the fastest
rate of growth in Bogotá due to that migration, there is simply no escaping
this.[65] If Usme has always been a zone of encounter and contest, then this
has only been further intensified by this more recent history of violence: it
has become part of the extension of warfare as everyday politics by other
means.[66]

In the most obvious ways, the echoes of this conflict are seen in the amputations suffered from land-mine explosions. They are heard when personal
stories of the "disappeared" intrude into otherwise benign conversations,
doing so either through tears that cannot be held back or through stories
whispered delicately behind turned backs. They are felt in the paralysis of
painful flashbacks that the presence of the national police can trigger, and
they are evident in the milieu of retired soldiers that fill the ranks of private
security firms. To be reminded every single day to "no dar papaya" is to be
reminded that many of the "demilitarized" groups have become part of a
new wave of organized crime, helping to make the urban landscape a constantly shifting array of unseen dangers to navigate.[67] The general disposition of distrust that this weariness could sow was both profound and plainly
evident living in Usme, and combined with migration, with its dislocation
from previous systems of social support, it can help to create a particularly
powerful kind of social isolation for many of Usme's newest members. It was
this isolation in fact that found itself at the center of so many stories of survivors and perpetrators of partner violence alike, as will later be explored;
alienation from one's neighbors, the seemingly infinite individuation of the
community in which one lived, all of it became a part of the experiences of
intimate abuse in a multitude of ways. It reflected one of the most internalized forms of fragmentation wrought upon the residents of Usme to be sure,
but distrust and dislocation were not the only means by which this district
has been further subdivided.

The fault lines that have emerged over the course of this history of conflict have even inscribed themselves in the most physical sense on communities, and nowhere was this more evident than the area of Usme Centro
where I lived.[68] Within only a half kilometer of the main plaza, now nearly
five hundred years old, was the arable land of small farms, apartment blocks

barely a couple of decades old, and most recently the rapidly constructed apartment complexes meant to absorb the continued waves of urban migration. Both within and between these more obvious frontiers, a finer handiwork of social differentiation could also be found. Looked down upon the most were the newest apartment projects—both figuratively and literally as they had been built down at the base of the ravine—and it was only by living in a sublet room of one of these apartments myself that I learned how not all complexes were looked down upon equally. On the one hand were the better-constructed ones that lay closer to the plaza; on the other were the subsidized homes that got placed at the very end of the dead-end road. "Don't ever go down there," I was repeatedly told, often by those who lived in the older houses and farms, "that's where the government placed many of the desmovilizados." With an almost whispered quality, that last word, meaning "demobilized," generally referred to any nonstate former combatant and carried the connotation of the ultimate transgression, the greatest threat of future criminality. To go around where desmovilizados lived was to court trouble, it was to "dar papaya" in the most foolish way possible. Again though, not everyone in Usme Centro is equally maligned. There always seemed to be another wedge to drive, and this applied to the demobilized as well.

As another confidante told me, while we were sitting in her living room at the edge of one of the older farms, there were the demobilized and the *demobilized*. There were those who had come from the old families of Usme, the lineages that had for generations done the arduous work of tilling the land, and then there were those who came from all other parts of the country, who had ended up in Usme only by some series of accidents of fate and the limited options they had been left with. The former were often quickly and quietly reintroduced into the everyday flows of life, but the latter were seen as the unceremoniously discarded, a burden for the community somehow to bear. The key therefore was not so much the actions of one's past as it was one's sharing of heritage, inclusion into earlier collective memories and experiences and, from them, the possibility of reintegration into existing social networks. It was a question of *comunitas*, and the distinction bore an early insight to the pitfalls that lie ahead in the implementation of peace accords with groups like the FARC. It was in this way that I learned that not all new housing constructions were equally unwelcomed, that not all demobilized were thought to be equally dangerous, and that across the crucible of Usme it is almost always possible to find another means of social differentiation. Even in this peripheral district there was always someone a little more marginalized, and one could always continue the work of elaborating the complex lines of fracture that spread within its space.

Beyond these contourings of social relations, also relevant to an understanding of partner violence in Usme are the more direct ways by which these histories have in one way or another worked themselves into the dynamics of this intimate abuse. Just how such a thing might happen is a subject of much active debate, and with regard to the legacy of the political conflict, this phenomenon of violence moving from spaces of open warfare into the spaces of intimate relationships is one that has been observed across contexts around the world. Overall, postconflict societies do generally seem to experience rises in partner violence following resolution of the warfare, and few urban areas have been shaped so profoundly by these legacies as Usme.[69] Some theories as to why this happens focus on the communication between militarized conflicts and gendered identities writ large, the building of "militarized masculinities" that creep from the more limited spaces of combat into more broadly held beliefs.[70] Others, including even Frantz Fanon, have focused on how male heads of household themselves carry into domestic spaces the experiences of their militarized lives and, in doing so, more directly mediate that diffusion of violence from zones of combat and into more quotidian places.[71] One of the most memorable reminders that I had of this came on a home visit that I made with a social worker from the Comisaría de Familia. Following up on a case of child abuse, she was making a routine visit to inspect the conditions of the home and conduct a brief interview with the man accused. He had close-cropped hair, spoke in short, direct sentences, and always ended his responses with a respectful "doctora." As we sat with him in his bedroom, and the social worker made her way through her list of required questions, he never lost his posture, his back always ramrod straight, eyes fixed straight ahead, and it was not until halfway through the meeting that I noticed exactly where his eyes had been focused. Across from him, hanging on the wall, was a picture of himself in camouflage fatigues, kneeling on bright green grass, with a grenade launcher gripped firmly in his hands.[72]

All of these different ways by which this conflict has woven itself into everyday life in Usme, creating a continuum between the exceptional violence of war and the everyday violence of partner abuse, are echoed in some way in the chapters that follow.[73] By situating this more recent influence on social life in Usme in the deeper histories that have constituted this district though, we avoid any simplistic notion that partner violence in Usme is merely epiphenomenal to the effects of the political conflict. From these longer histories we have seen the recursive accretion and contestation of many forms of power. They will all find themselves relevant to the intimate dynamics of abuse. From the paternalistic ideologies of authority to feminist resistances against them, from the contradictory means of consolidating domination to the fragmentation of social life, all of these will become recurring themes in understanding the lifeworlds of survivors of abuse, the perpetrators of it, and the professionalized work of those who are charged with responding to it. But reaching a fuller appreciation of the many ways by which these histories have worked themselves into intimate relationships will require a much finer lens into the lives of those involved. It is through a selection of their stories, meant to be illustrative and exemplary rather than representative or exceptional, that a more detailed exploration of these connections can be made. Without further ado, it is to their stories that I now finally turn.

CHAPTER 2

Possible

Cambiar de dueño no es ser libre.

—Jose Martí

Feminism is all about making connections.

—Angela Davis

Today the parking lot is empty, its small and undulating hills of brick devoid of life. One year ago when I first met Luz Elena, it was here on the tenth anniversary of the legalization of her barrio. In front of this packed row of houses, matches of micro-fútbol alternated with choreographed dances as "vallenato," "cumbia," and "salsa" sang out from a stack of speakers. She had taken me from this parking lot to walk around the community, down to the river and past the farms that lay just beyond the plaza. She taught me about the mining in the hills, what "arvejas" look like when they are ripe on the vine, and how Sundays are the best days to buy chucula, when the chocolate is freshly pressed with cinnamon and clove. A Scouts leader, community organizer, mother, seamstress, UNICEF volunteer, and impromptu caretaker of young children, Luz, more than any other person, taught me what it is like to live in Usme. Most often, these were lessons that she delivered on foot.

Today we are going to visit El Tuno, an area of recent settlement that she herself does not know. Approaching her home, the only person interrupting the vacancy of the lot is a woman, young, in her twenties, balancing an infant on her hip in front of Luz's front door. After she sizes me up, she begins into a litany of questions just as Luz calls down that she is ready to leave. Before Luz is out the door, I barely manage to find out her name, Katerin, and that she recently moved from Medellín and is staying with her aunt, who is Luz's roommate, Angelica, who herself was one of the first people I met in Usme. Luz introduces us again, and when Katerin asks how we know each other Luz gives her a measured look. A smile starts at the corner of her eyes, folding together those familiar grooves that have been formed over the better part of a century. Slowly that smile curls up the sides of her mouth: pure mischief. After a little hesitation, Luz leans forward and tells her matter-of-factly that she is my grandmother. Incredulous, Katerin eyes me again and when I confess that I am actually a student working in the community, she laughs off the strange little ruse.

When Luz and I turn away and start down the street, she immediately becomes more serious. "John, she has me exasperated. She has three kids and sometimes she just lets the youngest one cry. Why does she have children if she can't take care of them?"

I ask her why Katerin left Medellín in the first place, and when Luz tells me it was a problem with her partner her tone tells the rest of what she herself would rather not say. We push up the hill, past the grinding of mechanics and the wafts of freshly baked bread, losing our breath to the altitude. We change topics, pushing on from Katerin to some other neighbors of hers. As we roll past the last of the cantinas, we make our way along the edge of the valley, onward toward other settlements. Still, as we move forward, I keep thinking back to where we began. I am unable to let it go.

"Luz, why do you think you never had problems with your husband, like Katerin has had?"

Without hesitation she explains to me how she never would have allowed it, that had her husband ever started to mistreat her she would have either pushed back or left. When I ask her why some people stay silent or do not leave, she looks away to the hills beyond, lost for a moment. When she turns back to me, this time there is a new gravity in her look. She speaks slower, more deliberately, her brow furrowed.

"Economic independence is total independence, is it not?"

* * *

While there is more to understanding partner violence than economic independence alone, Luz's words cut straight to the heart of one of the main questions in understanding it: how is it possible, in the most basic sense, to commit this kind of abuse? In particular, how is it possible to commit this abuse *chronically*, in a partner-controlling way, and what keeps those who survive it from leaving? It is in asking this latter question that we find our-selves squarely in the realm of the kind of partner violence that is most unevenly gendered. Amid controversy over recent studies that have shown a gender balance in the perpetration of intimate violence, some have ar-gued that distinguishing between specific types of violence can clarify these numbers, to make them intelligible in light of our common experience.[1] And so while it is clear that simply gendering men as violent and women as victims is both inaccurate and unhelpful, in the case of *chronic, coercive* partner violence it is most often the case, as it was in my experience in Usme as well.[2]

When it came to that kind of chronic, controlling partner violence, what some have called "intimate terror," it was indeed predominantly men who perpetrated it and women who either survived it or were killed by their partners in the process. Hardly unique to Usme, in a global sense the num-bers behind this are staggering. The best current estimates put 30 percent of women around the world as having experienced physical violence at the hands of their intimate partners, and digging deeper into more local statis-tics presents a picture that is even more quantitatively alarming.[3] Within Colombia, the most recent estimates are that 37 percent of women have at some point experienced physical violence by their partners, and 72 percent have experienced some kind of controlling behavior by them as well.[4] This is also the case for Bogotá in particular, and delving into district-by-district comparisons in the capital city indicates that Usme is unfortunately one of the worst areas for violence against women. As the district with the second highest prevalence, in a recent community-based survey 82 percent of women reported some kind of controlling behavior by their partners and 47 percent reported some form of physical violence: 40 percent had been pushed, 32 percent were hit by hand, 9 percent were either strangled or burned, and 14 percent had been raped by their partners.

Against this daunting landscape, again where do we begin? How do we start to understand what makes this abuse possible, in the barest sense, and leads to these kinds of numbers? We can start by recognizing that while each person's experience of partner violence is unique, when talking about chronic, coercive violence there is, almost by its very definition, a single common denominator: control. Interrogating that question of control can be our point of departure. This does not necessarily mean that control is some rational or even intentional project on the part of its perpetrators; in-deed, they themselves may feel trapped in their own behaviors and the abuse that they commit. But the justifications that abusive partners make—the paternalistic pretenses behind their violence, the states of exception that they claim, the desperation they also feel—and how to understand them will be the topics explored in the following chapters. Here the question at hand is how the victims of violence experience that control, an experience that up to four out of five women in Usme have had.

Going behind the numbers and delving into some of these experiences, what starts to come into focus is that this question of control is also more specifically a question of sovereignty, specifically sovereignty on the intimate scale.[5] As such, it is not just a matter of understanding the social contracts that reverberate from family to state but a matter of understanding how domination over another person is sought through the construction of particular spaces and, frequently, the effort to contain the victims of that violence within them.[6] Located at the intersections of various dimensions of control—gendered, political economic, racial—these spaces become the everyday cages that survivors of violence are made to inhabit.[7] To see partner violence as a question of sovereignty then is to begin to understand it as an attempt at the architecture of space as much as the architecture of choice and, because these are only ever attempts at best, it is also to ask how these designs come to be contested. After all, it is in the daily resistances against these intimate regimes and, at times, their wholesale rupture that some of the greatest realizations are forged. It is for this reason that this chapter will focus on the stories of two women: Luz Elena, who avoided abusive relationships entirely, and Carolina, who was at the time that we met still surviving an intensely violent one. Theirs are stories of survival, if nothing else, and to begin to understand them is to begin to perceive the limits in the exercise of control as well as the paradoxes inherent to those efforts. At their core, theirs are the stories of how sovereignty is contested on the margins of the city.

"Total Independence"

From the very first time that Luz Elena invited me into her home and I saw the space devoted to her sewing machine, a full third of her own quarters, I began to appreciate what a central role needlecraft had played in her life. It was no coincidence then that after almost two years of knowing each other, when we finally sat down to record interviews, we would do so around that very machine. She had already taught me so much from this perch, with its panoramic views across the valley, like how the hills broke out into a brilliant saffron just before sunset and the tranquility that such a simple experience could bring. Here she had shown me the gifts she made for friends at Christmas time, the bulk orders she would fill whenever they came in, and the progress that she had made on making her own pants and jackets. It was from here that we had departed on walking tours around Usme and the neighboring districts of Kennedy and Ciudad Bolívar, where we had talked about everything from families to current affairs, historical icons like Jorge Eliécer Gaitán to her own views on feminism.

As we left her home and entered others, traversed neighborhoods unknown to me, and resurrected silenced histories, there seemed to be few boundaries that she was not willing to cross and fewer contours she felt obligated to follow. All of this time, her sewing machine never seemed to be left far behind. Making appearances throughout her stories, it would intrude like an unexpected but always welcome guest. Over time, I eventually came to understand that this vintage machine was her independence, and that she always in some manner carried it with her. It was nothing less than the enduring emblem of her ownership of her own direction. And so we sat by it as we burned through afternoons, talking late into the evening, retracing the stripes of her life. In those interviews she told the stories of her seventy-four years quietly but with confidence, punctuating them with her typical youthful laughter and that tight-lipped, eyes-wrinkled, mischievous look. Despite her mirth though, she had dealt in more than her own fair share of hardship, and even after knowing each other as long as we had I still found myself stumbling at times onto old scars and, on occasion, making them twinge again with a keener sting.

Rupture

Luz was born and lived her entire life in Bogotá, something that seemed a rarity in a city that has absorbed so many. During her childhood, the neighborhood of her birth, the Centenario, was on the outer limits of the urbanized area. Within the walls of her family's property they had, as many did, some space to grow a few crops—from fruits and vegetables to legumes—supplements to the groceries that they otherwise had to buy. She proudly told me about how the neighborhood was built during the period when Gai-

tán was the mayor of Bogotá, and that it was part of a program that he had
established to help ensure housing for all of the city's residents. In her mind
he had been a true politician for the people, and his belief in justice and the
role of women in achieving it were still unfinished business in the country.
When I asked her what she remembered most about her childhood, she said
that two or three events came to mind, but ultimately she wanted to tell me
about the one that marked her the most: the Bogotazo.

The Bogotazo was one of the most singularly defining moments in Colombia's twentieth-century history; on April 9, 1948, populist presidential
candidate Jorge Eliécer Gaitán was assassinated. With his life ended, and
with it his run for national office, the city was turned into a combat zone between protesters and police, eventually requiring intervention by the Colombian army to quell the impromptu insurrection. While the unrest within the
city limits was ultimately subdued, the Bogotazo is commonly seen as the moment of departure in which sporadic political violence—which had begun
since the end of the "Conservative Hegemony" in 1930—began to evolve into
the outright bloodshed of the period known today as La Violencia. During
this time, proto-elements of the enduring political conflict began to coalesce
and mobilize, setting the stage for the ensuing decades of multipolar civil war.

Even living on the outskirts of the city and away from the epicenter of
the violence, what Luz remembered most about that particular day were the
bodies of the dead, the guns, and the courage of her mother. With the threat
of martial law looming, she and her sisters were confined to their house for
the duration of the crisis. Even still, staying within the walls of her home
could not prevent her from watching the vans full of soldiers pass by her
window, and more than anything else that she saw on that day, and in all the
days that followed, this was what marked for her the end of the world that
she knew and the inauguration of some new order. As she put it, before the
Bogotazo the police in the city had been *policia civica* and to her memory
had not even carried guns. Today, fully automatic weapons are common-
place for the police, and as this militarization of policing has lived on, so too
have Luz's deeply engrained fears and mistrust of these agents. Even after
over sixty years, she noted that "that day marked me. It left me . . . if for instance a van of police comes close to me, I cannot move, I cannot move
myself, John. It gives me a lot of anxiety and I have not been able to get over
it. Still to this day I cannot get over it."

Far from a simple yearning for physical security, this repeated experience of fear for Luz has formed an ongoing basis of her questioning the very

legitimacy of the state that these armed actors represent, and with it the sovereign power that they uphold.[8] As such, to her the Bogotazo and the state's response to it constituted nothing less than a wholesale breach of the social contract that she had previously known, an undoing of the basic precepts on which civic life was supposed to be based. In this new world the threat of violence was constantly around the corner for her, and that this reality had replaced the promise of Gaitán was something that she could never fully accept. But as significant as this departure may have been, before the unrest of the Bogotazo settled and she was again allowed to leave her home, this contract with the state was not the only one that she would see broken.

Living through the Bogotazo for Luz and her family was about more than just surviving the events of that first day; it was also about being able to live out the following weeks. The first day of the riots happened to be the last day of a biweekly pay period for her father, which meant that with the stores closing down her family would not be able to replenish their dwindling food supplies on their normal Saturday of shopping. When her father arrived home late that Friday night, he brought back as much as he could possibly find, but it would not have been nearly enough to last their family for the foreseeable shutdown in the city. It was a frighteningly uncertain time to be sure, and as she explained this to me she did something, quite suddenly in fact, that I had never seen her do before—she began to cry.

When her tears subsided, she told me that what continued to affect her most of all about that day was the loss of her mother. Confused, I waited silently. As the moment passed I asked her what made her think of her mother's death: from what she had told me previously, her mother had lived for almost thirty years after the Bogotazo. She answered by telling me how her mother had guided them, spoiled them, that she had never mistreated them as children, and then she explained to me the connection that I still could not see. It was her mother who had gone back out that night during the city's shutdown, with two of her brothers, to travel the seven miles to Luz's grandmother's farm in the north of the city. Dodging the army the entire way there and back, they returned before sunrise with enough food for not only their own family but also their immediate neighbors as well, ensuring that no one else would need to risk their life until the shutdown had been lifted. It was on this note of reverence that she ended her story to me of the Bogotazo, not on the dead, the guns, or the fear, but with a thin smile and an almost whispered "my mother was a very special person."

The gendered juxtaposition that Luz offered here was stark. On the one hand, there was the terror of living through a crisis under a militarized state; on the other hand, the courageous generosity of her mother within that context. One was a heavily masculinized state apparatus, whose acts of violence delegitimized it in her eyes, and the other was a female role model who defied that same military by breaking curfew and leaving her home for the benefit of others.[9] One was associated with violence and fear; the other, with love and care. This is not to assert stereotyped gender binaries or even to imply that Luz did herself. It is to remember that genders, like any other identity, are thoroughly relational constructs that emerge through the course of political engagement rather than existing prior to it.[10] For Luz, her experiences during the Bogotazo were seminal events in her emerging consciousness of this, just as they were early departures in her development of the practices that would later protect her own independence.

Through her experience of the Bogotazo she found inspiration in her mother who, even in fulfilling her socially prescribed role of caring for her family, defied the orders of the state. Her mother who, risking her life by leaving their home while her husband stayed behind, actually broke through those traditional gender roles and with them broke the terms of the domestic contract that some have argued underlies the broader social contract of the citizen and state.[11] In a country where the constitution itself describes the family as "the fundamental nucleus of society," the importance of this rupture cannot be overstated. To break one necessarily threatens the other, and witnessing the subversive improvisation that her mother exercised during this moment of national crisis, especially when compared against the offenses of the state that her mother defied, was a lesson that Luz would carry closely with her throughout the rest of her life. To start to see one sovereign as illegitimate inevitably led her to eventually question the necessity of the other, and so it began for her the slow erosion of her faith in authority, be it at the societal or intimate scales.

Luz was not alone in this, and as she would go on to explain, these ruptures also foretold yet another one that unfolded over the years to come. In her eyes, her mother leaving their home in the late hours of April 9 also predicted a gradual softening of the spatial inscriptions of gender in Bogotá at the time. When I later asked her about how the collective silence on partner violence was eventually broken, she recalled that before 1948 few people would openly talk about what they knew, or at least suspected, happened behind closed doors. Few women would even leave the house. Again the

Bogotazo stood out to her as a pivotal moment, one after which she remembers seeing women in the streets like they had never been before. Over time this breach of social space gave rise to another intrusion, gossip, and as she remembers it, it was during the 1960s and 1970s that the taboo on talking about partner violence began to progressively weaken. Even still, it would not be until the 1990s that government agencies dedicated to intervening in these matters were instituted, or even that the issue began to gain significant traction in the published media. Whatever the timeframe that it took to transpire though, for Luz it began, as did so many other threads in the history of social life in Colombia, in the protean rupture that was the Bogotazo.

It was on this note that we finally left the Bogotazo behind, but still we continued to talk late into the evening about her life. The sun plunging quickly and softening the hills behind us, she continued on with this founding realization of hers, forged in the heat of that national crisis: always question those who might control you. For the next two hours that she talked I only listened, rarely intervening with a question, frightened that if I did I would break the careful concatenation of stories that she was laying out for me. Had I done so I might have missed it, I might have lost the thread that told the real lesson she wanted to pass on to me: her philosophy of freedom. Freedom for her from having to suffer the abuses of another, from losing control over her own direction, freedom from dispossession of whom she knew herself to be. This to her was her highest ideal, this was her total independence, and more than anything else she wanted me to know how she had gone about achieving it.

Weaving Independence

Her mother sewed. In fact her mother used for many years a machine very similar to the one that she would later buy, and she taught Luz all of the basics on it. After the Bogotazo had passed, Luz's father's work took him away from their home frequently, and looking back she saw the rest of her childhood defined by her mother's instruction. When she finally completed her *bachillerato* (secondary school) then, to start generating an income she began working as a seamstress in one of the clothing factories within the city. Doing so put Luz once again in the middle of an evolving national history, this one located at the crossroads of a global economy in flux. The jobs in clothing factories in Colombia had come about through a process of labor migration from the textile mills in New England to a rising industry of domestic production centered around Bogotá's neighboring city of Medellín.[12] Passing from the hands of capitalists like the Draper family in the United States to those of the Echavarría family in Colombia, the national production of textiles, and their further refinement into finished products, was not just a consequence of labor disputes in the United States. Manufacturing jobs like these were also the product of a growing trend in Latin America to replace imported goods with national production, a process commonly referred to as "Import Substitution Industrialization." While doing so gave Colombian companies the opportunity to upgrade to more capital-intensive operations, for Luz it was more simply an early opportunity to have her own income. On the one hand, doing so meant finding some measure of self-reliance through one of the main routes of employment generally available to women at the time. On the other hand it meant locating herself fast within the fabric of a global system of production and trade.

When I asked her about her first job in a factory, a bit to my surprise she told me that she very much liked it but stipulated that she only worked for a few people throughout her career. What defined that first experience for her was her boss, a man she described as a good and caring person, and for this she continued to work for him for nearly fourteen years. This was the factory where she worked when she married her husband, "in the church" and at the age of twenty, and it was the same place she worked after she had her first child.[13] Even when her infant son became ill and she took off several months, her boss guaranteed her a job and when she returned paid her weekly with some extra groceries. "This man was very humane," she said, an air of dignified respect in her tone, but she would not be so fortunate with her next company. There she worked under the direct supervision of someone less amicable, and it was not long before an incident led her to quit:

> I didn't last even a month there because one day, and I don't know what happened, I think I came in late, yes, I came in late. So he called me to his office and he scolded me, but scolded me in a very ugly way. . . . So me, being, spontaneous, like I am, I can be very passive but when, there are moments, I said that I am not dying of hunger, that I am taken care of and I do not need your work. Thank you very much, and I put my meterstick and scissors down on the chair and left.[14]

The sly smirk she flashed at "spontaneous" faded into firm resolution by the end, a sober testament to her will not to put up with being belittled before another person. But from whence did this security she spoke of come, and what did "taken care of" mean for her?

At the time Luz was not yet sewing and selling her own goods. The support that stabilized this transition for her from one job to the next, and allowed her to quit her job as suddenly as she did, came instead from her husband and her mother. Her husband at the time was also working, and from his income he paid for most of their housing and food, while her mother lived close enough to watch her son as she looked for and began her new job. With this net of support she could find a new position, but as she began to recognize the quality of work that she produced and the experience that she had accumulated, she also began to make demands at her new job. With a fellow coworker she secured both an early promotion in her new company as well as the opportunity to go back to the state-run vocational school (SENA) to learn how to operate newer equipment. Even still, she struggled to meet the demands that being a working mother imposed, further compounded by the fact that she had to leave home every morning at four o'clock just to get to her factory on time. Only with the additional support of her mother taking her children to school every day was she able to make it; only then could she stretch herself across the conflicting labors that she was expected to fulfill.

Over time though this small network came undone. First her mother died, leaving Luz to quit her job so that she could take better care of her sons. She found new employment as she always did, this time more amenable to her double duty as a working mother, but by then her relationship with her husband had begun to deteriorate. While the romantic affection she had for him had already diminished, the reasons she told me for why she left him were far more fiscal and paternal. As she explained, he had bought a car and begun working as a taxi driver, staying out later and later into the night and even at one point failing to take one of their sons to the hospital when he fell acutely ill. Over time Raul began to ask her to lend him increasing sums of cash, money that she said he never returned. "He knew that I had money saved, just not how much," she told me, referring to a separate bank account she had kept in her name throughout her years of employment. With those funds and her current job, one day she up and notified Raul that she would be leaving him and taking their sons with her to a new apartment, that he could see their children however much he desired but she would never ask him for a single peso for their care. Telling him that she was more able to *sacarlos adelante* (get them ahead in life), they left for a new home and she kept true to her word.

Given the almost insurmountable obstacle of getting a divorce after a "church" wedding, Luz and her husband never officially divorced, but their de facto separation was no less definitive. When I asked her how she felt at first about the separation she told me that emotionally she "never wanted to die of love for anyone," but in a more practical sense she was also not afraid to work hard, thanks especially to the early influences of her mother and father. Despite these lessons and the savings that she had accrued, without her mother's or her husband's support, the months that followed presented new challenges. Ultimately it was creativity, not just hard work, that got Luz through them. Early on, she used a portion of her saved money to buy herself a sewing machine and, on weekends or after hours, would fill orders for collars, belts, or whatever else shops requested from her. Beyond giving her more control over her working hours, this also replaced the other revenues that she previously had to cover transitions should she lose, or quit, her company job. Even with this greater control she still had to devise a new system to look after her youngest son while she was at work, and she would eventually rely on the support of close friends and her elder son when he came of age.

During this period of separating from her husband, her development of her own system of mixed incomes had the further felicitous effect of propelling her down totally new avenues. Telling me that she wanted to give herself the opportunity to explore other interests, something that she had put on hold since she took that first job in a factory, within a couple of years Luz became a leader in her son's Boy Scout troop. Doing so was the first indication of many that leaving her husband did not so much mark the end of a relationship as it was the first step of many in expanding her personal horizons. Over the following twenty-eight years this would eventually lead her to work full-time with the Boy Scouts and leave behind working in factories altogether, even going on to study and receive a diploma in sports and recreation from the National Pedagogical University in Bogotá. Through this new position she would become connected to other opportunities, like serving for a year as an outreach worker for UNICEF in a project on the outer limits of the district of Ciudad Bolívar. Retired by the time that we met, she continued to work with her local parish in "social pastoral" work where she led projects like *tejiendo redes* (weaving networks), a program built on putting other community programs into direct communication with one another.

Throughout these latter chapters of her life, the one constant has been the work that she has done on her own sewing machine, the very one that still looks out her window onto the valley in Usme. Regardless of her primary source of income, she has never lost control over this supplemental mode of production, using it to ensure that should she ever need to change direction she would be able to support herself through the interim. Even today when she is pensioned by the government and receives subsidies for monthly groceries, she continues to thread and weave, closing any gaps that may appear in paying for rent, diabetes medications, or just keeping food on her table. For Luz, this mechanical apparatus, this small piece of capital, is a paradox. On the one hand, she has used it to widen the purview of her life drastically and given herself possibilities that otherwise would not have been possible. On the other hand, it has increasingly become a singularly central emblem of her identity, a core symbol of how she sees herself. As she says, independence means not having to rely on another person, "to live out of their pocket," and this machine has consistently helped her to stake her independence in a number of relationships, from her husband to any one of her employers. However, independence should not be mistaken for autonomy, or worse for isolation, and from her personal welfare to the gifts she gives to others, so too has her sewing been a means of forging deep connections to others. Ultimately though her project of independence has not been one of material production, it has been one of respect, above all respect for herself. It was on these terms that she finally ended our interviews, instructing me,

> "One needs to have a morality, a respect for oneself. If you don't respect yourself, you can never respect anyone else, these are simple principles. . . . It's simple, if you do not care for yourself, for your body, whom are you going to care for? Whom are you going to respect? No one! No one. This is simple logic. And, yes, you can, yes, you can. Me, over twenty years single and *si se puede*."

Under No (One) Thumb: Interpositional Independence

The story of Luz Elena is about, if nothing else, the possibility of charting a path despite living at the intersections of multiple sovereign schemes. Hers is a potent reminder that, in order to understand the bare possibility of chronic, coercive partner violence, we must pay heed to more than just how isolation and vulnerability in intimate relationships are maintained. We must see also how they are contested and, sometimes, avoided altogether. Stories of domination are equally stories of resistance, and at the core of Luz Elena's was the enduring struggle for independence. Forged initially in the crucible of the Bogotazo, this was an ethos that kept her questioning any kind of social contract that might be imposed upon her, be that with the state, her employer, or even her husband. In turn she at some point rejected them all: distrusting the authority of her government even as she at times made good use of its financial support, quitting her job when an employer failed to treat her with respect, leaving her husband when she found the terms of their relationship no longer relevant to the life she wanted to lead. Each departure was a judgment, their sum a sustained critique of what she perceived to be unfair relationships in a persistently violent world. Through them, what she made explicit was that her struggle for personal independence was ultimately about opposition to the *monopolization* of power by others, and that the means of accomplishing this was a combination of her ownership of capital and her maintenance of a variety of social supports.

To be independent, therefore, did not mean that she did not depend on others. On the contrary, Luz was always intricately connected to, and in important ways always counted on the collaboration of, a great number of others: family, friends, employers, clients, and the government to name a few.[15] To be able to distance herself at times was not the same as rejecting them entirely, and each one at different points did help to sustain her in important ways. Her instrumental realization then was not in how to disentangle herself from all of the worlds of unequal power in which she lived. Whatever her creativity, she still remained embedded within the nexuses of political, economic, and gendered regimes, systems in which she typically found herself subordinate. Being relatively poor, living on the margins of the city, and a woman in a society that routinely privileges men, she did find a way to control some resources whenever she could, and she avoided stagnancy within these various spaces by moving between them instead. Ultimately her independence was, at its core, interpositional. That is to say that her self-professed independence emerged from her ability to weave together her available resources and never fully committing herself to just one. It was through this constant movement that she prevented herself from merely swapping vulnerable positions, from breaking through the barriers of the space of the home only to end up trapped with no further options in a system of debt relations, corporate hierarchy, or state dependency. Luz may have found herself frequently under the thumb of someone else, but she worked tirelessly to avoid at all costs ever being under only one. As another survivor of partner violence whom I came to know more succinctly put it, she "never wanted to enslave herself."

Instead Luz elaborated a continuously evolving, hybridized response to subjugation. For instance, when she left her husband and bought her sewing machine, she did so entirely with the money that she had previously saved. To own that machine free of debt was to keep at least part of her life outside of a whole field of sovereign relations, a political economic order predicated on the maintenance of power through the creation of debt.[16] Had she bought that machine on credit, in leaving her husband she would have simply been trading vulnerabilities, exiting one relationship that had the potential for abuse only to end up susceptible within another one instead. Afterward, though she continued to work for companies throughout the rest of her career as a seamstress, she maintained her own private business as well in order to tide herself over whenever she was between jobs. As her own business flourished, she voraciously sought new avenues for education, at first within her familiar field of textiles, much later in new areas such as child education. To expand her base of knowledge, she explained, was to invest in herself in a way that implied the ultimate form of ownership. The vagaries of the powers that be might threaten to take away parts of her material world, but knowledge was something from which she could never be dispossessed.[17] All the while her sewing machine remained there when she needed it, was left unused when she increasingly did not, but was always available to provide some stability during moments of transition in her life.[18]

With the added assistance provided by her family, friends, and, later in life, government subsidization, Luz built a life that expertly exploited the tensions that exist at the seams between these overlapping systems of sovereign relations. Doing so is no easy feat. As many scholars have observed, the global ascendance of capitalism was not accompanied by an inevitable equalization of power between genders, even though such an outcome might have been possible.[19] In what Angela Davis termed the "equalization-repression dialectic," rather than undoing the oppression of women, the historical result has generally been the creation of a mutually reinforcing "double inferiority," something not entirely dissimilar to Carole Pateman's observation of the sexual contract that underlies the social contract of the modern state.[20] Luz seemed to defy both of these to the greatest extent possible and, through her elaborate sequence of double moves between spaces, she was still able to chart a life that she at least believed to be distinctly her own. Eventually this meant achieving a form of escape velocity from both her previous forms of employment and her marriage, finding herself single and engaged in a series of careers in community that she found more meaningful than her previous work. It is in that mere possibility of willful movement that the truly radical potential of Luz's life praxis can be found. That is, to exist in any way outside of any given system of power, however temporarily, is to challenge its legitimacy in the most fundamental way. By living beyond its borders one shows that it is neither a necessary nor an inevitable arrangement of human affairs.[21] And while this never meant achieving full autonomy from those places and the power that they institutionalize, it did mean for Luz that she was at least able to avoid becoming irreversibly enclosed within them. She was able to escape the spaces, in either the home or the workplace, in which she would otherwise have been compelled into servitude.

Reproductive Coercion and Its Discontents

What happens when these strategies simply are not possible? What is the toll and how can survivors continue to mount a resistance? What could be its source? Enter Carolina, who despite living through most forms of interpersonal violence, had still found in herself a reservoir of fortitude, an unlikely ability to hold out hope. Unlike with Luz, I first met Carolina through one of the Comisarías de Familia in Usme. There she had presented to provide testimony in her own case of child custody, one where her ex-partner was accusing her of corporal punishment of their children.[22] When we met it was not in her living room or through meandering walks around the district, but in a windowless study room in a public library outside of the district. Away from the watchful eyes of neighbors and under the strictest promises of confidentiality, there she took me through the odyssey of her barely twenty-eight years, one that had frequently taken her, as she put it, "from Guatemala to Guata-peor."[23] Hers is a life that stands testament to the persistent possibility of staking one's self-worth, to keep finding a reason for

staying on this earth even after having passed through some of its most ru-
inous crucibles of debasement.

Broken Promises

Carolina was not born in Bogotá. Her family had moved from the province
of Santander to Boyacá when she was only a year old. So while she has no
memory of the region where she was born, she does remember quite well
what it was like growing up as the child of a migrant farmer on the altiplano
just north of the capital city. She moved yearly until she was twelve years
old, as her parents sought new employment seeding, cutting, and picking
anything available. Mostly they worked with coffee, and as she described it
her parents' employers were generally good to them, at least always providing a house in which they could live.[24] Even still, when thinking back to
those times there was one word that typically came to mind for her: terrible.
For one, the moving was usually a difficult, multiple-day affair in which
they would have to carry their belongings on their back until they found a
new position to sustain them for another cycle. When they were not on the
road, her parents were mostly in the field, Monday through Saturday, leaving her as the eldest of six children to play the primary caretaker. Between
the frequent uprooting and the time that she spent in the daily care of her
siblings, there was barely enough time to dedicate to her education, much
less to making and keeping friends. "*Soy solita* [I am alone]," she told me, as
we sat and talked about her life in light of those early years.

Despite covering more land in her first decade than most others her age,
life for Carolina did not exist much outside of her string of temporary homes.
Guarding the boundaries of those homes was her father, a protective figure
who, as she put it, never let anyone else harm their family. Within those
homes he was less providing, never giving her or her siblings any help in
buying clothes or school supplies, but otherwise treating them "well." With
her mother he was "terrible" though, and while he never hit her, he was verbally abusive for as long as Carolina could remember. When I asked if that
left an enduring impression on her, she said it definitely had, that one reason
she thinks she has been with abusive men herself is because her mother
never talked openly about it with her. Carolina never speculated on why her
mother did not speak with her about these things, or exactly how that lack
of communication led her to end up with abusive men herself, but what she

was clear about is that her relationship with her mother had always been unique:

> "We [siblings] would fight like kids . . . but now we are in contact with each other. . . . My mother though was very tough with me, I could never tell her anything like if I had a boyfriend because she would hit me. . . . I know that she loves me but I don't feel it. . . . My relationship with her is still different than for my brothers and sisters." The marks of it were still raw for her, and as we talked about her mother her voice often strained, and she would pause, hit a wall, and ask that we move on.

At the age of twelve, just out of primary school, her mother sent her to Bogotá to work even though she herself had always wanted to complete her bachillerato. In the end she had little say in the matter though and so, over the course of a year, she made her way slowly toward the capital city.[25] Arriving first in the small town of Chiquinquirá for a year, working as live-in domestic help for another family, she took the position because they had promised her that she while she lived with them she would be able to continue her studies. Not only did her host family fail to keep that promise, but what she encountered went far beyond a missed opportunity. The house itself was "immense," she recalled, and her *dueña* (female boss) was exacting in her demands. Between cleaning and cooking she also looked after their intellectually disabled daughter, a combination of obligations that would have her get out of bed at four in the morning and finish her day around nine at night. The work was exhausting but otherwise "fine"; what hurt her the most was her inability to study and the unwanted attention of her male employer. While the rest of the work was taxing, "putting up with the *dueño*," as she put it, was the real nightmare of it all. In talking about him she only ever went so far as to call him "dirty" but, with pursed lips and a downward stare, was reluctant to say any more. When asked if it was something that she wanted to talk more about, she quickly shook her head and again we moved on.

After that first year she was able to leave and finally go to Bogotá, this time living with an aunt of hers and under a similar pretense to her previous arrangement: that she would be able to continue studying while helping around the house. Instead what she found was once again more of the same, working from six to ten and attending to her aunt and son, no time left for her to go back to school. The three years that she lived there she described as painful, again for her unfulfilled expectations but also for her aunt's continuous verbal abuse and psychological degradation. Eventually she was able to leave and found work with a woman in the more affluent district of Chapinero, a position where she said, with a bit of relief, that she was finally treated with respect and, more importantly, able to go back to her studies. Over the next three years that she lived and worked there she was able to study up to the ninth grade and, in the process, she met her first partner. They met during a school fieldtrip and soon after began dating; not long after that she became pregnant with her first child. Slowly, the dream that she had been building began to unravel. First came the panic attacks, fitful episodes in which she thought she would die, and although her boss helped to take care of her at first, she soon gave notice to Carolina that she could no longer continue employing her. Unsure as to exactly why, Carolina was left assuming that it had to something to do with her pregnancy and her presumed "fitness" to work.

Left without income, she immediately moved in with her boyfriend who was working in a jeans factory at the time and living with his cousin's family. In spite of the precarious situation, she thought back to that period positively, recalling how her partner cared for her throughout the rest of her pregnancy and even moved them into their own apartment just before she delivered. Then, just fifteen days into life with her healthy new daughter, everything changed. By the end of her pregnancy she was already sleeping in a different bed from him and did not want to be touched or kissed, but when she refused to have sex with him two weeks after she delivered, he hit her for the first time and then raped her. It would not be the last time that he sexually forced her either. Over the course of their four and a half years together he would repeat it another four times, as well as continue to hit her on a more frequent basis. During that time his violence toward her followed an all-too-familiar pattern of abuse and apology, isolation and deceit. In his apologies he would promise to do anything to take care of her and their children, and when they visited family it would typically be his own. If she did visit her own family it was always accompanied by him, and during those trips he would become, as she would say, his charismatic self, charming her mother in particular.

In reflecting on those years, Carolina described her dawning of consciousness as a protracted one, that it took her years of surviving his abuse to become fully aware of her situation and the unlikelihood that he would ever change his treatment of her. There was a decisive moment for her though, and it came on the first birthday of their second child when he hit her during the party that they threw. Deciding in that moment that he would never change, she took her two children and left their home. Leaving him was more than a question of consciousness or will, however, and it was only with her brother's financial support in paying for an apartment that she was actually able to escape. In the time since she had come to the city her brother too had migrated to Bogotá and found work, along with most of the rest of her family, and with his job he was able to stake her in those early months that she moved to Usme. Even with this support though, Carolina never told him the specifics about her relationship, afraid that the truth would eventually reach her mother who, up until the day that Carolina and I first sat down to talk, still wanted her to return to this man.

This moment of assistance by her brother, and how Carolina mediated it, is the instance that brings into tragic relief just how isolated she had previously been. It was an isolation that began long before the abusive control of her ex-partner, a process that Carolina described as reaching back into her childhood, coming out of the void left by the relationships and resources she had never been able to build. She recalled how her father had never been a supportive figure and her relationship with her mother had always been characterized more by discipline and strict expectation than emotional nurturance. By the time that she was looking to leave her first partner, her lack of trust in her mother was so severe that Carolina even avoided disclosing details to her siblings for fear that they might find their way back to her. These early relationships of hers, and lack thereof, were not forged in a vacuum, however; they emerged in the context of continuous uncertainty that Carolina and her family constantly found themselves in: vulnerable and on the road. It was because of the long hours of her parents' work and their meager wages that her very first isolation was within her very own home, separated even from her siblings to a degree by her role as surrogate caretaker. Combined with her family's perennial displacement, she spoke of how making friends had never come easily to her, and most of the social support that she had ever had had come from within her own family.

Her migration to Bogotá had also happened within this same context. Having barely finished primary school, it was again the basic material needs of her family that provided the pressure for her to leave and begin working in the houses of others. Leaving on her own, Carolina had her isolation within her family's home traded for the isolation within her employers' homes. Through impossibly long hours, minimal pay, the broken promises of attending school, and worst of all the multitude of abuses that she endured, there was little recourse left to her other than to seek a new post whenever she could and to hope for something better. In fact, she eventually did find "better" when she began living and working in Chapinero, but the threadbare contingency of her existence was again exposed when she lost that job for the sole crime of becoming pregnant. With child and without income, this was the juncture where she ended up in the domestic space of a man who would ultimately become routinely and intensely abusive to her—psychologically, physically, sexually.

As Carolina retold it, much of that abuse was built through his progressive confinement of her within their home. And while she could list a number of ways that he himself sought to do so—control of their finances and lease, limiting contact with her family, leaving the care for their children solely in her hands—she was also careful to add that other aspects of her life compounded it. One of those was gossip. As she later explained to me, her difficulty with friends was a disposition that she adopted early in life, and that was reinforced through a few key experiences that she had when first making friends in Bogotá. In the few cases where she even tried, and confided intimate secrets about her life, her confidence was repeatedly betrayed when those friends spread her stories throughout the neighborhood. By the time we met, "friends" had become for her another entry on a long list of people not to trust, a list that included members of her family, employers, and intimate partners. That fear and mistrust extended beyond the people she knew too, and like many citizens of Latin American cities like Bogotá, Carolina had learned to maintain a healthy respect for the streets in which she lived. Citing twice being mugged, as well as verbal harassment by men whenever she left her home, the quotidian logic of "no dar papaya" had only further bolstered her isolation within abusive homes.[26]

Unintended Consequences

JOHN: How have you survived this? How do you keep going
        forward, fighting, and living?
CAROLINA: For my children. I always have fought for them.
        They are the motor . . . everything I do is for them.

As if it were possible, the second partner whom Carolina ended up with had been even more abusive than the first. She described the period between the two relationships as one in which she traded the intimate terror of her first partner for the grinding violence of working as an impoverished woman in the city, gone from seven to nine each day and hardly ever getting to see her children. In her almost nonexistent spare time she had found a new group of friends and began, for the first time in her life, trying things like drinking and smoking, and in the process she incurred a small amount of debt to them. In quick order though she lost her job, and when she attempted to withdraw from her new group of friends one threatened Carolina and her sister with a knife. Using the last of her rent money to pay back what she owed them, she found herself again without an income, now with two children to support, and so made the decision to move in with a man that she had only recently met, her current partner.

With him there would be no honeymoon period. Formerly in the military, he was at the time working as many men and women of the lower classes do, as a security guard in the more affluent districts in the north of the city.[27] Working two day shifts and two night shifts a week, Carolina spoke about the time that he was out of their home as a nothing but a huge relief, but when he returned it was complete hell. Whenever he was gone Carolina took care of her children—two more now from that relationship— and dealt with his constant stream of texts and calls, checking on where she was and what she was doing at all times. Early on in their relationship she had sold food on the street, a chance to get out of their home on some consistent basis, but after developing two hernias she had been unable to continue doing any work on her own. Caught in a bureaucratic quagmire of medical insurance and denials of authorization for any of her needed surgeries, she was at the point of desperation by the time that we met.[28] While she waited for a solution to help her get the care she needed, she left her home as little as she could manage. Mostly she tried to avoid problems with her partner if she could, always wary that intruding eyes could be keeping tabs on her movements outside of their home.

He first hit Carolina when she was four months pregnant with their first child, and she described their relationship thereafter as a mixture of verbal, physical, and sexual abuse. When he first hit her she did attempt to take her case to the district attorney's office that was bogged down with an impossible caseload already, so her case never meaningfully advanced and she lost hope for any legal avenues of recourse.[29] As with the case of her health insurance, she was again left to her own devices by the state. Too discouraged by her experience to want to try the Comisarías de Familia, she instead began to learn to walk on eggshells as best as she could during the times when her partner would be at home. By the time that we met, Carolina had survived this for over four years, and the cumulative toll of her life's hardships showed whenever she spoke about herself. Though not suicidal at the time, she explained how in the past she had wanted to die, and throughout our interviews she repeated one phrase in particular: "I don't matter." After decades of surviving life at the extremes of violent degradation by others, the value that Carolina held for herself had become all but totally debased. As she put it, she simply did not matter. And yet, despite all of her experiences, all of her misery and suffering at the hands of others, in between her narrations of her past she also spoke impossibly of hope. Hope that she could leave her abusive partner, hope that she could go back to studying, hope that if she could somehow get the operations for her hernias she could eventually go back to work. In none of these dreams was there space for another intimate partner though. After all she had been through, her hope was to leave behind not only her current partner but also partnership itself.

How after all of her years could she still hold out hope, something that can be so fickle, so delicate and ephemeral? From earlier when she had wanted to die, how had she begun the process of turning her gaze forward, of finding the fortitude to invest again in herself? By understanding how Carolina was able to do this, it is also possible to recognize one of the central paradoxes in the exercise of power: the unintended consequences of control.[30] In particular, her history of partner violence was not only about coercive control in a general sense but also about a very particular version of it: reproductive coercion. The idea of reproductive coercion can cover any variety of issues, means of control that range from the manipulation of reproductive planning to outright rape, the isolation of victims through the normative obligations of motherhood or the creation of financial barriers, making it harder for survivors to escape.[31] However we subdivide it, all of these forms of coercion reflect the abuses of the sexual contract par excellence, and in cases like Carolina's where all of her children were born from relationships characterized by repeated rape, it hardly bears distinguishing neat lines between them. But if reproductive coercion is woven into the broader dynamic of intimate control, then it may seem a bit self-contradictory to say that one of the unintended consequences of reproductive coercion would be the children themselves. The children are, after all, the very *point* of reproductive coercion and the means for its perpetrators to further isolate the partners they abuse. For them to become the fulcrum in undoing these designs would seem to be impossible, and yet for Carolina they seemed to be so.

If Carolina's life has been in part defined by the consistent experience of isolation, she has also simultaneously defined it through her roles as a caretaker. In every instance that she has been dispossessed of taking direction over her own life, she has found her riposte in finding purpose through the care of others. As a young child this meant playing the surrogate mother for her siblings, up until the point that she was expelled from her home to search for waged labor. Even then she found employment for the following seven years in attending to the needs of others as a live-in maid. Her work as domestic help ended only when she became pregnant with her daughter, and from this point on her attention shifted from siblings or strangers to her very own children. It was within these more recent relationships that she suffered the most extreme forms of violence, the most severe injuries to her very personhood and sense of self-worth, but through sustaining her children she also came to sustain herself. As we spoke about her second partner and she began to reveal her aspirations for a different kind of life, she told me about the decisive turning point for her in their relationship: when he began hitting her in front of her children and showing no remorse for the fact that they would see it.[32] Much like the case with her first partner who hit her on their son's first birthday, this was a major moment of consciousness for Carolina. In particular it was one that she took as an impetus to begin extricating herself from a situation that she could no longer tolerate, even with her undoubtedly high threshold of endurance. As she said, her children were her motor.

In propelling her away from her abusive relationships, Carolina's children have not just been a motivation for leaving. Her aspirations were not only for their education and advancement but also for her own—*she* wanted to finish her studies, find work, and live independently. Despite her repeated insistence that she herself was of no value, her hopes for her own betterment betrayed a more positive outlook. Against a continuous barrage of violence that had belittled and isolated her, her children had consistently been one of her principal means by which she resurrected and defended her self-worth. Through her care for them, she also cultivated a means of caring for herself, and as such the reproductive coercion of both of her partners had in fact been a source of their own undoing. Even as they sought to isolate her, limit her connections to a world outside of their homes—bolstered in those efforts by the broader context of her migration away from family, her history of continued material insecurity, the dangerous urban environment to which she moved—what they could not prevent was her connection to those who remained within those very domestic spaces, her children.

Through her survival she showed that biological reproduction in no way necessitates social reproduction, that is to say reproduction of the status quo; it is also, of course, a major site of resistance. Pregnancy can produce more than just further isolation for victims of violence; it can also generate a reservoir of renewed potential for their subversion of those intimate domains. In showing this, what Carolina demonstrated is one of the principal paradoxes of sovereign power, a central tension in its exercise: the greater the influence, the greater the unintended consequences. That those consequences are unintended at all could be one of the most significant reminders to those "in control" that there are very real limits to their ability to control anyone or anything. Not surprisingly, and especially when survivors of abuse attempt to leave, those unintended consequences can become the very reason that abusive partners escalate their violence even more. Triggering a rapidly deteriorating and downward cycle, these violent attempts at reclaiming power can actually, under the right circumstances, only further accelerate abusive partners' loss of control as their own actions delegitimize the appeals to authority that they had previously tried to make. If afforded the opportunity to leave, and safe passage to do so as Carolina had received before, this cycle can become the death knell of the relationship itself and the implosion of the domestic space that once contained it. And at its center, as was the case for Carolina, are the children who were otherwise supposed to hold it all together.

From the stories of Luz and Carolina, what comes across most clearly is that those who seek to maintain control over others must necessarily seek to inscribe boundaries into the social geography of everyday life, and to break those boundaries or to exist outside of them is therefore to challenge those systems in one of the most damaging ways possible.[33] Such was the case in Luz's history of women leaving their homes after the Bogotazo, a primitive rupture that preceded feminist movements decades later. Living literally outside the boundaries of control constitutes nothing less than a refutation of the sovereign power of others, both in their dominion over a given space as well as their right to define the contours of human connection. It is that connection with others that provides the basic experiential material against which consciousness emerges, and it is in this spatialized sense of power then that partner violence appears most clearly as a question of sovereignty: who has authority where, why, and how is that "where" constructed in the first place. To refute it though does not necessarily require leaving those spaces, as Carolina showed. Sometimes the limits of sovereign power can be breached not by reaching "outside" of the domestic spaces in which survivors of violence become progressively enclosed, but instead through the relationships "internal" to it. Despite her partners' intense efforts to reinforce her isolation—physically, socially, financially, emotionally—from those outside of their homes, what they were never able to account for was the influence of those who remained within them, their very own children. Infiltrating the limits of the spaces they controlled, it was through her connection with her children that Carolina repeatedly cultivated her drive, her self-value, her very consciousness of her situation, and came to question the limits of what she had to endure.[34] Against the abuses of her partners, her children remained her motor.

What both Luz and Carolina showed is that to see the possibility of intimate control through the lens of structured vulnerability or social isolation would be to see only the most obvious architectures of space and choice for those who become victims of violence. Through their various forms of resistance, each articulated creative tensions that transected the boundaries imposed by their partners, and along the way reconfigured them to reveal important vulnerabilities and contradictions inherent to those arrangements. Their stories are not just about contesting power within given spaces—be it the home, the workplace, or public places—they are about the insights that they have derived by living through those tensions that cut across these fields. They have shown that "empowerment" must mean more than employment, that independence is about more than just swapping vulnerabilities, and that even the most degrading exercises of power—down to the dispossession of control over one's own body through the acts of sexual violence—have the potential to lead to power's demise.

CHAPTER 3

Permissible

To do evil a human being must first of all believe that what he's doing is good, or else that it's a well-considered act in conformity with natural law.

—Aleksandr Solzhenitsyn

Sin mujer no hay revolución.

—Anonymous

Just because there is the possibility of exercising chronic control over someone does not mean that anyone will actually do it. Even when it works to privilege those who commit it, violence rarely just happens. Typically we need to either talk ourselves into it beforehand or at least justify it in some way after the fact.[1] How that is actually accomplished though is by no means an easy task, and for the perpetrators of partner violence that I came to know in Usme, their attempts to do so often put them at uneasy nexuses between overlapping fields of sovereign relations. In a dangerous sleight of hand they frequently found themselves borrowing from the ideologies of systems in which they themselves were the disadvantaged ones, trading this capitulation for a means to justify, in some way, their more intimate forms of violence. Beyond working to legitimate the violence that they themselves committed, moves like this also aligned them with the core social logics that upheld their own subjugation, stifling in turn their capacity for critiquing the very systems in which they were also injured. I refer to these systems, and their justifications, as paternalistic hegemonies, and the experiences of living within them, and through them, are vital to understanding how partner violence is made to be permissible.[2]

Focusing on a notion like "paternalism" might seem like an unusual point of departure into the ideologies of male-perpetrated partner violence, particularly in a Latin American context where frequently it is understood through the lens of another word, "machismo." Indeed the specter of "machismo" is pervasive in Usme, invoked everywhere from casual conversation to the chants of "forward women, back with machismo" that came from groups marching on the International Day for the Elimination of Violence Against Women.[3] From community residents to service professionals there appeared to be a general consensus that, more than anything else, machismo was a major culprit for partner violence. It was inescapable, and many were careful to note that not only machismo on the part of men but also "machista" from women had helped to co-create this damaging set of gendered expectations. But despite the undeniable salience collectively given to the idea of machismo, the problem was that none of the perpetrators of violence with whom I worked saw it in this way. Just as so many others had, the abusive men whom I came to know equated machismo unequivocally with what they saw as negative traits such as image obsession, the assertion of dominance, and posturing violence.[4] Most were careful to distance themselves considerably from them. Instead, the perpetrators of abuse whom I knew preferred to see themselves, and even their violence, through a different lens, a lens that we might call paternalism. Clearly there is more than machismo at play.

While the actual term "paternalism" was less frequently used, this did not detract in any way from its constant presence. It was there in the government reports tucked away in the district archive, emerging from between the lines of the pages that retold the history of Usme as an outlier to the capital city. There emerged a story of supposed benevolence, albeit a stern and forceful one at times, a regional stewardship that always presupposed the higher authority of Usme's neighbor to the north, Bogotá.[5] In the Comisarías de Familia, I would again hear the echoes of paternalistic pretenses but this time through the spoken words of the perpetrators of partner violence. During these audiences, when the lawyers at the Comisaría would decide whether or not to grant an order of protection, the survivors of abuse and those accused would both be allowed their legal right to speak. It was in these moments that I first began to learn how to appreciate the postures of accused men as well as the sometimes brash, sometimes subtle structures of the stories they told. Especially in the cases where men admitted to their alleged abuse, or even chose to speak at all, I had to quickly learn that there was always much more to hear in the arguments they made.

It might be tempting to neglect their stories, to take them as attempts at minimization that do not deserve their own scrutiny. And while they are stories that are often intentionally framed to face a forensic gaze, we disregard them at our own peril. Tossing them preemptively aside prevents us from hearing at least the poetic echoes of *how* abusive men legitimate both their own violence, not the least of all to themselves, and the struggles that to them are nonetheless very real.[6] Perhaps surprisingly, almost none of the men whom I encountered—from audiences in the Comisarías to out in the community and in the confidential spaces of our own encounters—justified their violence directly, making any categorical claims about their right to inflict violence upon their partners. Instead what came across most frequently in those pleas was that, one way or another, their abuse was related to the proper raising of their children, and in the months that I spent in the Comisarías de Familia, I never once witnessed an audience in which children were not invoked.[7] Though the details shifted based on the particularities of their situation, what remained consistent was the effort to present their violence as somehow related to their daily struggles in a difficult world and their efforts to give their children opportunities that they felt they never had.

Whatever the apparent differences between the two, paternalism and machismo both ultimately share in common an interest in masculine domination and are opposing facets of a patriarchal system. And while paternalism might appear to be the more palatable option between the two, invoking it creates an unavoidable paradox: how is a justification rooted in a presumption of benevolence then used to justify the use of violence? Insight into how perpetrators of abuse might smooth over these seeming contradictions is, of course, not something that can be made evident just from observation, even in a space like the Comisarías de Familia. It was only through the invitation of a few particular men to let me into their lives that I began to appreciate the simultaneously delicate and urgent work that was done to build a life, no matter how precarious, in light of these tensions. One key it seemed was to maintain not just the pretense of paternalism, a promise of benevolent authority, but also the ability to be the one who exercises the exception to that rule.

Great States of Exception

In the previous chapter, "Possible," one organizing idea that began to emerge is that partner violence is in some way a question of sovereignty on the more intimate scales, a matter of creating the spaces through which one can maintain power over others.[8] From the long and sustained deliberation over what terms like "sovereignty" actually mean, however, there are two now-classic ideas regarding the meaning of that word, ones that can help to clarify this more intimately violent work. The first is Max Weber's notion that sovereignty is the monopolization of the legitimate use of violence, and while Weber was referring to the governments of nation-states when he proposed this, what his idea makes clear is that it is not sufficient to legitimize violence, one must also *monopolize* that legitimacy as well.[9] The second idea is Carl Schmitt's, whereby sovereignty is the authority to declare the state exception.[10] It is by putting these ideas together that two possibilities emerge. First, the practical connections between the ideas of "sovereignty" and "hegemony" begin to come to light: power, as in the perpetration of partner violence, requires the simultaneous creation of the social spaces in which to exercise it, as well as the elaboration of ideologies to normalize it. Sovereignty is not just power exercised in a spatially inscribed manner; as Weber and Schmitt both point out, it is a constantly legitimized practice as well. Second, with their two ideas put together, how partner violence may be justified through the prism of paternalism becomes clearer: it,is not that those relationships are supposed to be manifestly violent, as violence in its most obvious forms is made to be the exception to the rule. Because it is the exception, and because declaring that exception is so necessary to staking one's sovereignty, it is only in those moments that abusive partners might claim a monopoly on its legitimacy.

Thinking about claims of legitimacy in such abstract and neat terms though comes at great risk. Chief among them is failing to see how ineffective they often are. While this might be most obviously true with regard to the survivors of violence—who have often rejected those terms long before they actually leave that relationship—it is also true for the perpetrators themselves. To see violent relationships as rationally planned programs of control would be a fallacy, and while ideologies like paternalism can sometimes be seen as preemptive justifications for violence, in practice they can just as easily be hasty pretexts concocted to make sense of one's own actions. If the promise is benevolence but the method is violence, how does one reconcile the two after the fact? Not even those who attempt to set the rules can always follow them, and when someone fails to meet their own expectations, what is left? What can come across as attempts for control can for perpetrators be every bit as much about feeling out of control; and what the stories of many abusive men show is that while their actions may come across as purposeful attempts for domination over others, they do not necessarily indicate the experience of mastery over themselves.

Sacandoles Adelante (or "Getting Ahead")

"I arrived around three in the afternoon. I got back [home] when a neighbor told me, 'Don't go to your house because people from Family Welfare are there.' 'Yeah? How so? From Family Welfare?' She said, 'Yes, that truck over there, there's a woman there with your partner.' Strange. When her daughter saw me, she cried to her mother, 'Mom, my papá has arrived!' (she calls me papá). 'No, mom, my papá is here.' Hmm. All the sudden they took out a suitcase and some bags, so I said to her, 'Where are you going, Luisa?' She said, 'Nowhere, nowhere, this doesn't concern you.' So she got into the truck and . . ."

He slaps his hands.

". . . Ciao."

"Where they went, I have no idea where she's living. They say that supposedly she's living in a house of 'family protection,' one run by Family Welfare. She's there in a boarding house. I got myself in a situation with the Comisaría de Familia. So on the twenty-fifth of last month I went to their office."

He laughs a little, nervously.

"So, well, I went to their office and a doctora told me that I, that I, how did she put it? That I had no right to know where Luisa was. So I told her, 'How can that be? Even if she's carrying a child of mine? I need to know where she is, what her situation is.' She said, 'Don't worry,' that Family Welfare, that the Comisaría de Familia is waiting on her and taking care of everything. 'You can't call her, you can't talk to her, you can't get close to her, you can't know where she is.' I said okay, because in the days before, after Luisa left, I had started to look for her everywhere. I looked and looked for her, called her phone but she didn't answer, looked for her everywhere and even went out to Villavicencio to look for her there. I called her family to find out where she had gone, but she wasn't with them either. I looked for her in the hospitals, I looked . . . I went to Family Welfare, asking them if they could help me. Nothing, nothing."

He draws a deep breath in and sighs.

"So one day arrived and I said, desperate, fed up, I told myself that I would go to the clinic where Luisa had been going for her [prenatal] care, to see if *maybe I could find her there. So one morning I went to, what is that clinic called? Javeriana, the clinic of La Javeriana on Seventh Avenue and Forty-Fifth I think."*

"Of the university? University of La Javeriana?" I ask him.

"Of the university, exactly. So I got to the counter and I asked the woman there, 'Could you do me a favor? I want to know if there's a patient here named Luisa.' 'Yes, one moment,' she told me, 'let me see if she's in the system . . . yes, she's here.' 'Yes?' How about that. So I asked, 'Can I see her?' 'And you are?' she asked. 'I'm her husband,' I told her. 'Yes, okay, one moment. Visiting hours are starting just now so you can go up.' So, they told me I could enter, so I did, but I didn't know she had an order of protection or anything like that. So I asked what room, she told me, and I went up."

He whistles and slides his hands together.

"When I got there, I went in and saw her lying down, she was eating an apple. I kept watching her until she got up. She stayed quiet until she said, 'You, Diego?' and I said, 'Yes, mi amor, what's been going on?' So I went in to greet her and she started to cry. She cried and cried and cried and the nurse came in and held her. I asked, 'What's going on here?' She said, 'No, you can't see her, you're not even allowed to know where she is.' And I said, 'Why can't I see her? Why can't I know where she is? I'm her husband!' She said, 'No, señor, she put an order of protection against you, you can't get close to her.'"

"Did you know at that time about the order of protection?"

"I didn't. I didn't know anything about that, absolutely nothing about the order of protection. They sent me to talk to a doctor and he explained to me everything that was going on. He called me in and sat me down. Explained to me, 'Don Diego, what is going on is that she has an order of protection against you and you're not allowed to know where she is, you can't see her, touch her, call her, absolutely nothing.' 'But why, doctor?' I asked. 'Because you have been mistreating her.'"

He sighs again.

* * *

This was the very first story that Diego told me. Before the long hours we spent talking about his growing up on a farm in Cundinamarca, coming to the city, and then meeting his partner; before we talked about his hopes, his fears, his frustrations, the things that made him feel ashamed; before I took my first trepidatious steps into his home or followed him to his work; before

I even had the chance to turn on my audio recorder during our first meeting, this was what he wanted me to know. Diego was the first perpetrator of violence to show me into his life, a connection made through one of the Comisarías de Familia in Usme, and when we first spoke on the phone his enthusiasm to meet and talk almost worried me. That excitement had not diminished in any way by the time that we first met at the public library, the bounce in his step and his boyish energy somehow at odds with his forty years of age and the gravity of the circumstances that had brought us together. In our conversations, Diego was above all a storyteller and would spend hours at a time taking me step by step through the paces of his life. He did so openly, eagerly, an oral autobiography delivered calmly and punctuated more by his ready laughter and wrinkled brow than by anxiety or anger. And yet he rarely spoke directly about the violence he committed. Even though he sought me out, as he said, as a means of reflecting on his actions, even though he readily allowed me to read through his file at the Comisaría de Familia, it was only with great difficulty that he ever spoke aloud about the physical or verbal abuse that he had committed against Luisa. In the few instances when he did, his whole manner would abruptly change. With his gaze dropped down to his lap, his shoulders hunched, hands clasped nervously, and always one knee bouncing, those seemed to be the only moments that he was eager to let pass on by.

Peculiar then that this was the very first story he told me, indeed insisted that I know before we could further test the waters of our new acquaintance. I say peculiar because in that story that he told, he was describing the detailed steps that he took in stalking Luisa after she left him. It was also not as though her flight from their home had been completely unanticipated. By Diego's own admission, it came at the end of a crescendo of his own violence, in particular after the very worst of their fights. But if his other acts of violence had made him feel ashamed, this one in particular did not seem to do so. On the contrary it was a story that he displayed with pride, if not also with exasperation, a saga through which he exemplified, by his estimation, the kind of concern that a good father should show. In telling it he made certain to call my attention to particular moments, for instance his stepdaughter's insistence on calling him "papá," and most of all that Luisa was pregnant at the time with their first child together. At the end of it all, when he finally appeared before the Comisaría to learn the specifics of the order of protection placed against him, this became his ultimate defense. It was his justification for his aggressive pursuit of Luisa throughout the previous weeks, from traveling hours out of the city to Villavicencio to arriving unsolicited at the clinic where she had been receiving prenatal care. "Even if she is carrying a child of mine?" were his words, as he retold them, his rebuttal to being told at the Comisaría that he would henceforth not be allowed to know where Luisa was living.

Whatever degree of justification Diego drew from his paternal role, this kind of behavior—his stalking of Luisa during the weeks before we met—was never something that he was able to categorically defend. Throughout every one of our subsequent encounters, in isolated interview rooms or out in the community that he called home, every time that he related a story in which he stalked an intimate partner he made certain to carefully justify why. Suspicion of infidelity constituted the first exception to his own rules, and acting in what he saw as the best interest of his children was the second. In this particular case, that meant tracking Luisa down, by any means necessary, so that he could provide for her the kind of support that he felt she needed during her pregnancy. It was a kind of concern that pervaded much of Diego's and my interactions up until, and even after, Luisa delivered the baby. Before the two reunited, whenever I would ask Diego what he was concerned about at the time, he would usually answer with some reference to their child's and Luisa's care. Even after the two began living together again, he would open our conversations with talk about Luisa's health and then continually rehash with me their options of where they would go for her eventual delivery.

Throughout Luisa's pregnancy, her delivery, and the childrearing that came after, the amount of self-worth that Diego found in his role as a father would be difficult to overstate and, as I would later learn, this sense of importance stood in stark contrast to the otherwise dismal situation he found himself in when we first met. At the time, he had just barely begun working again and was still uncovering himself from his accumulated debts, feeling also the constant pressure of loneliness from living in a community where avoiding everyday dangers on the street left him feeling cloistered away within his own home. Luisa's leaving was therefore nothing less than a total crisis of self for him, with the desperation that he felt while searching for her matched only by his desperation to frame those actions as born out of paternalistic concern. It was that framing that was so necessary to *his* ability to live with the consequences of his own violence and his subsequent responses to it. Against his own rules he was willing to find, and declare, exceptions, but only if the well-being of a child of his was at stake.

This is not to say that paternalism and its exceptions necessarily provide an explanation for all of Diego's violence against Luisa. In order to understand in greater depth what came before and what happened after that final fight will require a much longer foray into Diego's life and their relationship, something that will be considered more fully in this chapter. That broader picture was one that I only began to appreciate after a much longer engagement with him, one carried out over the course of the year following our first encounter. But even if all of Diego's physical violence cannot be made to fit under the rubric of the "state of exception," the abuse committed by many other men that I encountered in the Comisarías did. Though it was articulated in many different ways, having taken place in as many different situations, one of the giveaways during the audiences in the Comisarías was whenever accused men finished a thought with the saying "sacarlos adelante." It meant that they saw themselves as somehow better able to get their children ahead in life, because of either their financial resources or their ability to inculcate certain values. The logic went that if it meant a better future for their children, and so long as it was confined to discrete instances, violence against one's partner could be justified as a regrettable outcome, the effect of defending one's children from all perceived threats in the world, even including those from within their home.

Placed before the staff of a state institution charged with addressing partner violence, it would be difficult for aggressors to categorically justify their abuse, and indeed none of the men with whom I spoke in private ever did either. Absent such sweeping justifications though, they could at least attempt to portray those actions as exceptions to a more acceptable kind of conduct.[11] Supported by a hierarchy of vulnerability in which children were imagined to require the greatest protection, these states of paternalistic exception became the heated arithmetic of prioritization, of robbing the rights of one to benefit another in the context of a challenging and unfair world. To view these as cynical and disingenuous claims made before others—be it agents of the Comisaría or an outsider ethnographer—would again be to deny them of their full meaning and audience. As I came to more intimately know some of the men behind the abuse, and the intricacies of their reactions to their own violence, one thing that became clear was who they were really speaking to when making these kinds of claims. Beyond any Comisaría staff, their neighbors, or even their partners, what became increasingly evident was that in justifying the violence that they had committed, perpetrators of partner violence had one audience above all in mind: themselves.

"I Drink So That I Can Cry"

Justifications are not always successful, even when those who make them have a vested interest in believing them. Those who are in positions of power are often unmoved by their own ideologies, even when they are directed mostly at convincing themselves. When they fail, and when perpetrators of violence lose the partners upon whom they have become dependent, what then are they left with? Frequently, as the case may be, they are left with alcohol, and certainly the relationship between the use of substances and partner violence is a phenomenon documented around the world.[12] Colombia, and specifically Bogotá, represents no exception to this rule, and in one audit of presentations to the Comisarías de Familia, alcohol use on the part of the aggressor was cited as an instigating factor in at least one-third of cases.[13]

The possible uses of alcohol in particular are legion, and the potential connections to partner violence just as many. Be it a means of social engagement or self-disinhibition, emboldening for posturing performances or coping with boredom and isolation, quieting painful memories or intrusive thoughts, even more simply a means of coping with chemical dependency, there are almost innumerable instrumental uses of alcohol as well as its unintended effects. Indeed many of these were represented, some even plainly visible, in the quotidian rhythms of life in Usme. Down the road from Usme's central square it could be seen through the open fronts of cantinas, gathering spaces where mostly men sought company, sitting for hours around small tables overrun with emptied bottles of Poker beer. In the more urban neighborhoods to the north, it could be smelled seeping out from behind the closed doors of discos and seen in the liquor ads that covered their outside walls. During the weekdays it could be heard in the lamentations of Comisaría de Familia staff, those who claimed that their workloads always seemed to swell after public holidays and the binging behavior that the holidays had brought.

Amid this multitude of social uses of alcohol there was one dynamic in particular that I did not expect, one that I first began hearing of during my early months in the Comisarías. This was a self-reported pattern from some perpetrators of violence in which they described how their alcohol consumption drastically increased only *after* their separations from their partners. These insights were not easily offered up by abusive men though; usually the lawyers and psychologists on staff extracted them only with the greatest of care. Alcohol as a legitimate excuse for violence had already lost its cachet, it seemed, at least within these particular spaces, and for the accused men there seemed to be very little attraction to further admitting any of their dependencies. When revealed, these admissions carried with them a mark of desperation, a brief and tightly guarded window into the difficulty that that person might be having, and with it a reminder that what many perpetrators experience during their separation from their partners amounted to an intense and intolerable loss. One man in particular, Nicolás, the worker in the quarries of Usme who had left his home at the age of eleven to escape an abusive stepfather, said it the most clearly. Later during our own private interactions, when I asked him why he started to drink more after his partner left their home, he told me simply, "I drink so that I can cry."

Alcohol provided for men like him not simply an exception to the ideologies that otherwise were meant to justify the violence that they committed against others; instead, it provided an exception to the violent set of rules that they made for themselves. In addition to the other instrumental uses of psychotropic substances, one might add their ability to open up windows of time in which those who use them are able to express emotions that are otherwise considered unacceptable. The man who told me that he drank so he could cry was more than aware of these multiple uses. After running away from his childhood home, alcohol had provided a way for him to both momentarily subdue the memories of his own abuse as well as mimic with his friends what he imagined adulthood to be; alcohol was a means of separating himself temporarily from his past but also of sharing experiences with those around him in the present. Later when *he* became the one who battered, the one who raped, when he was the one who had to live with the recognition of his own violence, alcohol again became his means for forgetting, but it also became his means of coping with the boredom and isolation that he felt when he found himself alone within his home. There, in the solitude of his own room, he was continually confronted by the fact that forgetting would never be a possibility for him and, confronted by that fact, confronted by his continued ruminations on what he had done, alcohol provided him the exception for adhering to dominant masculine norms. Even in the secluded space of his own room, it was still only in an intoxicated state that he could allow himself to express his sadness, his shame, his desperation and fear, to let himself do the one thing that to him men are never supposed to do: cry. When repression, even to one's self, is not successful, exception may be seen as one of the few avenues of recourse left.[14] And so to think of partner violence through the rubric of states of exception does not refer to only the violence done against others. For some, it has just as much to do with the states of exception declared with regard to domination over one's very own self.

An Ideology Divided Against Itself

Taken altogether, what these experiences show is that when it comes to partner violence in Usme, there is clearly more at stake than machismo. The instrumental role that children play in the lifeworlds of abusive men beckons us to recognize that masculine domination is not upheld by any one-dimensional belief. Not only is machismo itself a complex notion that goes beyond violent displays and intoxication, as others have shown, but children and the imagined paternal role can be central features in partner violence as well.[15] This is particularly true when perpetrators declare their children to be their primary purpose in committing that violence and, through their prioritization, a valid state of exception to the just treatment of their partners. The problem with states of exception though is that not everyone believes in them equally, and when they are used to validate violence against others there is no guarantee that survivors of that abuse will believe any longer in the legitimacy of their partners. It is only through the discordant stories that retell any such relationship that we begin to perceive the inevitable parallax that arises in them. This is the self-defeating trap into which many abusive men fall, and it is why it is so critical to understand masculine domination as a multifaceted object. From some angles, some might view it as paternalism—an ideology of benevolent authority—but from others it is a more plainly violent system of control. This was the contrast that one lawyer in the Comisaría de Familia offered when comparing the two: both paternalism and machismo are core features of a system that privileges men, but paternalism pertains to the provision for others whereas machismo is that same system when it causes suffering instead.

Hegemony fundamentally refers to how power over others is maintained, and Hannah Arendt famously proposed that violence is not the tool of its maintenance but rather a reflection of the loss of control. That the intensity of violence in abusive partnerships often escalates when survivors attempt to leave would certainly seem to support this idea, but there is more to the picture than just reactive violence.[16] As explored in the previous chapter, acts of violence can themselves drastically accelerate that very loss of control, and it is in understanding this dynamic that the view of an entangled paternalism/machismo is most useful. Paternalism is not only a fantasy for benevolent authority: it is the search for legitimacy in intensely unequal relationships, and as such it is also an attempt to efface from view the violent potential of what is more often associated with machismo. The escalation of violence in partner abuse—from verbal to physical and sexual forms—is therefore not just a reflection of the loss of control but is itself an actively counterhegemonic practice. It is the undoing of the control that paternalistic justifications, and their related states of exception, sought to achieve. Indeed in my experience, as with the experience of many others, the escalation of violence was generally the primary reason for people to present to the Comisarías de Familia in the first place. In a context where survivors of abuse have the ability to find support, or even a means of escape, violence itself becomes the force that rotates the object of masculine control and widens the discrepancy of the parallax between the people involved. Perpetrators desperately seek to justify these acts then as valid exceptions to the rule, but those who bear the brunt of these acts more easily discern them as violence without justification and, if they can, often refute those arrangements by leaving them entirely.[17] In leaving, everything that abusive partners sought to maintain suddenly comes undone, and for them what is left in its wake is often intolerable. No one made this clearer than the men who admitted to drinking more *after* their partners left them, not so subtle indications of just how emotionally dependent perpetrators can be on the very people whom they abuse.

Finally, what an eye to paternalism helps us to see is that the ethical and logical systems tied up in partner violence are not so easily "otherized" to areas on the margins of society. What this means is that just because an area of a society might have higher rates of violence—as is the case for partner violence in Usme—we cannot so easily assume that it is because of some peculiar cultural pathology, an implication that many try to implicitly or explicitly convey when invoking the term "machismo." The moral frameworks implicated in this violence are not "backward" philosophies alien to the "modern" centers of society. On the contrary, they cut to the core of them. The first implication of this is that paternalistic partner violence in Usme actually adheres to broader moral systems, ones that are even played out on national and international scales. What it also means though is that in using these justifications in their intimate relationships, abusive partners on the margins of the city are capitulating themselves, at least in part, to ethical systems that are central to other forms of their very own subjugation. By borrowing from these social logics and substituting their positions within them, they become active surrogates in these broader systems. It is therefore not just a question of the domination of one person over another, but how that intimate practice plays a role in stabilizing other sovereign schemes (political, economic, or otherwise)—systems in which abusive partners are not only implicated but also frequently subordinated as well.

Paternalistic Hegemonies and Surrogate Power

As previously discussed in the history of Usme, there persists a certain "geography of imagination" in Colombia, indeed in the rest of Latin America and the entire hemisphere.[18] As the imagination often goes, at the cores are cities or powerful countries, and at the margins is violence. At the hemispheric scale, Colombians have lived with this for quite a while now, plagued still by the ignominy, the *mala fama* of a supposedly distinct "culture of violence" vis-à-vis their neighbor to the north.[19] As a half-Colombian growing up in the United States, I myself was only too aware of this dynamic any time that I discussed my dual heritage. From elementary school assemblies to medical school seminars, encountering the presumption that Colombians are somehow preternaturally predisposed to an exotic and pathological ethos has been a sadly consistent experience of mine. This exotification is not just a product of crossing national borders though: within Colombia itself these kinds of imagined geographies have been major influencing features from colonialism to the present day.[20] The continued labeling of Usme as a zona roja, a racy and transgressive area within the limits of the capital city, is only one of the many indications of it.[21] Be it the histories of extractive industries and their primitive accumulations, the ownership of rural haciendas by urban elites, or the inconsistent presence of a centralized state, the creation of "peripheries" has always required the creation of "cores," and since their moments of inception the lines between the two have been nothing more than imagined distinctions.[22]

The sense of violent "otherness" though that has been projected onto "peripheries" goes well beyond the lines of political insurgency or economic exploitation. When "machismo" becomes the oft-invoked explanation for an uneven epidemiology of partner violence, it carries with it the implication of cultural lag, that the values in one place fall behind the currents of progress already made elsewhere. In doing so it betrays a deeper belief in difference, in the fundamental separation of one area of society from another. By seeing partner violence also in terms of "paternalism," rather than just "machismo," we help ourselves to see beyond these false distinctions. The purpose is not to deny uneven distributions of violence but to recognize that the ideologies that underwrite intimate abuse, even on the margins of Bogotá, continue straight to the core precepts on which broader social relationships have been built. Paternalism, it turns out, is the pattern that carries all the way down this fractal of violence. Beginning with Usme and working our way back, we can come to see what that has actually meant.

From Margin to Center

As a peripheral district of the federal capital itself, Usme is a bit unusual in how directly its history is tied to both municipal and national politics. Regarding the political geography within Colombia, one thing that the history of Usme illustrates is that the maintenance of cities themselves, Bogotá in particular, has been a central feature in establishing national sovereignty in an otherwise frequently contested land. As the history of Usme, outlined in Chapter 1, shows, when Usme was annexed in 1954 along with six other municipalities, it was more than a question of local urban redistricting. At stake was the creation of the largest city in the nation, a capital district without equal, one whose exceptional status could allow it to continue to serve as the seat of government control during Colombia's ongoing nation-building project. That was no trivial matter, considering that it was accomplished at the tail end of the massive shock that was the Bogotazo and La Violencia. Yet despite the importance of Usme at that historical juncture, it did not mean that residents of this municipality-cum-city-district were treated any more as equals. What happened instead was more or less a continuation of the same, the part exploitation, part neglect, part infantilization of its people, even while nominally it carried all the equal status of any other part of the city.

Again, much of this dynamic had long been established prior to the mid-twentieth century, a relationship that goes back to at least the colonial era. Fals Borda referred to this process as the "Catholic subversion": the original conquest of the land that later turned into Colombia rested as much on the pedagogy and proselytization to the indigenous and rural poor as it did on anything else.[23] Considering the role that the Catholic Church played during this era, perhaps it comes as little surprise that a system of governance emerged that was based upon the presumed intellectual and moral authority of those closer to the organs of the state.[24] Given the Catholic origins of the very term "hierarchy," the doctrine of a "father" above, and the institutionalized privileging of men within the Church itself, it takes little imagination to see how Catholicism played one role in establishing gendered regimes of power that continued through to the formation of an independent Colombia. When that state became imagined as a national "family," the power within it and the obligations to protect and provide also took with them the notion of a paternal legitimacy.[25] As such, as was the case in the founding of so many other modern states, the social contract that bound Colombia as a polity was, from its outset, inseparable from the presumption of certain gendered relations on the more intimate scale.

Far from a relic of the past, such symbolic roots find themselves still woven into everyday experiences in Usme in a multitude of ways. In perhaps the most banal sense, this is seen in the limits of what political participation in the district really means, limits that I saw most clearly displayed during community meetings with elected officials.[26] Such attitudes are demonstrated in other ways though, ones that, despite their apparent benevolence, still signal the continued justification of unequal relationships through more subtle exercises in authority.[27] I came across an example of one of these during a meandering walk around Usme's countryside with a friend of mine, a member of the community, as we passed an old hacienda that had since been converted into a meeting space for campesinos in the community.[28] As we passed by, I made a comment about how I found the reappropriation of space interesting and, turning back toward me, my companion told me with a wry smile about how that was the building that they used for educational workshops for farmers. Amused, she pointed out the irony that she saw in government representatives teaching farmers how to grow their crops or protect natural water supplies. As she saw it, it was campesinos who were fighting in the first place for the preservation of arable land and protection of the páramo that supplies their farms, and the rest of Bogotá, with fresh water.[29] Fighting against the continuous encroachment of housing projects and the erosion produced by ever-expanding quarries, it was her belief that the campesinos themselves should be the ones teaching the government representatives about the "real" farming issues in Usme, not the other way around. Instead, educating people about a vocation that they have long held displays a striking presumption of superiority, in this case an intellectual one, one that clearly echoes the colonial era even if its religious tones have been traded now for technoscientific ones relating to contemporary agriculture.

To add further irony to the situation, such educational programs reek of the same dynamics that have constituted the long history of Colombia's relationship with its neighbor to the north, the United States. The main distinction between these experiences has been that in these more global relationships, it has been the whole of the Colombian people, and by extension its national government, that has typically been treated as the infantilized "other." The history of the United States' presumed exceptionalism and general superiority is a long and storied one, and its emergence and maintenance depended heavily upon its relationship with the Latin American states with whom it has shared its hemisphere.[30] Since the founding of the United States, its political leaders have traditionally adopted a downward gaze toward their immediate neighbors, best epitomized by words that John Quincy Adams wrote, saying that "[Latin Americans] are lazy, dirty, nasty and in short I can compare them to nothing but a parcel of hogs." From the time of that writing to when Adams became secretary of state, his views had scarcely changed, and when it came to recognizing the newly liberated Gran Colombia in 1820, he took again to his diary to declare that "there is no community of interests between North and South America."[31] Whether or not this turned out to be true depends on our definition of a "community of interests," but either way the following two centuries have been characterized by both the assertion of U.S. superiority—epitomized by the Monroe Doctrine and its later interpretations—as well as the intricate involvement of the United States in Latin American politics, organized ostensibly around the pretense of democratic stewardship in the region.[32]

Although the United States fashioned itself as a guiding light of liberty and good governance in the hemisphere, by the beginning of the twentieth century it was increasingly clear that it had taken on that mission under the precept of the "white man's burden," as the educator to nations that were frequently portrayed as younger, racially inferior, and generally less capable in their self-determination. And even though the U.S. policies enacted during this period make that clear enough, the political cartoons published during the day also make it all too painfully obvious. One such cartoon, called "School Begins" and published in *Puck* in 1899, showed Uncle Sam standing at the front of a classroom with stick in hand, small brown-skinned children labeled "Philippines," "Hawaii," "Puerto Rico," and "Cuba" slouched over in a bench in front of him while a Native American sits in the corner and a Black American washes the windows. Another, entitled "Wilson Teaches Latin America" and published in 1914, unsurprisingly showed Woodrow Wilson standing in front of a blackboard with the words "we can have no sympathy with those who seek to seize the power of government to advance their own personal interests of ambition," with child-sized people in sombreros that read "Venezuela," "Nicaragua," and "Mexico" before him.

If many in the United States saw their country as exceptional, and by that reasoning a legitimate authority in the region, then they also rarely hesitated to invoke states of exception to that putatively benevolent guidance. Hemispheric sovereignty was staked not just under paternalistic pretenses but also by the frequent use of violence, accompanied by its incumbent justifications.[33] For Colombians this became all too clear in the U.S.-backed secession of Panama, when the "big stick" portion of Theodore Roosevelt's foreign policy was employed to ensure the realization of what he deemed to be an economically necessary project, the construction of the Panama Canal.[34] Memorialized in political cartoons like the 1903 "News Reaches Bogotá," which read "Teddy tosses a spadeful of Panama dirt on the capital city of Colombia," and the 1905 "The World's Constable"—itself a play on Roosevelt's earlier position as New York City police commissioner—these almost casual commentaries still serve as powerful reminders of the violence that always lay just beyond the "benevolent guidance" of the United States to the region.[35]

Just as the logic of paternalistic governance "internal" to Colombian affairs has continued into the contemporary era, U.S. paternalism toward Colombia and the rest of Latin America still occurs as well. Similarly, unlike its more crass early iterations, the United States has also had to continue this program of dominance under a softer guise, this time as technoscientific advice giving, material aid, and training of other forms. One example of this was the intervention of U.S. scientific advisors—and later institutions such as the nascent USAID and those that would eventually merge into the World Bank—in reshaping the modes of production for coffee cultivation after the collapse of the hacienda system in Colombia during the era following the Great Depression.[36] In collaboration with the Federación Nacional de Cafeteros (FNC; National Federation of Coffee Growers), these advisors succeeded in promoting mono-cropping of coffee and more capital-intensive practices such as using fertilizers and pesticide. Beside re-yoking coffee farmers to systems of international debt through the use of these tools, these projects had the additional effect of reconsolidating much of the previously redistributed land into progressively larger operations, ones that could sustain those new forms of cultivation.[37]

On a more regular basis, contemporary U.S. involvement in Colombia has been characterized by the provision of material support and military training. Beside coffee, cocaine has been one of the continued reasons for U.S. interest in Colombia, and the waging of the "war on drugs" has to a great extent been exported internationally. In the year 2000 it reached new heights as Plan Colombia, intended to curb the exportation of drugs and the activity of militarized groups, made Colombia the greatest recipient of U.S. aid in the Western Hemisphere, second only to Israel on the global scale.[38] Rather than dispatching its own soldiers, the United States has more typically engaged in training Latin American special forces, particularly Colombian ones, through an institution known as WHINSEC (Western Hemisphere Institute for Security Cooperation). Formerly known as the infamous School of the Americas (SOA), in the first decades after its founding in 1946 it was repeatedly accused of teaching otherwise prohibited military tactics, ways of mounting "dirty" counterinsurgency efforts against leftist guerrilla groups. How were those contradictions maintained? Mostly by exporting the training to liminal spaces of U.S. governance. Founded originally at Fort Gulick in the Panama Canal Zone—a territory that simultaneously pertains to the United States without being fully incorporated into it—the Canal Zone in this instance served as a sort of *space* of exception. Just as the Guantanamo Bay detention camp has more recently provided a space of exception for torture or detainment without habeas corpus, the Canal Zone provided the perfect space for U.S. policy makers to attempt to contain the exceptions that they made, contradictions against what was otherwise the officially promoted project of fostering democracy and good governance in the region.[39]

"Surrogate Power" and the Undoing of Hegemony

What these various histories of paternalism combine to tell us is that violence in Usme is not just the product of some exotic or in any way discrepant ethos. Be it at the interpersonal, municipal, national, or even global scales of social relations, the same motif is made manifest at all layers of the fractal of sovereignty: the projection of benevolence and the practice of exceptional violence. Rather than representing a peculiar cultural pathology, a marginal practice, the intimate violence that some men on the margins of Bogotá commit lies directly at the core of how our entire hemisphere has been made.[40] If not so easily "otherized" though, what do we make of the unusually high prevalence of partner violence in Usme, and where does this fit into the broader picture? Viewed from one direction, it helps to clarify the social positions that abusive men in Usme occupy, the historical justifications for them, and therefore a starting point to understanding what the stakes are for men who commit partner violence on the margins of this city. While partner violence is often discussed in terms of the control exercised within an intimate relationship, what other research and to some extent common sense shows is that those who commit that violence often relate it to the very lack of control in other aspects of their life. That is to say, when these men feel most out of control, the most belittled, they become the most violent in the few situations in which "control" still feels like a possibility.[41] None of this though is intended to advance a facile interpretation of partner violence whereby the "real" culprits for it are those who wield power on a hemispheric scale, nor is it an attempt to find some compromise on a continuum of culpability between the agency of social actors and the supposed structures in which they live. Adjudicating that particular kind of blame simply pales in comparison to the imperative of engaging directly with perpetrators of partner violence, and the purpose here is to begin to find new apertures in which to do so.[42]

Taking this approach offers instead a space in which to appreciate the frequently paradoxical, and as such precarious, situations that many abusive partners in Usme inhabit: using those ethical frameworks to justify, at the very least to themselves, their exercises of power over their intimate partners at the same time that they are also marginalized or exploited under them. There is a profound tension here, one that can be productive of a great many different ends. While one of them is the instigation of violence against their partners, another consequence can often be the mitigation of how abusive men criticize these broader sovereign systems. Notably absent from my conversations with Diego, and indeed any other perpetrator of partner violence who let me into his life, were the kinds of incisive criticisms that had become the common substance of my discussions with people like Luz Elena and other survivors. Even after the extensive hours of our interviews, after Diego had allowed me into his home, taken me to his place of work, shown me around his community, when I prompted him more directly and asked him about what ideas like "injustice" meant to him, the responses that he gave were always considerably constrained. In them, he would turn back to stories he had told me about the few times when he had been treated disrespectfully at work or the frankly criminally low pay that he had received along the way.

Displays of disrespect and low wages: that was about as far as any abusive partner that I knew went in speaking about what was unjust in their lives. Unlike the critiques by Luz and survivors of partner violence, the complaints of these men were thoroughly lodged within the logics of those economies, but they did little to rethink them. The problem it seemed was not that their bosses had institutionalized power over them, but that the problems arose only when that power was abused in some way, either through verbal offenses or unfair pay. Through their own reliance on those logics, Diego and other perpetrators of violence had become invested in those very systems that continued to injure them. By contrast, when Luz spoke of iniquity what she meant was the concentration of power in the first place, and through both her explicit philosophy and her living as praxis, she repudiated the fundamental bases of those arrangements. Just as one survivor of partner violence had vowed to never "enslave herself" to a company, Luz made certain through the diversification of her own personal resources that no one person could ever hold determination over her life. This difference in word and practice from survivors to perpetrators of partner violence is significant. Even though early iterations of social contest are often articulated within the logics of those existing systems, at some point viable alternatives do need to be proposed.[43] Without them, any lasting or fundamental change would seem to be unlikely.

It is in this aspect in particular in which men who abused their partners seemed particularly limited. Through their capitulation to paternalistic ideologies, used to privilege themselves vis-à-vis their intimate partners, they significantly constrained their imaginations for a more broadly different world. Straightforward criticism of inequity is not the grounds on which more drastic social change is built, and it is in this respect that those who had been most multiply marginalized showed the greatest creative potential. Their critical imaginations, the alternatives that they proposed, were born out of the crucibles in which they had lived, forged in the urgent practice of self-preservation against the overlapping regimes of power that they had learned to simultaneously contest. But it is not simply that they were marginalized along a number of dimensions of power: so too were Diego and other abusive men. It was by not co-opting those ideologies into a means of violent control within their intimate relationships, including toward their children, that they avoided surrogacy to social logics like paternalism. In doing so they left themselves open to cultivating both the insights and practical knowledge of how to effectively evade and even undo these abusive systems.[44] Through their everyday practices they made real a vital set of refutations against these violent forms of domination and lit beacons in the fog for others to follow away from the mutually abusive logics that uphold them.

As such, this issue of co-optation and capitulation is a question of hegemony in the Gramscian sense: the maintenance of sovereign power by cultivating ideologies into which the subaltern can at least partially invest themselves.[45] It is also, however, a matter of tying together in a meaningful way different regimes of power—be they gendered, state, economic, racial, or otherwise—and binding together these various axes through the process of constructing sovereign control, be that on the intimate or hemispheric scales. By bringing these axes together under a core set of logics about what supposedly "benevolent" operations of power look like, and introducing to them the concept of the violent exception, paternalistic hegemonies represent one of the vital processes that serve to unify the mutually reinforcing systems that make up our world.[46] Even the strongest critiques of this kind of hegemony have allowed for at least two possible instances in which ideologies might maintain this kind of power: first, when people are denied any social interaction with one another (an exceedingly rare circumstance) or, second, when there exists the possibility of future advancement within that unequal system.[47]

What the interpretation of partner violence presented here allows for is a third possibility: surrogacy. This means that these kinds of ideologies can be effective—they can strengthen hegemonic positions—when some of the people disempowered within them can in turn co-opt them, using them to their own relative advantage in other aspects of their lives. This has nothing to do with delayed gratification, of holding out hope for future advancement within a given system. It has everything to do instead with capitulating to the power of a sovereign, provided that one can immediately re-create those dynamics on a smaller social scale.[48] It is a surprisingly viable mechanism of manufacturing consent, and what it means is that through each daily exercise of intimate violence, perpetrators of abuse, like Diego, invest themselves more fully into these ideologies and, through doing so, make themselves into surrogate agents in their own subjugation. But surrogacy does not imply passivity or rote mimesis of abuse. Surrogacy by contrast is an active role and, in performing these arrangements, perpetrators of partner violence experience firsthand the paradoxes that emerge from the positions that they occupy. It is in these uncertainties in the webs that they themselves have helped to spin, and their confrontations with some of their consequences, that their own potential for creative transformation may be found.

The supposed strengths of a system can also be its greatest weaknesses. In fact, because systems rely on these putative strengths, to address them is to potentially provoke these forms of violence into precipitating their own collapse. In the case of paternalistic hegemonies, this means working directly with perpetrators of abuse like Diego, those who occupy considerably unstable nexuses of power and who experience firsthand the contradictions that emerge from in between these various regimes. Theirs are the stories about the unintended consequences that come from the search for sovereignty. Theirs are the parables about how its violent practice can inadvertently capitulate oneself to broader ideologies, and in doing so become the glue that binds these forms of violence into a mutually reinforcing whole. But just as their violence against their partners progressively weaves them more deeply into these series of arrangements, gave them active roles in their maintenance, and invested them with surrogate power, so too could their experiences lead them to turn against those ideologies entirely.

The men who elected to open up to me about the abuse that they had committed did so for a reason. In large part it was because, faced finally with the full force of the negative consequences of their actions, their ambivalences over the basic precepts on which they had built their lives had deepened considerably. Faced with crisis, they chose to seek a space in which they could reflect on those underlying assumptions. By calling critical attention at such moments to these basic justifications of power, and providing opportunities for abusive men to realize new forms of self-appreciation and respect, it may even be possible for men like Diego to become the most unlikely of accomplices in projects to rework our social worlds. Doing so will only be possible, however, by working directly through the justifications that they make for their violence, not reflexively dismissing them instead. By engaging with perpetrators of violence like him, from in between the lines of that which has been made permissible and that which has been experienced, something else entirely might just emerge: a new vision of what is possible. If we are ever to get there though, we must also first understand what is at stake for perpetrators in the violence that they commit.

CHAPTER 4

Stakes

Ya es anunciado una batalla
Como todos los días
Solo hambre, guerras, muertes
Que acaban con la vida
Como en busca de poder
El hombre se auto-destruía . . .

—Alma de Negro, "Profecias"

Violence can only be concealed by a lie, and the lie can only
be maintained by violence. Any man who has once
proclaimed violence as his method is inevitably forced to
take the lie as his principle.

—Aleksandr Solzhenitsyn

As before, just because something can be made possible, and even tenuously permissible, still does not mean that it will ever come to pass. With regard to partner violence, the question of "possibility" points us toward how vulnerability is structured and the limits it reaches, and the question of "permissibility" points to the self-contradictory ideologies at play. While both are indispensable aspects of how any violent system comes to inflict harm, neither actually uncovers why someone would come to commit a violent act. In order to begin to understand as much, we must instead delve into the most interpersonal levels, and we must ask what is at stake for the perpetrators themselves. In this case, doing so requires a deep engagement with the lives and experiences of abusive men. With those whom I came to know, that kind of engagement consistently pointed in one direction: if chronically abusive relationships are fundamentally a question of control, then they also emerge from a deep sense of dependence that the perpetrators themselves feel toward the very partners that they abuse. While often the focus in partner violence is on how its victims are made to become dependent on those who commit that abuse, the opposite is equally true and, if anything, this is the great contradiction of this intimate form of terror. Acts of control are also reflections of dependence, and not only is this a seeming contradiction, but it can be a deeply shameful one at that. When the webs of mutuality that inevitably make up our existence are made instead into sources of shame, violence often becomes the most ready means of obscuring that truth.

The purpose of this chapter is to explore this contradiction through the life of Diego, the first perpetrator of abuse who was willing to speak with me about himself and, after we finished with our series of interviews, also the first to invite me into other parts of his life as well. If the previous chapter departed from my very first encounter with him, when he began laying out for me his paternalistic justifications for his violence, then this one will have to proceed by probing much more expansively into the arc of his life. Doing so opens windows into not just his worldviews but also the experiences from which they emerged, his fixations, his fantasies, his emotional investments, how they ended and to what effect, and what brought him joy, sadness, meaning, and shame. And even though the nature of shame is to hide things from view, it was through both the negative spaces left from what he was not willing to share, as well as what he would eventually come to reveal, that Diego sketched an outline of some of the social origins of dependence, its denial, and consequently its devolution into cycles of violence of the most intimate kind.[1] To remain open to hearing his story is to also hold open a belief in the potential for a less violent life.

Of Desperation and Disconnection

The first time that I go to meet Diego in his home, I get to his front door and scarcely have an opportunity to knock before he has opened it and invited me in. Coming in from the late morning sun, the kind that presses down with a palpable force, his living room is dark, still cool like the dew that started the day. As my eyes and skin adjust, Diego steps around excitedly, telling me where to put my bag, asking if I want to take a seat, introducing me to Luisa, his partner, and her daughter, Diana. Luisa pokes her head out through the narrow door of their galley kitchen and greets me with reservation; Diana hides but smiles at me from behind her mother's leg. I walk over and thank Luisa for having me in her home. She nods and gives me a calculated smile, then turns back and focuses intently on the arepas frying on the stove. Diego wastes no time in showing me around their house, the rooms on their first floor, and various home improvement projects that he has under way. I find myself eyeing instead a meticulously crafted model of a DNA spiral sitting on their table with Luisa's name on it, wondering how she made it so neatly and noting by the date that she must be keeping up with her nightly classes. Soon he is leading me up the back steps of their narrow shotgun-style house to a partial second floor where a single bedroom sits, from the looks of it recently vacated and not yet put back to use.

As we continue up to the rooftop, Diego starts to fill me in on the story of the subletter who had stayed in that room. She was a friend of Luisa's, one that she made at the refuge house when she had originally left a few months back with the help of the Comisaría. Up on the terrace a sheet of plastic shades us, protecting us from the sun and shielding the laundry hung up there from the inevitable rain. Among the drying clothes and odd tools lying about, Diego gazes off above the surrounding rooftops into those resplendent hills, squinting into the sharp rays that the landfill retches back our way. His face is calm, relaxed in a way that I have actually never seen before, devoid now of the nervous energy I had come to automatically associate with him. Here he seems composed, and with a brief sigh he begins again into the story about their subletter, Luisa's friend.

"She wouldn't do anything, que pereza, so lazy," he tells me.

When I ask him what he means, he tells me about how she had moved in with her two small children for several weeks after leaving the refuge house, emphasizing to me his willingness to let her stay in their home. The one condition that he had, he explains, was that she could not at any time have her ex-partner come over to the house. He did not want any "drama" with a man that sounded to him to be particularly mean. Once she was there, their coexistence sounded more like mutual neglect, each keeping to themselves, always using shared spaces like the kitchen at different times.

"She would not get out of bed until eleven in the morning: when were her kids going to eat? How could she let them starve like that? And when she did cook she would let her food spoil, leaving it out on the stove, not even bothering to reheat it every day to preserve it."

I realize that what I'm hearing is that this person was most likely depressed, but Diego saw it as simple laziness, a sort of ineptitude at life contrasted against what he portrayed as his own industrious nature. When I ask him about this, if perhaps all of this was because she was depressed in the wake of everything that had recently happened to her, he gives only a small shrug and lets the conversation go with an air of indifference. Still peering off at the hills, he finishes his story by telling me that after she did call her ex-partner and he came to the house, a violent and mean guy, he adds, he was forced to ask her to leave. After helping her move her few belongings to her brother's house, he lost track of what happened to her and had little interest in finding out.

We check the hour and realize that we are almost running late, given the unpredictability of traffic we have to leave early; otherwise, he faces a heavy fine. Making our way out he grabs his work jacket and, after saying goodbye to Luisa and Diana, we're off at a quick clip.

"I like your home. It's good to see that you've been able to start those projects you were telling me about," I offer.

He goes on to explain that he is building on it slowly, arranging what he can and saving to add another floor on top, slowly building their home up as everyone else in Usme does, story by story. While he seems proud of being able to do so again, thanks to his new job as a bus driver he is no longer behind on his debts, he does lament how thin the walls are between the houses. It seems to him to be the one irreparable part of his home.

"Everyone can hear everything that goes on; they're like paper. We don't have any privacy," he complains.

His consternation is suddenly interrupted and his gaze shifts to the community church that we are passing. He tells me that only a few days ago a young man was killed outside of there, but he adds that I shouldn't be worried, that the really dangerous part of the neighborhood is further down the hill toward the river. As we wait for and pick up the bus, he changes the subject to an earlier conversation of ours, the difficulties of his job and the many ways that his superiors could dock his pay. While we jostle down the narrow streets, gears grinding as we wind our way to the Avenida Boyacá, Diego lists all of the ways that he can be punished at his job: if he arrives late at his final stop, if he detours from a traffic jam without authorization, if he looks at his cell phone, if he takes a drink of water, if he responds negatively to an irate passenger—the list goes on and each offense carries a potentially hefty deduction from his paycheck. The sum total of it, he says, is that he has no desire to work his way up to driving larger buses or taking on managerial roles. Mostly he wants to keep his post long enough that he can pay off debts and possibly save up enough to open his own store in his neighborhood.

As Diego looks out the window, living for a moment in his daydream, another group of passengers climbs up into the bus, one by one paying their fares. The mood changes. Just before a young man starts speaking, a strange quiet falls over the bus, as though each passenger has kept doing whatever they were doing before, only now a little more intently. The passenger begins his speech to the crowd benignly enough—he is in between jobs but believes in God above, so instead of turning to crime he goes on buses and hopes for whatever little money people can spare. No one responds, no hands go outstretched. His voice dips lower, and everyone else gets a little more intent on doing nothing. He says that before he was working in the family business, but now his father is in jail, that he hurt a man real bad, and while he says that he himself would never do the same, something in the way his voice cuts the air starts to suggest a different story. Hands start to go into pockets now, grasping for whatever change they might find, and just like that he leaves the bus as quickly as he mounted it, barely waiting for it to stop. The strange little episode, another daily moment of uncertainty, what threat there really is, if any, is over. Everyone goes back to actually doing nothing, and Diego and I go back to chatting.

Eventually we get to where his company stows their vehicles, right up against the very western limits of the city. Unlike Usme, where the transition to the countryside is gradual, where barrio fades into farm and farm into forest, here there are apartments and then there are fields. Beyond one there is only the other. No sooner do we walk past the rusted metal that encircles the lot than Diego spots a coworker of his and at once we're drinking sodas and smoking a cigarette before his shift starts. They compare schedules, talk about who got the better routes, complain about traffic and how unruly passengers are getting. Diego asks him about how his "mujer" and he are doing. The timer is running down though, we have to be off in less than ten minutes, so we bolt down the rest of our bottles and check over Diego's vehicle, looking for any damage he might have to declare. Prep work done, Diego registered in the onboard system, we climb up, his friend and I picking the choicest seats in the empty bus. We lurch forward with a hearty belch of diesel, and as we pull out into the city I catch a glimpse through the rearview mirror of Diego behind the wheel. Eyes squinting against the sun but face slackened, he has donned the

*same calm that I had seen just an hour earlier on the roof of his house. Up
until today, it would have seemed so unfamiliar.*

✱   ✱   ✱

Before Diego invited me into his home, before I met Luisa and could not just
put a face to but also hear a voice behind the other side of their story, he and I
met for an extended series of interviews at the local public library. In this
somewhat neutral space, tucked away in an unused room, it was there that he
first opened up our conversations by telling me about his odyssey to stalk Luisa, eventually finding her at the prenatal clinic where she had been receiving
her care. From that very first moment, jealousy and his desperate fear of loss
became, sometimes intentionally but most often not, the common thread that
wove itself through all of his stories, histories that he would gladly spend
hours walking me through so that I might better understand his life. The purpose at the time though was not for Diego to have a space in which he might
simply justify himself and narratively reassure himself of his violence against
Luisa. We had framed these meetings as providing a space for reflection—
though again not a formally therapeutic one—and over time they became a
place where he could tell his story as fully as possible, bringing forth and
finding connections to his violence that he may not have previously seen.
Such was one basis of his interest in speaking with me at all, and what was
true then is also true now. It is never passive, listening to the stories of perpetrators of abuse, for they too are complex persons formed through extensive lived experiences.[2] There is always a purpose, and in this case it is not to
apologize but to better understand where Diego's jealousy, and the dependences that underwrote it, came from. It is to understand what drove it and
what was at stake for him throughout his repeated cycles of violence against
Luisa. By doing so, it just might be possible to uncover points of purchase,
fulcrums for transformation in light of his experience and those of others.

Fear

Diego was not born in Bogotá. He grew up in a small town in the department outside of the city, Cundinamarca, as the youngest son in a family that
not only possessed their own land but were relatively well off compared to

other members of their community. Though not wealthy, they did enjoy the
security of growing both their own crops for subsistence and coffee for an
income, a kind of system that put them squarely within the norm of the
post-hacienda era of coffee production. So while they were not the hacendados of the bygone era, with their possessions they were able to cultivate a
stable situation and even a place of leadership among their peers. This early
period of his life was one that Diego always spoke of with a bittersweet nostalgia, recalling how his father had become a de facto director of the coffee
trade in the area, organizing other growers to collect the fruits of their labor
to sell in bulk to the traders who would take those goods global. It meant
that his father was often traveling or working off of the farm, a place that his
mother and older siblings took charge of, but to Diego his father's absence
was more than compensated for by the times when he would return. Despite
being one of the youngest siblings, he always felt as though he was his
father's favorite, and whenever his father would return from trips he always
brought him a special gift, unique from the ones that he gave to his other
children. On one occasion, Diego beamed to me, his father even told him
that he was his favored son.

The joy that he showed recounting this to me was quickly tempered
when he told me that, when he was seven years old, his father was killed.
Unlike many Colombians who have lost loved ones through more intentional forms of violence, Diego's father was killed by accident when a truck
he was riding in tipped over on a country road. Though others riding in the
vehicle were only injured, his father was crushed and quickly succumbed.
The damage done to Diego, however, would not be so brief, and that his
father's death was an accident and not the result of the conflict did little to
mitigate his grief. Even thirty-three years later, Diego immediately with-
drew inward when talking about this with me; shoulders collapsed forward
but eyes turned upward, it was the only moment that I ever saw him close to
tears. In the wake of his father's death he found himself living in a family
that seemed inhospitable, indifferent at the very least. It was his mother
who carried on the family business afterward, but as a woman in a male-
dominated community she was denied the central and privileged position
that her husband had attained. As their income suffered for it, Diego's older
siblings became even more important in their family's financial solvency,
and together with their mother they worked to avoid selling off any assets
that they owned. In these lean times though, the scarcity that Diego remembered was more than material. Speculating that this was because of his

father's favoritism, following his death Diego felt that his relationships with the rest of his family were unusually frigid and strained, and this apparently continued for some time. When we first met and I asked him how those family relationships currently were, he said that there was only one brother that he might call just to talk to, but the others, including his mother, would only ever contact him if they needed to borrow some money. And so this was the basic state of affairs that he remembered for the rest of his time in Cundinamarca: chores and school, some time with friends, but a considerable degree of loneliness even while in the presence of others. This was at least up until he had his first romantic relationship, a classmate of his in secondary school. For a brief moment his eyes brightened while talking about her, a sense of excitement showing through in an otherwise muted part of his life. Again, that joy instantly faded. Within a year of them meeting, she died of cancer.

Her death triggered for Diego a vital juncture in his life: it was the moment that he decided to move to Bogotá.[3] Like many others, this was a gradual process of transition and not a migration made all at once.[4] Having quit his schooling early, to both support his family and leave his town, his options were moderately limited. He was nevertheless able to find a position as an assistant in a grocery store, making sales and stocking shelves in a town just outside of the city. When he finally did make the final move to Bogotá, seeking better prospects for employment, what he found instead was a total shock. What he remembered most of all about arriving in the city was the constant fear he felt: fear of being hit by a car, fear of getting robbed, fear of not being able to make it. Though he had since acclimated to life in Bogotá, learning to appreciate what it means to "no dar papaya," that sense of wariness toward any stranger, had never left him. And so when he arrived, though he found a modicum of personal connection through his new place of employment—working again in a grocery—he quickly found himself isolated from the rest of the world around him, a world that he everyday found to be increasingly hostile. In this unfamiliar sea, his first life raft was his boss at the grocery, a middle-aged man that he still remembers fondly as a friend first and employer second. In learning to navigate this strange and new social terrain his boss was a friendly source of helpful advice; whenever Diego requested an absence from work he was gracious in his accommodation. According to Diego, he infrequently made these requests during the beginning of his time in Bogotá, but after he met his first partner, Yesica, they became a more common occurrence in his life.

When I asked him what it was like for Yesica and him in the beginning, he sighed deeply and smiled, looking off somewhere beyond the corner of our room and into a buried recess of his mind. The tenor of his voice lifted and his muscles relaxed, relieved from the accumulated stress of retelling the story of the death of his father and its aftermath. In the beginning, he told me, everything was wonderful. Hearing this, I cringed. I had heard this trope too many times before from survivors of abuse. I had also become only too familiar with where it typically led. What was most wonderful, he elaborated, was the affection they shared, the intimacy of their connection in a world where he otherwise perceived a threat in almost any other person that he encountered. When exactly his interest became fixation, when fixation became dependence was never entirely clear, but after knowing each other for about a year they found an apartment and moved in together. I asked him when their relationship began to change, when they began to have problems; his answer was when she began to get "restless." In a calm and measured voice, he told me about how he was working long hours at the grocery, trying to bring in as much money as he could to support the two of them in their new home. Being gone most of the time, he began to worry that maybe she might become "bored" and, with all the patience of a carefully reasoned conclusion, he told me that one day he decided that it might be best to "give her a baby."

I was never able to ascertain what kind of level of coercion might have accompanied that decision of his, but what was clear was that Diego believed, with no small measure of certainty, that having a child would help to keep them together. Read another way, it would help to keep him from losing her. During her pregnancy, he began to ask for more small breaks off from work, a few hours here and there to go back home and bring Yesica food or anything else that she might need. After their son, Eduardo, was born, those visits continued but the reasons he gave for them were now to check on Eduardo and to make sure that Yesica was taking proper care of him. Their first major fight that he told me about was on one such occasion. He had come home in the middle of the day to find Eduardo alone in his crib, Yesica visiting a male neighbor in the building. Though he denied any kind of physical violence toward her, he made clear that it was after this encounter that his jealousy began to take full force, and from the sound of it his employment did not help. Rather than his obligations at work putting some limits on his ability to keep tabs on Yesica, it was actually his boss who would encourage and facilitate Diego making surprise midafternoon trips back home. Thus became a pattern of suspicion, stalking, and constantly devolving jealousy, a period that Diego alternately described either as motivated by fear of her infidelity or as justified under his paternal obligations to protect Eduardo from accidental harm. Regardless of whether or not Yesica had other romantic relationships in the beginning, their fighting became more frequent and likely continued to push her away to the point where, having stalked her all the way to the north end of the city one day, Diego eventually found her meeting with another male friend of hers. Even though he meticulously related this history of stalking her in great detail, what he presented as a sort of odyssey of his own victimhood in an attempt to discover the truth, he never admitted to physically harming her in any way.[5] Devoid of other resources or documents that might tell another story, I was never able to learn to what extent that was the truth. What did seem certain was that following that revelation, Yesica left him, took custody of Eduardo without needing any formal order of protection, and began living a life outside the sphere of Diego's control.

Losing Yesica from his life, as well as his son, was devastating. It is difficult to overstate just how deeply invested he was in keeping them in his life, and if his stalking was not indication enough, then his trajectory afterward helps to further clarify. In the time that followed their separation, he began drinking and even left his job at the grocery store, giving up his last tie to Bogotá in order to go back to Cundinamarca and live with his family. If Diego's story is about intense and desperate jealousy though, it is largely because it is also first and foremost about loss and isolation as well. And even though isolation is frequently an issue associated with victims of abuse, Diego's experiences show that it can be every bit as relevant to perpetrators as well. And what following the long arc of those experiences tells us is that these losses are not just elemental fixtures of childhood, ones carried into the present through memory and habit. They are losses that can propagate in chains, that isolation must always be contextualized because it is not just a question of whether or not someone has experienced it. It is a question of where they are isolated, from whom, and how. Isolation is not just a state of being but rather a repeated process of dislocation and disconnection. The violence that can result from it always happens somewhere, and both the "somewhere" and the path to there matter.[6]

It would seem vanishingly unlikely that the death of his father, followed later by the death of his first girlfriend—not one but two losses of significant, affectively important attachments—did not leave lasting psychic scars and an enduring fear of further loss. It would, however, also be too easy to point to these early experiences and straightforwardly link them to his obsessive preoccupation with Yesica's fidelity, his attempts to control her as a means to avoid experiencing the loss of another relationship. In between those points in time he had also migrated to an unfamiliar city in which everyday fears for safety and the deeply ingrained lesson of "no dar papaya" shaped his general avoidance of most other people. Combined with his removal from the town where he grew up and his remaining family support, however meager he might have perceived that to be, it is not difficult to see how Yesica became to him an uncommon human connection in what he otherwise saw as a hostile and lonely world. And so it was not just in these primordial experiences of loss but also in the chain of dislocations to which they contributed that we can begin to understand what was at stake for Diego throughout his violence, what helps us to see it as the consequence of many different junctures and their enduring influences.[7]

It is also what helps us to begin to appreciate Diego's violence as a reflection of his dependence on his partners. Despite the apparent paradox that relationships of chronic coercion are supposed to be about control, what Diego began to illustrate is that they are indeed every bit as much about the intricate forms of dependence that perpetrators have on those they try to dominate. For Diego, as it was for other abusive men that I came to know, this was one of the more shameful secrets that he desperately sought to maintain. It was only by appreciating the presence of that shame that I was able to start to make sense of why he always assumed an excessively calm and measured tone when telling me about fights that he had with his partners, minimizing the violence he committed, or why he would so adamantly claim that he was accepting of Yesica leaving him, his own actions to stalk her notwithstanding. Related with paternalistic overtones that suggested that he knew best, carefully summarizing the reasons why he was right and they were wrong, the stories he told of his fights with his partners consistently deflected from his own fears and vulnerabilities by fashioning himself to be a detached and rational benefactor instead.

Even if Diego remained relatively reticent on just how afraid he was to lose those relationships though, he was always at least willing, even eager, to talk about why he was so invested in them. As such, exploring these topics became a crucial means for us to approach talking about his violence and to do so in a manner that was simultaneously empathetic but critical as well. So long as initially we did not directly label them as forms of dependence, they could serve as points of mutual exploration for us to connect his other experiences throughout his life with the violence he inflicted. Insights like these he readily explored, and over time they even became gateways for him to take steps toward considering how he might be less controlling of his partners, how such forms of reliance need not be shameful but sources of strength instead. Going from previously assuming that Yesica needed to have a child to "keep her occupied," and implicitly keep her in their home, he began asking questions like if he should support his new partner, Luisa, who was also pregnant at the time, in going back to school to get her bachillerato. Asked as if looking for permission to support Luisa's education, he actually became a major proponent of her pursuing opportunities like these, ones that could potentially give her more independence, even as he continued to still cyclically inflict violence against her. Indeed this conflict became as clear an indication as any as to how nonlinear the search for alternatives to violence can be, how complicated the entanglement of control and dependence really is. In order to better understand it, the intricacy of this contradiction, we would need to delve deeper again into the nuance and evolution of Diego's relationships; and compared to his relationship with Yesica, which I only ever learned of through his recollection, his current partner, Luisa, was someone whom I also came to know.

Shame

Diego met Luisa only because he began to work for the public sewage system. It was dirty work, but work nonetheless, and having left his family for a second time, returning to Bogotá, it was the only opportunity for a job that he could find. At first it was simple work, maintenance of tunnels around the city, but with his growing experience he was soon asked to take on more independent projects. This new role would take him outside of the city, for short assignments at least, between which he could come back to his home in Usme. It was on one such trip out to the Pacific Coast city of Buenaventura that he met Luisa. With a bit of a sheepish grin he told me about how they met in a bar, how he had almost been too shy to approach her, but with the days counting down on his assignment how he had found the urgency to finally go and introduce himself. Within barely a couple of weeks not only was Diego returning to Bogotá, but so too was Luisa and her seven-year-old daughter, Diana, and that she would upend her life so quickly perhaps speaks to the uncertainty of her own situation at the time. As I would later learn from Diego, as well as their case file in the Comisaría de Familia, Luisa's life in Buenaventura was not just a matter of making ends meet through sex work: she also "ran errands" for some illegal groups and by the time that she left she had ample reason to worry about her own safety. Whatever her precise motivations to leave Buenaventura on such short notice, what Luisa found on the other end of that journey to Usme was no safer than the situation that she had just left behind, and to add to it all, within the year of her relocation she would also find herself pregnant.

Even by Diego's recounting of the year that they had lived together, it had been a general devolution of escalating fights, the details of which were often difficult to elicit. Talking about the actual details of those fights were unquestionably the most labored moments of our relationship, when Diego would transform from his usually eager storytelling self and draw immediately inward. Leaning forward with his eyes down, one knee nervously bouncing and arms clasped across his chest, he only reemerged when he could begin to talk about them from a more detached position. Finding his voice by explaining to me the content of what they fought over, not what he did, was the only way that he could really speak about their disagreements. Inevitably these were explanations that betrayed the presumption that he knew best, that one way or another he could not always trust Luisa or her judgment. More than just superficial veneers though, thin façades for justifying or obscuring his violence, these expositions of his became his way to communicate his deepest concerns and, over time, even speak directly about the things in his life that gave him the greatest shame.

What he repeated the most was his preoccupation with what those around him saw and thought of him. For Diego the specter of gossip was both omnipresent and terrifying, and it manifested itself in different ways.[8] The first had to do with what Luisa did in public and how others saw her, and one of the more common stories that he repeated to me was the case where he would give several thousand pesos to her and her daughter for taking public transportation, only to find on their return that she had not spent it. What bothered him, he said, was not that she had not spent it, suggesting maybe that she was saving money somewhere that he did not know. What bothered him was that if she had not spent money on a bus it meant that she had probably found transportation by hitching a ride in the cabin of a commercial truck, one making its rounds within the city.[9] As he explained, his fear was based in the fact that she had previously made a living through sex work, but it was not that he was afraid that she was continuing to make money in that way so much as he was afraid that others might see her and think that was the case. It was never evident who exactly those other people were, or how they might possibly know that Luisa had previously been a sex worker, but what was clear was how salient this fear was to him in his everyday life.

Superseding these more public concerns were his preoccupations with keeping what he thought should be "private" properly within the home. That came through in his repetition about how thin the walls of his house were and how easy it was for neighbors to hear what happened in each other's homes. It was a theme that he would bring up throughout our discussions of his and Luisa's fights just as it was his ready reply when I visited him and commented on his own home improvement projects. Of all the features of his home that he dreamed of repairing or renovating, this was the one that seemed the most resistant to his efforts. Less persistent but no less troublesome to Diego was another issue, one that he revealed to me only after I asked him directly what things in his life made him feel the most ashamed. With a drawn-out sigh he relaxed back into his seat and told me about how during his previous period of unemployment he began to feel increasingly isolated again and would resort to drinking alone in his house. Using the little money that he had left, he quickly found himself behind on his bills and taking on debts that he was still paying back when we first met. Further compounding these residual debts was the more recent loss of his job, his employment with the sewage system, at a time where he was financially supporting not just himself but also two others, Luisa and her daughter. The low point for Diego in all of this though was not just when he began getting harassing calls from a friend who had earlier lent him money, it was when the utilities began posting notices of the cessation of his services on his front door. His period of unemployment might have injured his self-respect, the resulting debts might have given him something to worry about, but it was the publicly visible notices that he said actually brought him the greatest shame.

It was in this context of Luisa's pregnancy and Diego's unemployment, mounting debts, and door notices that "the fight" happened, the big one, after which Luisa went to the Comisaría, took out an order of protection against Diego, and fled to the refuge house. It took place one day when Diego came home and, as he told it, saw her on the bed and asked if she had found some documents he had asked her to locate. When she did not respond he asked her again, and when she responded quietly the second time he became angry and a fight ensued. At some point, as Luisa became more vocal and began raising her voice, Diego clamped his hand against her mouth to keep her from yelling. He admitted in hindsight that he could see how that would be a frightening experience for her and also, considering that she was already pregnant at the time, how that could be an especially dangerous thing for him to do.[10] Even still, he maintained that it was something that he did not out of direct aggression to her but out of his fear that the neighbors would hear their commotion. To him it was less about the intent of harm and more about secrecy: whatever transpired between them should stay within the boundaries of their home. Against this version of what happened that afternoon are Luisa's words, as she put it on the day she sought the order of protection, and they are worth quoting at length:

> The day before at 9 P.M. I was in my house, where I live with my partner, when he came home and became infuriated because I had not found some documents of his. He started to say "where are the fucking papers" he needed, he repeated it a number of times and when I did not answer him he began to treat me badly saying, bastard, bitch, did mice eat my tongue or was something else keeping me from talking, and he grabbed my arms and twisted and put his fingers in my mouth to open it, saying he would find where the papers were by hook or by crook. [Three days before] he also mistreated me, called me a fucking bastard and he tried to suffocate me.

Luisa also noted in the many check boxes on her form that causes for Diego's violence included poor communication, economic difficulties, and alcohol consumption. When asked if there was any kind of dependence in their relationship, her response was clear: she felt no particular dependency toward him, but he did depend on her. Where asked to clarify his dependence, she wrote off to the side one word: emotional.

Several things happened in the period immediately after Luisa first went to the Comisaría. For one, she and Diana went to live in a refuge house for survivors of abuse, a place where they traded their safety for the stringent rules that governed taking shelter there. Soon thereafter Luisa returned to the Comisaría, this time with the support of a lawyer from the refuge house in order to give a more extensive recounting of Diego's violence and receive an official order of protection. In that meeting she expanded on what had happened that night, saying that after Diego calmed down, he lay down in bed with her, began touching her in a sexual way, and would not let her get up to leave. When he asked her in the morning to forgive him she told him "no" and decided in that moment to go to the Comisaría. Though she stopped short of accusing him of penetrative rape, Luisa did go on to say that on other occasions he had twisted her arms and legs, even bit her face, called her names such as "bitch" and "prostitute."[11] Beyond acts of control these were also clearly actions of degradation, ones that even included calling her the very thing that he feared other people around them might think: "prostitute."

If leaving Diego and speaking openly about what he had done was an act of rebellion by Luisa against his control, for Diego it was a complete crisis, a confrontation with the unintended consequences of his violence against her.[12] In seeking to contain her he had pushed her away instead, out from the boundaries of their home, and, in doing so, brought down the walls that enclosed his private sovereign domain. Unemployed and again having lost an affectively important relationship, he fell back harder on the same solution that he had found many times before: he drank even more. Diego described this period before he once again became employed, this time as a bus driver for the public transit system, as a period of loneliness more than anything else. There were a few people with whom he might meet up and share a beer or two, a friend who lived in another district or even occasionally a brother of his, but most of the time he found himself emptying bottles of Poker or Club Colombia beer with nothing but his empty apartment around him. In that silence his desperation only grew. Detached from Luisa, he either began hatching plans of how to track her down or found himself paralyzed in his own ruminations and regret. As the overdue bills continued to accumulate and more utilities notices shut him in, he would continue to play over those last moments with Luisa, alternatively berating himself for crossing another line or planning what to do differently should she ever return.

This was the juncture where I first met Diego and eventually entered into both of their lives. Off and on over the course of two months, we met a half dozen times in public libraries, often for hours on end tracing through the broader arcs of his life and the minute details of how he experienced it. Even during this relatively short period of time, the first of several major transitions happened: Luisa moved back from the refuge house and into their home. Her move was nominally voluntary. After the incident at the prenatal clinic, Diego had not had any more contact with her or her daughter, Diana, and the refuge house had not ejected them for breaking any rules or running out of available space. Her voluntariness has to be understood though in the context of living a highly regimented life at the shelter, a place that even those who work in the Comisaría readily admit is hard to tolerate for extended periods of time. Once out of the shelter, Luisa was sufficiently estranged from her family so as not to fall back on their support, and also she was insufficiently prepared or connected to quickly find work. Edged out of these other possible paths, she returned "home" to live with Diego, and for a time it seemed that the situation she returned to was not as hostile as before.

As Diego explained to me, his desperation at losing her and their unborn child was matched only by his relief at her return, and it appeared that from that relief followed a period of quiescence all too familiar in the cyclical patterns of partner violence. If fear and shame had previously played roles in his violence against Luisa, for the moment at least they instead put a thin lid over it. Diego also had a job at this point, and with it a stable income with benefits, allowing him not just the opportunity to resume repaying his debts but also a window of opportunity in which to mend his own self-respect. Within this window some new possibilities began to emerge. Soon after Luisa's return, he began bringing up in our conversations her desire to go back and finish her secondary school studies, hopefully even receiving her diploma before their son was born. With tones that echoed his preoccupation those many years before about his partner Yesica being "restless" in their home, Diego sounded hopeful about this possibility. He thought that perhaps getting her degree was the kind of thing to occupy her and give her some fulfillment, implicitly also making it less likely for her to want to leave again in the future. Even if I could hear Diego searching for ways to avoid repeating the recent rupture in his world, without first upending his entire understanding of what caused it, Luisa going back to school sounded like a positive step. At least, as other survivors of abuse I had met had said, education was something from which no one could later dispossess them, and I in turn also encouraged Diego to support her in that endeavor.

Whether or not my words carried any weight, Luisa did go back to school through an extension program just a few blocks away from their house, and over the course of the spring she finished all but the equivalent of her last year's worth of studies. It was during these months that I first began visiting Diego in their home, taking tenuous first steps into that contentious arena, one of continued danger to Luisa, and incidentally began to build a connection directly with her. It surprised me how quickly she relaxed some of her defenses, and compared to her understandable reservations the first time that we met, by the second time she had already begun joking with Diego while I was around. Wagging a finger at him or shooting him a glare, she would admonish him for offenses both past and potential. Once, early on, I asked Diego generically just "how things have been." Poking her head out from the next room, she quickly chimed in: "oh, he knows he can never do anything like that again. If he even tries I'll be out the door. I have a bag ready and everything." "Oh, I know, you have it all planned out," Diego lobbed back, rolling his eyes and laughing all the while Luisa retreated back into the other room.[13]

Luisa was also at the time in the last trimester of her pregnancy, and within a few short months of when I began visiting them, she gave birth to their son, Luis. When I saw them in the days after they returned home from the hospital, Diego explained that the name was intentionally a derivation of Luisa, that he wanted him named after her even if he could not explain exactly why.[14] It was the happiest I had ever seen either of them, Luisa beaming through her exhaustion, Diego regaling me through an interminable smile all the details of how quickly Luis was already growing and putting on weight. Whether known to them at the time or not, in their delirium they were already passing through an inflection point in their relationship and, like the experiences of so many other survivors of abuse, it was in the period following Luis's birth that problems again began to appear on the horizon.

I caught the first intimations of this just a few weeks later when I returned to visit them. Greeting me at the front door this time was Diana, Luisa's daughter, and under the weight of her baby brother she was carrying she seemed just about to crumble. Beyond her I caught the sight of Diego waving me in, and as I stepped through the door I shot a quick "hello, how have you been" out somewhere into the dim living room beyond. Before my eyes could even acclimate, I heard Diego approaching me with an audible "ooooof!" that told me I was about to hear a story retold in dramatic rendition. "Difficult," he said. Just two days before he had come back to the house to find that Luisa had gone to the store nearby and Diana had carried Luis out into the alleyway of where they lived. "What if one of the neighbors saw her and called Family Welfare? What would they think of us as parents?" he asked. Clearly he was not worried about Diana carrying Luis, because she was doing that the whole time that we spoke. What worried Diego was that someone else might see her carrying him around, away from the house, and judge them as a result. In his worst-case scenario he envisioned this even instigating a series of events that would see him having his newborn son taken from their home. "I came so close to hitting her," he told me, only this time he was not referring to Diana. By "her" he meant Luisa, for leaving the two children unattended and for permitting Diana to in some way, as he saw it, put them all at risk.[15]

On that particular occasion he had managed to step outside and calm himself, a strategy he had discovered in the preceding months, but his worry that he might not succeed the next time was plainly visible. As he paused, Luisa interjected, stepping fully into the living room and standing resolutely upright, facing both Diego and me simultaneously. What worried *her* most of all, she said, was that Diego might "return to his old ways," but it was not until the next time that I visited their house that she elaborated more on what that actually meant. This time, for the moment, she left her words hanging in the air and quickly we all found ourselves talking more about Diana and how she was adjusting to having a little brother, coping with the loss of attention. As we chatted, the three of us sat down and settled into the sweetened coffee that Luisa had prepared, steaming cups of Colombian honey, a gracious invitation against the drizzle that had begun outside. Nestled into our chairs, we never returned to the topic of violence the rest of the afternoon.[16]

Over the following month and a half, I lost touch almost entirely with Diego and Luisa when the phone number that I had for them became inactivated. I had been careful never to visit their house uninvited but, in desperation, with my days in Usme nearly numbered, I found myself knocking at their front door unannounced. This time an unfamiliar face was on the other side, an elderly woman who peered back at me puzzled, confused probably as to what a gringo was doing outside of her door. Behind her Luisa appeared and exuberantly welcomed me in, introducing me to her mother and her sister who were visiting from outside of the city.[17] No sooner had I made their acquaintance than Luisa was ushering us back to the room to check on Luis, and once she had him back in her arms we started into small talk about life with their infant son. Repeatedly though we hit a wall, the shadow cast across it was the question of just how "stressful" it all had been recently: had Diego "gone back to his ways" as Luisa had worried about before? Eventually her mother and sister moved into the kitchen to clean the dishes left over from lunch, and with a hushed voice, and Luis still in her arms, Luisa began to speak a bit more freely. "He hit me again, twice, over the head the other day," she whispered as I nodded quietly. "I don't know what to do, I know that he has been under a lot of pressure and there are things that I should have done to be more helpful, . . ." she tapered off. Almost under my breath I expressed that no one deserved to be treated that way, to which she looked down silently at Luis. "What do you hope can happen? What are you afraid of most?" I asked her. What she told me then spoke volumes about the complicated situation in which she remained, one that even in the close presence of her own family she felt she had to keep hidden just in order to maintain some minimal control over it. Her biggest desire, she replied, was simply that Diego stopped once and for all. She did not want to lose him: she just wanted him to stop the violence. Her biggest fear was that she would report him to the Comisaría and they would take him away to jail, against her will. "I know that I have to report him, we have a meeting this next week and I know that I should report what he did. But I depend on him now more than ever," she told me. I asked her if she meant "dependence" in the financial sense, now that Luis was born and they had new expenses to bear, but to my surprise she only dismissively agreed. More than anything else, she said, she depended on him emotionally now too.

Before Luisa could elaborate, we heard her mother and sister come in from the kitchen and suddenly her voice took on its normal pitch. Sitting down, we all continued with our pleasantries as Luisa rocked the baby back to sleep. Diego arrived just a short while later and, even with him home, we never revisited the topic of his violence. With Luisa's family still present, any chance of that seemed to be a foregone conclusion, and even had they not been there I am not sure that Luisa would have broached the subject again. As it stood, she was looking down the barrel of a momentous decision: to report or not to report Diego. A few days later, the day before that meeting, I left Bogotá.[18]

Control

How does one begin to interpret the intricately complicated reality of an abusive relationship—is it possible or even fair to try? Given Luisa's situation, perhaps the only thing that can be said with any certainty is that "fairness" did not factor much into it in the end. Her frustration at feeling that her options amounted to little more than a series of false dilemmas was palpable, one endured beneath the very same weight that continued to mute her voice. And yet to not try to make even some amount of sense of what led up to her impossible decision, or the continued issues that Diego himself struggled against, would be the greatest ingratitude to the generosity with which they opened their lives to me. Ultimately though, it is worth reiterating that I knew them both primarily through Diego, from his retracing of his own past to the details of how he carried on in his current life, and what follows should always remain framed as such.

What Diego first reaffirmed to me, intentionally or not, is that chronic, coercive partner violence is indeed fundamentally a question of sovereignty, of creating control through the construction of social space, and that the search for that kind of power over others is about, if nothing else, the desire for boundaries within which they might be constrained.[19] For Diego this was centered on his home. It was reflected in his desire for thicker walls, his need for protection from prying eyes and ears, and his preoccupation with gossip and what others might think of Luisa and, by proxy, of him as well.[20] In its most extreme instance this is what drove Diego to almost kill Luisa, nearly suffocating her once during a fight, violently silencing her in what can only be understood as the severest form of policing the "private." This creation of limits though goes beyond the bare necessity of creating a space over which one can preside; it extends also to the complicated feelings of shame and fear that are woven into that search for sovereign power and how that search for power leads to the construction of violent fictions like "the home." Shame, having to do with being seen, especially when one does not want to be, beckons the question of why someone would so ardently desire that kind of privacy and go to such violent lengths to defend it.[21] What was Diego really trying to hide? Asking this again takes us back to the most significant secret about control: that beneath it is, by necessity, an underlying dependence.[22] For Diego, it was the shame of that reality that only further fed the desperation of his violence, not only to contain his partners but to conceal his reliance on them as well.

It is possible to understand Diego's experience of this contradiction between control and dependence in at least two ways. First, his intense emotional dependence on his partners—first Yesica, then Luisa—provided much of the impulse for him to attempt to control them in the first place. Just how deeply invested Diego was in his relationships was abundantly clear, from the changes in his demeanor when talking about them to Luisa's own words in her application for an order of protection. Just as another perpetrator of

violence I knew said that he would drink so that he could cry after his partner finally left him, so too did Diego find himself drinking more, alone, in
the aftermath of his abuse. The chains of loss and isolation that brought him
to those junctures are what made his partners more than companions: it
made them life rafts of connection in what he perceived to be an otherwise
hostile and isolating world. Jealousy for him was not just a fear of loss but an
almost totalizing preoccupation. One could contrast this dynamic with the
diametrically opposed manner in which he instead tried to present himself:
self-reliant, composed, a provider. Seeking perhaps to take after the image of
his father—gift-giver, provider for his family, leader in their community—as
desperately as Diego sought to keep his partners from leaving him, he also
sought to project the image of the benevolent, assured patriarch. If only
behind the latter the former might be concealed; if only he could convince,
at least himself, that he did not depend on his partners, they depended on
him. Failing that, he relied in turn on violence.

The second meaning this contradiction had for Diego then was in its relationship to the other experiences of shame in his life: notices on his front
door, his debts, his unemployment.[23] Against his gendered self-expectations,
and his perceived failures to live up to them, exercising coercive control
within the last remaining place available to him became his penultimate attempt at recovering some modicum of a certain sense of power. He might
have been minimized and injured by his position in other parts of his life,
but at least within his home, through his intimate domination over Luisa, he
might feel momentarily in control. By staking his self-regard in any way in
his control over her, however, he actually became dependent in another way
on domination itself: his identity became intricately entwined with, and dependent upon, his position of intimate power. Again the problem with this
is that to be in control, to exercise power *over* another, is not supposed to
also mean being caught in a web of dependences, and yet for Diego it certainly seemed to be. Relations of domination, patriarchy chief among them,
are not supposed to have dependence at their core. And yet they do. That
direct internal contradiction, that driving tension, has the potential to produce a great variety of ends. What Diego repeatedly created from it was violence of the most intimate kind.

What Diego's story so clearly illustrates then is that the impulse to commit partner violence cannot be reduced to a matter of displaced rage, even
though experiences outside of that relationship certainly affect it; nor is it
simply a matter of social learning, even though early exposures might shape

why specific forms of aggression are later used.[24] Even by locating it within the realm of the question of "control" we put it beyond the pale of ideas like psychodynamic notions of eros and aggression, interrelated concepts originally introduced by Freud but later carried forward and modified by others.[25] What Diego's experiences help to illustrate is that this violence itself cannot be contained within these principles; even in partner violence, it is a question of far more than just frustrated eros. After all, even though the concept of eros/aggression shares a common theme of the desire for connection, coupled with similarly directed violent reactions, relationships of chronic, coercive violence go beyond just those specific acts of aggression. They are by their own definition a matter of long-term domination, and as such they are not just a matter of violent outbursts: these relationships are a matter of routinized, systematized control. In order to understand them we therefore need to take them on this basis, we cannot see them as merely the sum of a series of aggressive acts. Diego's story also helps to show that we cannot understand what is at stake for perpetrators by focusing only on their eventual loss of control, an issue that has already been intermittently explored throughout the previous chapters.[26] While it is well established that violence in intimate relationships can escalate dramatically during the process of separation, this does not help us to understand either the many instances of violence that happen before that separation begins or more importantly why control is sought in the first place.[27]

Looking beyond the singular issue of control, it is also a matter of dependence, and especially its denial that bends the vector of violence back toward the very people on whom perpetrators depend the most: their partners. By necessity, any relationship of control reflects an underlying dependency and, as it is in other systems of violence as well, the contradiction that this creates forms one of the most important bases of violent partner relationships. In order to really begin to appreciate why someone might seek to control their partner, and why they might violently maintain that relationship, we need to see it as such. To seek to understand it on any other terms would be to miss the depth of the reliance—instrumental, emotional, existential—that aggressors have on the very people that they abuse. To take the issue of control at face value would be to miss the forms of dependence that both precede and result from those very efforts to control, their complex social origins, the forms of shame associated with them, and the realization that the resulting violence is often an effort to, at the very least, obscure their existence in the first place.

It would also be to miss a critical moment for intervention. Humans are vulnerable, fragile beings, and interdependence may be one of the few defining aspects of the entire human condition, but this does not mean that all forms of it are equally conducive to our well-being.[28] When our webs of mutuality become instead a means of exploitation, or when the base acknowledgment of our dependence is somehow made to be shameful, this fundamental experience shifts from being one of our greatest potentials for collective strength and into one of our greatest wellsprings for inflicting violence against one another.[29] By framing chronic, coercive partner violence in terms of a dependence that has been made to be hidden, we identify one of our most important targets in addressing it. What Diego was the first to teach me, whether he meant to or not, was that in order to engage with what is at stake for many perpetrators of partner violence, we must above all embark on a project of finding meaning through our reliance on others. For those who commit this violence, we must make the act of depending on others something that is itself permissible.

CHAPTER 5

Contradictions and Consciousness

Revolución mental
Lucha por autoridad
Dominio facultad para mandar o ejecutar . . .
Poder manipular centros nerviosos
Emociones de otro ser, y así tener
Al imagen de cualquier tipo de situación
Este es el objetivo de tanta revolución
Guerra mental, guerra (guerra guerra)
Guerra mental, guerra (guerra guerra!)
—Alma de Negro, "Guerra Mental"

Tensions are not just a part of life: they are its very vitality. Life *is* tension. When I first arrived in Usme, I found myself repeatedly coming up against a wall, one whose question was something like "why does it feel good for people to exercise power?" In trying to understand what kinds of motives there might be for the exercise of partner violence, what might be "at stake" for the perpetrators of it, I kept fumbling around, trying to think in terms of how such a thing could be desirable in some way. Only eventually did I realize that I was asking the fundamentally wrong question. I was trying to understand it in an embarrassingly reductionist way. Had I understood this from the outset, I might have sooner realized that, like any human experience, acts of intimate violence are deeply uncertain affairs.

Seeing it this way, soon I began to see the tensions everywhere, all of the time, tensions that shot straight through the thresholds of the social frontiers that we often assume: the self, the home, the society. The question was no longer *if* there were tensions that could help to understand the perpetration of violence. The question was what was in tension with what else, why, and to what effect.[1] Curiously, I found myself remembering my lessons from cellular biology of all things, the generation of the action potential for neurons to be precise. This minuscule example served as a reminder that what is actually important about tension is not just the poles that pull away from one another, or even the resulting midpoint on that continuum between them. What matters most of all is what do those tensions *produce*, and what they produce is often something that shoots off perpendicular to the line between them, even orthogonal to the plane on which they began. When taken to higher levels of complexity, such as the threads that permeate the mind of a person and the social worlds in which they live, these directions become even more indeterminate, even less predictable.

Once I finally started to see partner violence through this lens, the social fabric that I had been trying to dissect began to disappear. In its place was a vast vibrating web, unfixed, reproducing, shifting, pulsating electric strands articulating and repelling, sending off new strands from their moments of contraposition. Though it may be tempting to think of ambivalence and tension as paralyzing, holding us trapped somehow between opposing forces, the truth is quite the opposite. These tensions are instead profoundly productive, a common generative motif played out at all levels on the fractal of life, something vital in every sense of the word.[2] If this evokes a sort of dialectical imagination, then that is no accident, but what the experiences of the people in the preceding chapters demonstrate is that the tensions from which violence emerges are anything but binary. Even if they are contradictory, that does not mean that they are diametrically opposed. They are polygenic, they are pluripotent, and if we are ever to imagine new ways to rework them, we must first break free from the narrow confines of dialectical thought.[3] It is by thinking in these terms of polyvalent interactions that we more faithfully honor the unpredictability and indeterminacy of the worlds in which we live.[4] It is only by momentarily framing these instances of articulation, and asking more openly what they might produce, that we allow ourselves to see instead these more complicated motifs, their repetition across the scales of social life, and therefore help to organize our woefully and wonderfully imperfect appreciations of its complexity.

If we are to understand why partner violence is committed then, we need to appreciate the contradictions out of which it emerges, and it was only on these kinds of grounds that I was able to engage directly with the men who commit it. To be able to enter into the lives of abusive men, and to

do so both empathetically and critically, I had to understand it as the product of tensions, as a network of multisided oppositions that not only beset
but also continuously put into motion those who committed this kind of
abuse. Their very existence was one of the only reasons that an outsider such
as myself was able to engage with perpetrators at all, and especially to do so
in a manner that promoted at least some amount of self-reflection, not just
an echo chamber of self-assurance. By working directly through those tensions we have the potential not only to engage productively with these violent men but also to begin the process of undoing the underlying ideologies
that perpetuate those relationships. In doing so, if tensions are indeed one of
the constitutive motifs of life, then we must realize that the goal is not to
categorically resolve tensions so much as it is to help perpetrators articulate
new ones, ones that lead to less violent lives against themselves and their
partners. In other words, when we see intimate abuse as the violent means
of stitching back together the webs in which people have suspended themselves, then we must consider how we can engage in the work of bringing
together new strands. What follows here is my effort to bring together, in
light of all this, some of the themes that have cut across the preceding chapters. By putting them into conversation with one another I hope to better
explain what a "tengentic" approach might mean and what it might look
like: a means of understanding and, in this case, a means of engaging with
perpetrators of violence.[5]

Of Personhood and Power

The brilliance of ideas like Arendt's notion that violence follows from the
loss of power is that it frames this common human experience as effect and
not some primordial cause. Unlike the tendency to see violence as some essential element of "human nature," an instinct, a hydraulic force in the elaboration of human affairs, such theories of violence-as-consequence allow us
the much-needed space to open up the phenomenon and try to understand
it, all the way from its generation to its most reflexive self-perpetuation.
Such views should not be confused with naïve optimism for its elimination
though, and those who have shared this approach with Arendt have come to
similar conclusions.[6]

Seeing violence as the product of particular tensions does exactly the
same; it frames this pervasive experience of the human condition as ineras-

able and yet nevertheless neither inevitable nor immutable as well. In fact, the very first field of tension introduced in this book was not a form of domination but a form of resistance against it. Luz's interpositional independence, or as she called it her "total independence," proves, at the very least, that there are very real limits to any project of control. Despite living her whole life on the margins of the city, and at the intersection of multiple fields of sovereign relations, what Luz demonstrated was the possibility of independence without autonomy, the potential to weave some amount of liberty, rather than subjugation, out of the complex nexuses in which she lived. The creativity of her strategy came through how she engaged the various threads that socially positioned her, her cultivation of diverse systems of support, including her own homegrown sewing operation that meant she was never beholden to any one person's whim. Indeed one of the most ubiquitous tensions in the exercise of power is the ephemerality of its effect, the temporal tension of impermanence whereby any measure of domination must be continuously renewed in some way. What Luz made abundantly clear is that when sovereignty is interrupted, even momentarily, it can have catastrophically subversive consequences.[7] But these systems of sovereignty are not only vulnerable to the resistances made directly against them: they are also susceptible to the instabilities provided by the very contradictions that make them up. From the stories presented in the preceding chapters, there are a few in particular that merit reprise.

Control, Unintended Consequences, and Social Support

We live in a world that each of us is woefully underequipped to understand. One of the many consequences that we must confront because of this fact is that any action that we undertake is likely to have unintended consequences, and this has certainly been true in the stories of partner violence as previously explored. Among them, Carolina's experience, discussed in Chapter 2, stood out as perhaps one of the most severe, both for the intensity of the violence that she had managed to survive and for the irony in the undoing of her partners' control. In both of her relationships, in particular in her second one, she had lived through repeated rape and reproductive coercion, but even at the extremes of attempted degradation it was through her caring for her children that she was always able to find in herself a powerful source of self-regard. With her children as her "motor," the inflection points in both of her relationships seemed to be when her partners' violence began to involve her children as well. It was once the children became directly exposed to the violence inflicted against her that she decided to risk leaving those relationships altogether. As such, reproductive coercion, one of the many mechanisms of control that her partners had wielded over her, indeed one of the most violent and potentially damaging of them all, in the end became one of the greatest sources of their relationships' undoing.

What was true in the extreme for Carolina is generally true for many, and it is a demonstration of how the escalation of violence can itself undermine the forms of authority on which abusive relationships have been built. Even if perpetrators of violence attempt to claim permissible states of exception to the ideologies on which their sovereignty is maintained, it is hardly any assurance that others will accept them. When that violence delegitimizes their authority instead, and in the case of partner violence pushes survivors to leave, it betrays how violence is not just a reflection of the loss of control but can itself be a counterhegemonic practice. At least this is the case in a context where the victims of that violence have a means of escape; without it the opposite can just as easily be true. Left without recourse, completely enclosed within a violent relationship and with no viable way out, the ability of some to endure and further self-silence can be truly astounding. Others are even less fortunate still, and as the existence of intimate partner homicide reminds us, not everyone survives this form of abuse. In the settings where survivors do have the support—material, emotional, practical, legal—to extricate themselves from these relationships, where there is a perceptible exteriority to the boundaries that have been imposed by abusive partners, it means that each act of intimate violence has the potential to instigate its own crisis instead. It is the availability of this support—held in simultaneous tension with violent acts and their unintended consequences—which gives rise to this possibility, and it is its absence that directs the product of this tension to very different ends.[8]

For the perpetrators of abuse themselves, when separation does happen it represents a crisis that is nothing less than existential. To the extent that chronic, coercive partner violence is fundamentally a question of control, by intention or at least by effect, then there is no greater indication of the limits of one's control than being confronted by the unintended consequences of one's actions. Moreover, the greater the exercise of power, the greater these unintended consequences have the potential to be. Caught in the confrontation between the need for control and the forced realization of its limits, the response of many abusive partners is in turn to escalate their efforts for that very same control, a cycle repeated ad infinitum, or at least until the whole arrangement breaks. Taken together with the contradiction between control and dependence, this kind of self-accelerating dynamic helps us begin to understand why the process of separation is so significant for perpetrators of this violence and is also a great time of danger for the victims.

Control, Dependence, and Shame

Unlike the previous two, the tension between control and dependence is perhaps the most inevitable, as close to an *aporia* as we are ever likely to find in the perpetration of partner violence. Every act of control, every act of domination, however forceful, is by its very own definition also an act of dependence. If it appears to be a direct internal contradiction, however, it is only because of the simultaneous loading of shame that shapes this dynamic into one of violent self-effacement. Rather than a self-contained duality then, this contradiction also represents a dense nexus of social process instead. As the stories of perpetrators and survivors alike have illustrated, the social origins of both these forms of dependence, and the ways in which they are made to be shameful, are many.

We see it in the most mundane of ways, a consequence of a gendered division of labor in which men are kept from certain domestic obligations, but equally so incapable of fully taking care of themselves on their own. When working in Usme this was sometimes told to me as a joke, with a wink and a laugh about how helpless some men would be if it were not for the partners in their lives. At other times it was revealed by the pride that the men who did cook, clean, and generally defenderse (that is, fend for themselves) showed for having those basic abilities. The dependence that lies beneath control came through in graver ways too though, such as the profound emotional dependence that many perpetrators of abuse, like Diego, had upon the very people whom they sought to control. For Diego, rooted in his own experiences of prior loss, migration, isolation, and loneliness, it was his intimate relationships with his partners, and his role as a father, that provided such significant meaning and value to him. Otherwise alone in the city, fearful of its everyday insecurities, shamed by his meager wages and accumulating debts, there was a certain desperation in how he staked his well-being on those intimate relationships. To lose them was intolerable and to openly acknowledge how much he depended on them was almost just as bad. Whatever the forms of dependence, what unifies them all is that whenever a person stakes a part of their identity, a part of their means of self-valuation, or their position of domination over anyone else, they have inextricably tied themselves to them: they have come to depend on that very quality of that relationship.

When such forms of dependence are made to be shameful then—through assumptions about gendered roles, autonomy, strength, or anything else—rather than be the basis of a robust and mutually supportive interdependence, this shame demands a means of keeping that basic truth hidden. As such, any declaration of sovereignty, however intimate in scale, is precisely in that same moment also a denial. To declare oneself sovereign is to seek to erase from view the very real forms of dependence that one has on others. It is in this manner that sovereignty becomes the lie, coercive control its violent concealment, forming a sort of closed-loop contradiction that routinely feeds back upon itself. Despite how this might sound, this dynamic is still a precarious one and requires constant tending, made all the more so by the fact that partner violence itself carries its own forms of shame as well. Understanding this violence might be so much simpler if only those who perpetrated it were completely devoid of any concern for others, or even a basic ability to empathize with their partners. That is, however, almost never the case, and the reticence of many perpetrators to talk about the abuse that they commit can be in part understood as a reflection of the shame that they feel for those very actions.[9]

While realizations like this in no way mitigate the accountability that we must demand for acts of intimate violence, recognizing the many different roles that shame plays in these relationships does begin to open doors to working directly with the perpetrators themselves. Contrary to common phrases such as *hombres sin vergüenza* (men without shame), it appears that partner violence is not so much characterized by a lack of shame but by a preponderance of it. Seeking ways of addressing such abuse therefore needs to be attendant to this, not dismissive of it as a false appeal for sympathy. Shaming violent men out of abusing their partners seems to be as reasonable as trying to guilt someone out of addiction, sometimes a reflexive response but likely counterproductive in the end. Moreover, just as survivors of partner violence cannot really begin to process the trauma of their abuse until they are within a safer environment, it is unlikely that abusive men will be successful in projects of personal transformation until critical spaces are opened up that allow them to confront, in a productive manner, the forces that shame them on a daily basis. In other words, in order to make it possible for abusive men to critically encounter themselves, we must first open up spaces in which they can more critically encounter the worlds in which they live.

Surrogate Power, Sovereignty, and the Creation of Social Space

The powerless becomes the powerful, if only for a moment. The dispossessed becomes the possessor, if only at home. When the means of control and respect are rent away from oneself and economized, made contingent on premises nearly impossible to attain, the response by some is to search for the one space in which they can instead still be "in control." Rather than excuse partner violence, or even suggest that it is restricted only to those who have been the most marginalized, this once again serves as a reminder that its perpetration does not just happen in a vacuum. It is intricately woven into broader fabrics of power and suffering and not defined only by gendered relations. This also means that it is no "Russian doll" either, a bounded phenomenon contained within a larger context. To think of partner violent relationships in such a circumscribed manner would actually be to perversely honor the myth that these are somehow "private" affairs. The same threads, and tensions between them, can hold true no matter how we scale our thinking and, through doing so, obviate any real meaning that we could otherwise give to demarcated "spheres" of social analysis. This is precisely the purpose of concepts such as "surrogate power," to make clear that even the most intimate forms of violence can be perpetrated along the same dynamics, justified under the same pretenses, as other forms of violence played out at the global scale. In the case of partner violence in Usme, this means grounding that understanding in paternalistic ideologies of authority and their violent states of exception, understanding how these acts are reproductive of broader paternalistic hegemonies. More than any of the other previously described fields of tension, this provides a means of not just scaling across violent systems and finding the contradictions along the way but also of locating the confluences that bring together gendered, political, economic, religious, and racialized regimes.

Such nexuses give rise to equally complex arrays of contradiction, existing in the many forms of sleight of hand that perpetrators pull when they employ the justifications of their very own subjugation, using those same ideologies in order to explain the partner violence that they commit. If the borrowing is itself deft work, managing those contradictions is no delicate task. It is a daily and violent affair of desperately trying to hold together the resistant threads that they have attempted to weave together, and it means that abusive partners often come to occupy considerably unstable nexuses of sovereign power that are as much violent parody as they are any semblance of authority. In doing so, all of the faults in those broader systems, the ones that they themselves might otherwise have criticized, become their own to obscure. And it is then, in the quotidian work of this hiding, the violent silencing that must be done, that the illusions of social boundaries become constructed. The home becomes its own reified space, the person its "own" subject. Instead of seeing the processes that penetrate the frontiers of these entities—the internal/external, private/public, person/society—we are left instead with the violent fiction of their reality. Space, like identity, does not precede the struggle for power but rather emerges through it, and it is in this struggle, the search not just for power but a place in which to exercise it, that again we see sovereignty brought into being.[10] But it is through this process of contouring the social worlds in which we live, erecting frontiers that cut across and divide them, that we also begin to see something else as well. It is through the search for sovereignty that we also come to see how consciousness emerges and how it is shaped along the way. It is this final tension, one indelibly relevant to partner violence, that now warrants its own attention.

Of Sovereignty and Consciousness

Throughout the preceding chapters, one of the most consistent themes has been that of sovereignty: the question of how the assumption of power is spatially inscribed, and how those socially constructed spaces mediate the exercise of that power. In Chapter 2, this idea of power-in-space was most self-evident in intimate relationships. It came through the isolation of people like Carolina within their homes, the limiting of their contact with those outside of them, the enforcement of gendered divisions of labor within them, and the monopolization of control over their resources. The concept of sovereignty, however, is more than the realization that any form of power is institutionalized through the creation of social space. Max Weber called it the monopolization of the legitimate use of violence, Carl Schmitt took it to mean the ability to declare the state of exception, and both of these ideas were central in understanding the paternalistic pretenses for violence, all the way from the intimate to the global scale of social relations. This was the focus of Chapter 3, as abusive partners sought to justify their violence as urgent states of exception, aberrations in what they otherwise claimed to be benevolent exercises of authority. What all of these frameworks had in common was the underlying assumption of control, that control is what chronic, coercive relationships are ultimately all about. And while inverting the relationship between control and dependence—as was the focus of Chapter 4—certainly helps to destabilize this assumption, it does not go beyond it entirely.

In the end, if we are to really upset this dynamic, if we are to understand the full extent of partner violence and its implications, we need to be able to see past these kinds of oppositions as well. To do so requires asking what, other than just overt acts of violence, do the tensions that constitute abusive intimate partner relationships produce? What else do the social processes, as examined across the previous chapters, generate? To ask these questions is to finally move beyond the confines of thinking about sovereign power only in terms of control, or at least "control" in any traditional sense. Many others, of course, have already sought to do something like this, chief among them Michel Foucault who argued that power, including sovereign power, does not only function through repressive means. In order for power to be truly effective it must be productive as well. In the case of sovereignty in particular, this means that control is a matter not just of imposing rules— spatial, material, moral—but also of shaping the emergence of broader world-views and patterns of being.[11] Sovereignty as a productive process then extends out to the cultivation of consciousness itself, and it does so for all of those caught within its web. Seen through the prism of partner violence and the spatial inscriptions it takes, it becomes evident how this is true for perpetrators and victims alike.

Houses are built, homes are constructed, and in the case of violent relationships their walls are made as much of shame and the fear of reprisal as they are of the sand and clay taken from the earth. Though the term "domestic violence" has largely fallen out of favor in recognition that partner violence does not only happen within the heteronormative home, this change in language also reflects a recognition that to even call it "domestic" would be to validate this violent fiction of the home. It is through these processes of delimiting the world that sovereignty comes to have consequence for the emergence of consciousness, and in order to understand the relationship between the two we must first recognize that consciousness is far more than a simple synonym for "awareness." While an extended exploration of

such an enormous concept is simply not possible here, we might at least begin by saying that consciousness is that peculiar phenomenon that occurs
when the mind's eye is turned outward and inward at the same time. Out of
this juncture, previously disparate elements are brought together through
inward reflection and strained to be intelligible to, or at least in light of,
the outward world. It is the product of the tension of this multidirectional
gaze, the moment in which the infinite beyond and the infinite within
come into contact, and it is in these moments that new assemblages—mental
or social—come into being.[12] Consciousness is therefore a question of connection, but more specifically it is a question of *configuration* and how those
reworked assemblages emerge out of our encounters with one another.[13] It is
a process of perpetual becoming, of engaging a world that constantly resists
our understanding, and it is out of this struggle, this continuous search, this
critical will to consciousness, that we come to make and remake our worlds.
Consciousness, be it personal or collective, is always a matter of articulation, and that occurs through the process of experiencing the larger world
around us.[14]

It is in this sense that the relationship between sovereignty and consciousness begins to come into focus, and where another notion of its meaning begins to appear: sovereignty is the shaping of consciousness; it is the
etching of the contours through which it emerges.[15] Indeed we might even
say that it is the shaping of consciousness that is sovereignty's ultimate task.
For survivors of abuse such as Carolina, her partners' efforts to confine her
to particular spaces and cut off her contact with those who might support
her were not just exercises of power for their own sake. They were acts of
establishing sovereignty but they were also acts aimed at limiting the extent
of her social encounters, the very base material on which consciousness is
cultivated.[16] Her partners' wishes to prevent her connection with others
were part of an effort to prevent the intrusion of perspectives that might
work against them and that threatened to undo the normalization of violence that they were trying to achieve. As such, the process of normalizing
partner violence is not just a matter of espousing a particular set of ideas
and brutally enacting them, it is a question of actively managing the influx
of competing views. To do so is to influence the shape of the social consciousness that emerges, and even if the isolation of survivors of violence is
never truly complete, the effects of these efforts can still be profound.

As explored in Chapter 3 though, sovereignty is not just a matter of
shaping the consciousness of survivors of abuse. To say that surrogate power

is a means of investing people in the justifications for their own domination is to claim that it is a matter of limiting the emergence of critical consciousness on the part of perpetrators as well. Those who commit this violence are, inevitably, witnesses to their own actions, and the many acts of violence that they inflict upon their partners constitute important experiences for them as well. Paternalistic justifications then, the rationalization that violent episodes are merely the state of exception, are every bit as important for perpetrators as well; they are bulwarks against the recognition of the implications of what they themselves are doing. The lines that are drawn in the search for sovereignty cut through people themselves, and in doing so they can serve to shape the consciousness for perpetrators of violence in such a way that it avoids forging certain critical connections. Were this not the case, very different outcomes might be possible. For example, for Diego it could have been that his moments of most intense violence against Luisa represented fundamental ruptures for his worldview as well, moments in which the ideologies he employed began to ring hollow and he started to question the basis on which he had built a significant part of his life. Instead, in spite of the cracks in these justifications, ones that showed through in Diego's remorse and the typical cyclical pattern that his violence took, in the end Diego was never able to make a full departure from the moral frameworks that upheld his abuse. By the end of my time living in Usme, Luisa was once again faced with the decision of whether or not to report him, and his views on allowable power had changed very little, if they had at all.

To say that the search for sovereignty is the shaping of consciousness though does not make us beholden to the designs of those who commit it. Understanding the resistances against this violence—the daily work that women like Luz Elena and Carolina both exemplified—is to recognize that, for survivors of this violence, the search for sovereignty and with it the cultivation of consciousness is as much about their refutation. This refutation though is not necessarily of the terms set forth by those who commit it, that is, the ideas, the habits, and patterns of life; it is refutation of their right to *monopolize* the setting of them. Agency does not always have to mean refuting specific ideas: it is not contingent on always living in direct opposition to the particular terms set forth by various regimes of power.[17] It is a matter of who has the power to set them, and undoing the concentration of sovereign power is therefore a question of undoing another's monopolization of that right. In the case of partner violence these refutations can come in many forms: from simply not believing in the legitimacy of an abusive partner's violence to taking out orders of protection, even leaving partners and the spaces that they have attempted to build. Of the many ways in which these potentially conflicting processes play out, the will to consciousness and the search for sovereignty, it is all too frequently that in their contest we find violence of the most intimate kind. And if the picture painted in the previous chapter by Luisa and Diego's story is discouraging, an all-too-familiar pattern of reconciliation, quiet, and then the repetition of abuse, it is not the only one. Sovereignty, like consciousness, is never fully a fait accompli. In its incompleteness possibility springs eternal, and not every abusive relationship remains caught in the same cycles as theirs did.

Return to Center

Against the experiences of Diego and Luisa were those of another man, Jairo, someone I also initially came to know through the Comisarías de Familia. We first met in the immediate aftermath of the audience that decided his order of protection, a meeting that he attended with his partner and during which he implicitly admitted to the violence that he had committed. His enthusiasm when we first met was almost startling, a bit like it had been with Diego, and from that very first moment onward I began to appreciate the energy that he brought to so many endeavors in his life. Over the course of a year I would see that vitality everywhere from our closed-room conversations to the mobile locations of where he worked, but unlike with Diego the one place I never met with Jairo was in his home. That place, his home, was still clearly in its own way a central pole in his life, but for Jairo social life did not just exist in reference to it. His attention was frequently focused elsewhere, on places and people unfamiliar to him, the settings for the kinds of new experiences that he almost obsessively sought. This curiosity of his quickly became the common interest that drew us together, the means by which we would repeatedly come back to the same questions we had already asked, hoping to mine them again for new materials. In many ways that same propensity of his was also what formed the central tension between his partner, Valentina, and him, a key feature to understanding both the genesis of their conflict and Jairo's transformation in its aftermath. Just as with Diego, in order to understand why this was so important to Jairo, what was really at stake for him throughout his violence against Valentina, we have to glimpse back briefly at the longer arc of his life.

Like so many other people, Jairo did not grow up in Bogotá. His birth-place, and where much of his family still resides, was in a small rural town in the department of Meta just to the south and east of the capital city. Like so many other departments—Tolima, Guajira, Putumayo, and Chocó to name but a few—Meta has enjoyed its fair share of "mala fama" (bad fame, or ignominy) on a long and nebulous list of "hot zones" throughout the history of the political conflict. To whatever degree this ignominy has been true, Jairo always portrayed his childhood in a more idyllic hue. The specter of the conflict was there to be sure, he remembered, a shadow lurking somewhere beyond his immediate horizons when he was growing up, but, when seen again through the prism of memory, his enduring impression of his youth was that it was a tranquil one. More relevant to him than the threat of armed actors were the threats of chores and homework, the joys of long afternoons spent playing by the river, and the absence of his father to whom he gave a sort of conspicuous indifference. He knew who his father was, he could point to him as a member of their community and would run into him from time to time, but he never had a relationship with him. It was his mother, he explained to me, who played all roles as his parent, who cared for him, who taught him discipline and the value of hard work, who instilled in him a strong desire to learn.[18] It was through these sorts of small moments that he remembered his childhood, not through the seismic shifts of catastrophic loss or victimization from overwhelming experiences of violence, and it was a much more peaceful recollection of his upbringing from what I had gotten used to hearing.

When I asked him once when he thought that he became an adult, he paused, intrigued by the question, and then, as if struck by a revelation, told me that he felt he became a full adult only when he did his time of required military service.[19] If his mother was disciplined, he said, the military was strict in the most scrupulous sense, and if his mother had brought him through childhood, then it was the military that brought him into adult-hood.[20] Joining the military was not just the time when he began to fully assume adult roles, however; it was also the first time that he ever traveled away from his hometown, and after it there was never really any going back. Though Jairo spent a few short months back with his family after his time of service, he did not linger for long and soon found himself moving to Bogotá and enrolling to study to become a nurse. It was a profession on which he would go on to build the rest of his career, contracting himself out to corporations for extended field deployments on large-scale projects. Combined with his military experience, his degree in nursing helped him to easily find positions as a field practitioner for anything from mining to petrol to infrastructure development projects all around the country. As with Diego's experience working for the sanitation department, these positions would take him away from Bogotá for weeks on end to a constantly changing array of disparate locations. Jairo, however, never seemed to mind. To the contrary, whenever he spoke of his previous work to me he would always emphasize how much he loved every bit of it, relishing the opportunity to continually meet new people, see new places, and satisfy a deep-seated urge to strike out beyond his present horizons.

This seemed to work well for him for over a decade until he met Valentina, and together they had their first child. Her pregnancy had not been planned, according to Jairo; in fact at the time neither one of them particularly wanted to have a child nor were they certain about what they wanted their future together to be. As we talked about their relationship he made it clear that one of the major reasons that they had stayed together at all was so that their son, and later their daughter, would have both a maternal and paternal presence, something of which he felt that he had been deprived. For another ten years Jairo tried to live both lives, still working as a field nurse on repeated deployments, but now returning to a home in Usme that he shared with Valentina and their children. It was a balancing act that carried its own significant difficulties: infidelity, absence, guilt, returning to a home where his lack of presence undermined the authority that he wanted to have as a father. One might think then that when he was fired from his contracting service and returned home on a more indeterminate basis that the tensions behind these difficulties would have resolved and life would have become much easier. If anything though, it all became much worse.

Jairo's permanent return to Usme was a transition met with dire consequences. As a psychologist involved in the aftermath of the order of protection against him would note, with his unemployment and increased time at home, Jairo began fighting with renewed urgency for authority within his family.[21] Ultimately there was one episode in particular that prompted Valentina to seek the order of protection, but as she noted on that initial encounter at the Comisaría, it was certainly not the first time. As she indicated, Jairo had for a long time been controlling of her, even hitting her once right after their daughter had been born nine years before. After he lost his job and returned home to Usme permanently, that physical violence had not only restarted but had been building to a crescendo ever since. On the most recent occasion, he had grabbed her by her hair and hit her head up against a wall, all for her interjecting into an argument he had been having with their son about watching television rather than doing his homework.[22] Throughout the months that followed, neither Valentina nor their kids ever moved out of the house that they shared, but she did visit the Comisaría de Familia, the attorney general, and the department of forensic medicine in order to document what he had done.[23] At their joint audience two weeks later, Jairo did not contradict a word of what she said.

It was at this point, in what was, emotionally speaking, an especially ambivalent time for him, that Jairo and I first met. It was a new low for him as he tried to reckon with his most recent violence, and even though he did not turn to alcohol in the way that Diego had, it was still clear that his own actions had begun to weigh on him as well. Early on when we first began talking he would repeatedly comment on how incongruous his actions were, contrasting them against either the love and respect that he had for his mother who single-handedly raised him or his role as a caregiver through his work as a nurse. Pursued constantly by these ruminations, he one day showed me how he found some solace from them, using a very peculiar device that he had contrived. Pulling out a small change purse from his pack, he explained to me that in that small bag he kept all of his worries. As he would reflect on those challenges that he was facing, and eventually find a means of working through them, he would "take them out" one by one from his purse, usually to replace them shortly thereafter with some newer concern.[24] At the moment, he said, figuring out why he hurt Valentina was taking up most of the room in his bag. Buoying him to some extent throughout all of this was the fact that he found a new job recently after we met, and the excitement of this new outlet injected him with renewed optimism. His new posting put him with a public health outreach group, and after a couple of months of interviews he began inviting me to follow him around with his team. The project he worked on was a novel one for Bogotá: provide mobile health services to the city's most marginalized members, who struggled with homelessness or addiction or were working as street recyclers or sex workers. For Jairo it was everything that he had loved about his previous employment, but with the added benefit of taking place within the city where he lived, allowing him to continue his work as an outreach nurse and still be close to home.

Walking with him one Saturday morning, we were on our way to a meeting hall where his team was about to host a forum for parents on the topic of adolescent drug use. We had left with plenty of time to spare, but one by one the street-side shops began opening their shutters for the day's work and on every block Jairo would find one to duck into, saluting the owner as if he had happened upon a long-lost friend. In between them, as we hustled on to make up for lost time, he extolled the work of his team and especially the leadership of its founder, someone who had used her high-reaching political connections to create the program in the first place. When we finally arrived at the hall, almost late at that point, I saw in action his esteem for their team's director as he traded his earlier ebullience for a more subdued, deferent tone. Working with the director and the team's doctor, both women, he moved quietly in the background, jumping from group to group. When two parents became overwhelmed telling the story of their teenage son's addiction, he consoled them, took them to another room, and left their side only when the team psychologist arrived to take over. It was a picture so starkly at odds with that of a man who had thrown his wife's head against a wall: there, he was caring, gentle, not just deferential but reverent to his female superiors. I have to admit, I even found myself doing double and triple takes. And while that is precisely the dissonance in so many cases of partner violence, what victims experience and what others see outside the home, seeing Jairo at work beckoned the question of whether or not there was indeed some kind of deeper change under way for him, one that transcended a mere pause in his violence.

By Valentina's account, there had been a change. Three months after she obtained the order of protection, she came back to that same Comisaría de Familia, this time for an individual follow-up. When asked about her situation, she told the social worker that everything had changed. Jairo had found work, and through his job an opportunity to reflect on his family. There was harmony, they were working to come to agreements, there was no more yelling, no more violence, and he was helping her in what she needed around the house. She felt calm. At the half-year mark she returned, this time for a routine series of questions meant to gauge the likelihood that Jairo would return to any of the forms of violence that he had previously committed against her. Again, across the board the picture that she painted was a positive one: there was still no more violence. In its place there was dialogue, and through therapy Jairo had continued to reflect on himself. Even almost one year after she took out the order of protection, there was still no indication that Jairo had gone back to his earlier ways.

What happened? Why, when so many other perpetrators of intimate violence repeat cycles of abuse, was Jairo able to avoid doing so for so long? For one, something had flipped. Now home on a more permanent basis, Jairo's desire to reinsert himself into the lives of their children was constantly counterbalanced by his persistent desire to also get out of that very home and continue exploring outside of it. Previously that tension had created for Jairo a kind of dire urgency, a need to reassert his paternal authority within their home whenever he was actually there. After the order of protection, Jairo began bringing their children outside of their home to explore around with him, showing them parts of the city that he had come to know through his work on the outreach team. In doing so he was able to fulfill what he felt were his paternal obligations to them, not by fighting Valentina for authority within their home but rather by taking their children outside of it and showing them the broader world that he himself was getting to know. Additionally, Jairo and Valentina had also gone to therapy, something that was frustratingly uncommon according to those who worked in the Comisaría system. For a transformative process to work though, in this case one defined under a particular "therapeutic" paradigm, there must be a window of opportunity for it to be effective, a context in some way permissive to the difficult work of critical self-reflection. Frequently the basic willingness of a person to engage in such a process is considered to be one of the most influential of these, and to be certain Jairo had all the appearances of being a highly motivated patient from the very outset.[25] Even still, it is worth asking if there had been anything else that had opened up that window of opportunity for him, any other reason why he was so positively predisposed.

According to Jairo himself, it came down to one thing: *conciencia* (consciousness). It was only toward the end of my fieldwork, when we were taking another aimless walk around his neighborhood, that he directly laid out for me how that change had come about for him. Ambling down the hill away from the main avenue, cutting through a neighborhood playground, I asked him simply how his work had been going: nothing special, nothing directive, just a reflex of sorts to get us talking. Work was uncertain, he told me, because, with mayoral elections coming around in the fall, there was never any certainty that the program he worked for would even exist in the new year. Still, he continued, in the short time that he had been on the team it had already made a significant impression on him. Surprised, I asked him why. Pointing back at the children running around the playground, he explained to me how though it was his job to provide care and health educa-tion, he felt that he was actually the one who had been taught the most throughout his work. The stories of his patients stuck with him, he said, the stories of those who had grown up in homes beset by violence, the stories of those who had fled their homes and found drugs as a way to escape their memories of them. Their stories made him worry that he was doing the same thing to his own children: that if he did not change, and quickly, that his own children might one day follow down a similar path. And so just as so much of Jairo's violence against Valentina was built on his investment in his children, so too was his motivation to change. It is not only alternative models of being that check ideologies like paternalism; through the contra-dictions in its practice paternalism sometimes even checks itself, or at least provides a sort of "hinge" in the process of change.[26] As Jairo put it, "it is a question of consciousness," and as Valentina herself explained during a fol-low-up meeting of hers, it is a consciousness that emerges in particular spaces, prompted by the kind of crisis that sometimes only an order of pro-tection can properly provide.

For Jairo that space of transformation was his place of work, and given his job description that meant a multitude of locations out in the commu-nity, from schoolyards to underpasses, all of them far beyond the walls of any clinic. Instead of walls, in his job Jairo had around him a multidisci-plinary team, one in which both the majority of its members and those at the top of the ladder were women. It was not just mere exposure to the life stories of other people: it was face-to-face encounters with them, in unfa-miliar spaces, and with a particular cadre of colleagues around him at the time.[27] These were the experiences in which he found himself unmoored, uncertain of himself but not made to feel ashamed, the spaces in which he found the kind of material through which his consciousness could continue to grow. Consciousness though can be fleeting, and where we find ourselves during its brief moments of reconfiguration can drastically shape where it leads to in the end. In Jairo's case he found himself bolstered by being gain-fully employed again, by having a role in which he was able to serve others while being on a team where the principles of care and interdependence were its founding pillars. It was at this peculiar juncture, this unlikely ar-ticulation of circumstances, that the change that Valentina observed began to occur. If psychotherapy also played a role, at the very least it cannot pos-sibly be understood outside of the context of his broader experiences at the time. Just as our understandings of the violence committed in the first place cannot be divorced from these connections, our assessment of possible routes of redress cannot be either.

Metamorphosis *is* possible. Jairo's story reminds us of as much, but it also reminds us that in order to achieve it we need to create permissive conditions in which it can unfold. We need to recognize that consciousness is more than mere awareness. It is a complex social experience that emerges from the milieus in which we are immersed. Ultimately, if we are to achieve these changes, we need to open up critical spaces in which to realize this work, spaces not unlike the one that Jairo found himself in during a pivotal moment of his course. If we are able to create them, and if we are able to bring abusive men into them in ways that do not inherently shame them but instead offer opportunities for growth, for the cultivation of consciousness, just as Jairo did we just might find that intimate partner violence can indeed come undone.

CHAPTER 6

Response

No es amor
No es crimen pasional
En feminicidio
Es asesinado!

—Anonymous

When I finally confronted my fear and took a concrete step
for social justice, the accumulated shame began to dissolve
in a new sense of self-respect. For me, the real victory of that
encounter with the Jim Crow system of the South was the
liberation of my mind from years of enslavement.
—Pauli Murray

I am sitting in the reception office with Cristina, the young psychologist-in-training, as one by one she receives the visitors for today. Outside of her office, people wait on blue plastic benches and huddle against the interminable cold. A few mothers stay busy by keeping track of their young children as they run around the waiting area, but most others are sitting alone, avoiding eye contact with one another and ignoring the telenovela that is on the TV. Stuck inconspicuously into a long row of businesses, there are precious few windows here on the first floor and the only natural light that finds its way in is through the small glass door that the security guard watches. An endless flow of people comes in and out of Cristina's incandescent domain, where she quickly hears their stories and directs them on to the next steps in their journey. Half of the people it seems are sent on to other agencies, and most of them complain that they have already been remitted from somewhere else.

One woman comes in and, as soon as her daughter goes back to the waiting room, bursts into tears as she tells Cristina about how her ex-partner spends his money on alcohol and leaves her struggling to feed her daughter. She feels humiliated, she says, frustrated, exasperated, she is at her very wits' end. A few follow-up questions, printed pages, directions, and kind words later, she is sent to the Defensoría de Familia. Next, a father. His seventeen-year-old daughter left a few days ago with her boyfriend and has not called. He is sent to the Defensoría. A woman who says she has an order of protection tells us her ex-partner has been calling and harassing her, but it turns out her order was never finalized because she had not made it to a follow-up meeting. When she hears her next appointment was already scheduled for a month from now, she sinks her head into her hands, sighs, then thanks Cristina and leaves. Now a woman in her thirties, who carries her head high, sits straight in her seat and tells us with confidence the story of her separation from her partner. He had been verbally abusive before but now he was threatening her life. She wants to make a denuncia and get an order of protection. She laughs when Cristina asks if he had been controlling or verbally abusive before the split. Yes, yes, he had been, his insults used to be her "daily bread." Moving now with quick, precise motions, Cristina grabs a clipboard, hands her the paperwork, and enters her into the computer system. Next.

*   *   *

Who comes to the Comisarías? The desperate, the despondent, the indignant; the "punted" and the confused; those in need of financial support without which they may not survive. I learned early on though from the days that I spent in reception that those who come here are not just seeking support for partner violence. The people who work here address a much broader range of issues. Even still, this office, hidden in plain sight along a major artery in Usme, is a primary point of attention for anyone looking for government assistance in this kind of abuse. It is impossible to understand the response to partner violence in Bogotá without examining its existence.

Usme has two Comisarías, and by conducting fieldwork in both of them I was introduced to these issues in the community in the first place. During my time there, the people who worked in these offices became crucial partners and provided some of the closest relationships that I built. They not only opened their doors to me, but they started to show me what it means to routinely enter into experiences of intimate terror. And yet understanding the development of the Comisaría de Familia system in Bogotá, and the work that the professionals who operate within them do, does not just open up a window into the difficulties of addressing partner violence. By exploring the process by which these institutions were established, and subsequently invested with some of the tools necessary to actually address the needs of survivors—legally, financially, psychologically, and emotionally—we see quite clearly some of the limitations that have emerged from this professionalized response.[1] Rather than being blind to them, through their daily frustrations those who work in the Comisarías are as aware as anyone of their limits. There is a constant yearning to reach beyond them. Perhaps for this reason, my most rewarding moments in working with Comisaría staff came when we were able to talk openly about the kind of work that they *wished* that they could do. In those aspirations, and the search for collaborators who could help to realize them, we start to see the possibilities of what more critical approaches to this violence might be. And we desperately need them.

Wherever partner violence exists it is a blight on us all—be it through its infliction, its endurance, its justification, or its redress, even our indifference to it—and the responsibility to address it is beyond any one entity. Institutions such as the Comisarías are but one step in this process, particularly useful in triggering crises for the perpetrators of that violence and with them crises for the broader systems of power that their acts come to condense. In order to operate, however, they have necessarily made a number of capitulations along the way, and if we are to use partner violence as a starting point from which to remake a better world then we must ultimately be able to work ourselves past them. Some of the people who work within them already are. As they know, be it legal or therapeutic, the sum of services provided will never amount to justice. As absolutely necessary as the Comisarías de Familia are, as valuable as they can be in rebalancing the scales, they are not the settings in which critical consciousness can be cultivated in earnest—at least not as they are currently devised, and that consciousness is one essential exteriority to which we must continuously strive. To search for it we still need the intrusion of institutions like the Comisarías into intimate affairs, and before we can take steps beyond them we must first come to see how they function from the inside out. From their regulations and from their frustrations we can start to look onward: it is the very limits that bind them that can serve as our guides.

What Are the Comisarías?

Though the total response to gender-based violence extends to many other state entities, civil society, and, of course, less formal networks of support as well, the Comisarías de Familia of Bogotá are most explicitly charged with addressing partner violence. As a municipal agency under the mayor's office, they represent an important instance of a state-based organized response to this form of violence, the development of which has been slow to progress over the course of decades of repeated demands. The regional movements that helped to eventually build institutions like the Comisarías de Familia did not begin in Colombia, as previously discussed in Chapter 1, nor did those movements even directly address gender-based violence from their outset. Beginning instead in countries such as Chile and Argentina, some of the initial mass mobilizations by women in Latin America were made against autocratic regimes for their abuses in their respective "dirty wars."[2] Leveraging their identities as mothers, sisters, and wives, women in these mobilizations used more traditionally recognized gender roles in order to make claims against their governments to acknowledge or return their "disappeared" relatives. These encounters eventually became the basis of coalitions that evolved to make more direct and subversive claims about gender norms themselves and eventually link them to addressing gender-based violence.[3] One major transition point for this came in July 1981 with the first encuentro of the Feminist Conference of Latin America and the Caribbean, convened in Bogotá, during which November 25 was set as the International Day for the Elimination of Violence Against Women. With its declaration, the forms of violence under scrutiny were no longer just those of repressive state regimes but also the daily abuses by intimate tyrants. The marker for addressing gender relations themselves was effectively set.

Over the course of the ensuing decade these mobilizations would continue to mature, and in Colombia new opportunities emerged to bring in global human rights discourses, especially with the social upheavals that culminated in the drafting of the constitution of 1991, the "Constitution of Rights."[4] During this period came not only the acceptance of the new constitution but also the institutionalization of some of its undercurrents through the passage of other laws. For the Comisarías de Familia, this process predated the constitution itself with Decree 2737 of 1989, the "Code of Minors," which established the ability of cities to set up commissaries for the specific purpose of addressing "family violence."[5] That framing of the mandate in terms of *family* violence was no accident either, as two years later in Article 42 of the new constitution the family was officially consecrated as the fundamental nucleus of society.[6] Over time, the roles of these institutions would be further clarified, their legal powers expanded progressively to allow them greater efficacy, and as everyone I knew in the Comisarías would tell me, their mandate eventually came to include four specific forms of violence: partner violence, child physical abuse, child sexual abuse, and child neglect. Knowing the history of laws that expanded their mission, however dry it may seem, is actually no academic matter. The invocation of laws, decrees, and accords, and knowing them by their numbers and years, is part of the art of both working in and effectively consulting the many bureaucracies that order everyday life in Colombia. Whether or not it is what one of the country's founders, Francisco de Paula Santander, had in mind when he said, "Colombians, arms have given you independence, laws will give you liberty," it is difficult to deny the impressive front that a working knowledge of them can create. When Comisaría staff hurriedly recite these genealogies during their audiences, as if rushing through a mythic story of their institution's genesis, the laws that have built these systems of response once again leave the pages of legal tomes and become the animating force of a performed authority. To understand that authority, and the work that it can do, is therefore to see beyond this legal history. To understand what the Comisarías really represent as an institution of redress, we must have some actual institutional memory.

Reconciliation or Bust

Of the people that I came to know within the Comisaría system, few were better able to provide that background of lived history than Marta. Trained as a lawyer, Marta had worked in the Comisarías since their inception and risen quickly to be the head of one of the branches, before moving on to work at the central level of administration for the city's system. As she explained to me, there were really two major periods in the life of the Comisarías, and they were currently on the precipice of a third. In the beginning, it was all about reconciliation, as she bluntly told me: "That was all we were able to really do. A woman came in whose husband beat her? Reconcile them! We did not have the power to do anything else." This logic of reconciliation was not just a by-product of underdeveloped legal authority at the time, however; it came from a carefully delineated theory of conflict. Outlined in full in a federal report called "Conciliación y violencia intrafamiliar" (Conciliation and intrafamilial violence), the fundamental proposition was that conflict is not only inevitable but perhaps even vital to life, and that only violence can and should be avoided.[7] The authors begin the report in this way:

> Conflict is a part of the dynamic of life. Everyone plays a role in the conflict and the different forms of approaching and resolving it.... Men, women, children see the world in different ways. Depending on where they are situated, of their personal and particular psychological history, their position of power, their social position, age, sex, culture; depending on their own unrepeatable identity, among other things. The family, constitutionally consecrated as the fundamental nucleus of society, constitutes a topic of particular concern for the makers of laws and public policy, to the extent that it is necessary to surround it with the means to guarantee its unity, harmony, and survival.

According to this, Marta's early experiences of working in the Comisarías and her frustrations at being unable to do anything other than reconcile partners were built directly out of a normative mandate to maintain the integrity of the family. The system in which she worked was originally devised only to supervise and negotiate conflict and to try to maintain it within certain bounds and keep such tensions from exceeding the threshold into violent behavior.

To be fair, the same authors also adopted a view of violence that framed it as the instrumentalized force used in maintaining unequal relations of power, and they explicitly promoted a view of family relations that was built on more equitable grounds.[8] This was made most clearly evident when they contrasted the "traditional model" and a "model of cultural transformation" of family relations. In the column of the former were appropriation, competence, submission to authority, obedience, control, verticality, imposition, and exclusion, while the latter included participation, cooperation, reflection and constructive criticism, accord and consensus, horizontality, self-determination, and respect. In this way then the original Comisaría system might be seen as an attempt to preserve the family unit but to do so by promoting its transformation to a new paradigm of gender relations and conflict resolution. Without useful instruments like the orders of protection, however, personnel were at best ineffectual at realizing this objective. At worst they were routinely imposing unwanted solutions onto those who sought their assistance through something that could be called the normative violence of reconciliation.[9]

Though the introduction of tools like the order of protection has certainly changed this in the system's current form, there are still strong undercurrents of this kind of logic in the guiding philosophies of some of the functionaries. In some of the audiences that I was able to witness in the Comisarías in Usme, I was often shocked at the explicit messages delivered to the people who had placed a denuncia in the first place. In one instance, a young man in his early twenties came in to request an order of protection against his mother, who he claimed had pulled a kitchen knife on him during a recent argument. His parents had previously separated so he had since left to live with his father and at that point in time wanted nothing more than permanent separation from his mother and the legal protection to ensure it. While the lawyer granted the order, so too did she mandate family therapy sessions for the two, justifying it by saying that no person could go the rest of their lives without the presence of their mother and that what was best would be to learn to resolve their differences more peacefully. On other occasions, women who had taken out orders of protection against abusive men, and had already separated permanently from them, would be told during meetings about child support that the visitation rights of the father would mean that their ex-partners would never be entirely out of their lives. In such cases they would usually also be lectured about how, during these encounters, they should take care not to fight with their ex-partners, cause conflict with them, or speak poorly of them behind their back as doing so might have a damaging effect on the children that they shared.

Orders of Protection, Measures of Separation

Despite these pervasive tendencies, the *medidas de protección* (orders of protection) have been the source of the single greatest transformation of the Comisarías and mark, according to Marta, the second major era of its exis-

tence. Originally created through Ley 294 of 1996, it was only through subsequent modifications such as Ley 575 of 2000 and Ley 1275 of 2008 that
lawyers in the Comisaría system gained the full authority to place immediate orders of protection, as well as have more authority to impose consequences to infractions. It was not until Comisaría staff were able to grant
and enforce these orders that the system came into its contemporary form.
This is because the orders of protection, though imperfect and limited as all
legal tools are, offer two things that were previously not possible: a means of
deterring further violence as well as a real possibility of separation. I say
"possibility" because obtaining an order of protection does not necessarily
even mean physical separation of the people involved. The orders of protection therefore are not restraining orders that necessarily mandate a given
distance of separation, although some of them are; they are most fundamentally an instrument that is meant to help shift the balance of power back
to the survivor of abuse so that she has greater power in the determination
of her own future. While this ideal is not always realized, and sometimes
even actively abated through the interactions between functionaries and
citizens, it is nevertheless demonstrated at a number of points in the process.

When someone first comes in to make a denuncia, she is asked to fill out
a form that gives her basic information, a brief account of the events for
which she is seeking protection, and a series of questions about the future
steps in the process.[10] The first question is whether or not she wishes to be
placed in a protective shelter. If she elects to do so, a member of the Comisaría will take her to the shelter once the rest of the paperwork for that day is
finished. Most women elect not to take this option, and given the restrictions that are presented to them perhaps this is not surprising. As one psychologist explained to me, going to the shelter does mean protection but it
also means not being able to go to work and likely losing one's job, not letting one's children attend school, having a limited ability to leave the facil-
ity, and not being allowed to have visitors, including any contact with the
person against whom she has made the denuncia. The second question that
she is asked is whether or not she would like the accused perpetrator of violence present at the meeting to establish the permanent order of protection.[11]
Most women choose to have this meeting together with their denounced
partner and in my experience the psychologists who work in reception sometimes actively encourage this by counseling that having this audience together will hasten the completion of the process. The reasons for choosing to

have this meeting together go beyond these suggestions though, and on the intake form there are open spaces for people to explain why they have made these decisions. Not infrequently these spaces are left blank, but when people fill them in the answers that they give can be quite telling. For instance, one woman who was not even certain yet if she wanted to permanently separate from her partner wrote, "I want him to see that I have more in my life, that it does not revolve around his." In these spaces, one finds everything from justifications based on practical matters to nothing short of small declarations of independence.

From this initial encounter, those making denuncias must return for a meeting with the Comisaría's lawyer in order to discuss the events in question, allow a space for the accused to voice his version of events, for both to present other evidence or testimonies to what has happened, and ultimately to finalize and sign the order of protection. The conditions of this final order are largely dependent on the desires of the person making the denuncia, who may want anything from an official warning to their partner to a permanent separation with cessation of all contact. What surprised me greatly, the more cases that I observed, was how often the former was the case. More frequently than I would have ever anticipated, women making denuncias did not want immediate sanctions or separation but rather something more along the lines of an official warning, something that would let them still live with their partners but hopefully deter future abuse as well as give them more immediate recourse should it recur. Depending on the case, from this point on a series of meetings then follows with the psychologist on staff in order to discuss other issues such as child support or options for therapy and, over the course of the following two years, periodic follow-ups with an assigned social worker. At the end of those two years, unless the person who made the denuncia renews the order of protection, it expires and the case is considered closed. Contrary to the original system where the only recourse effectively was to reconcile couples, those who present to the Comisarías now have a much wider range of options that include, but crucially are not exclusive to, separating from their partner. From their initial presentation to determining the order of protection itself, and up through the renewal (or not) after the standard two-year term, built into this process are a number of steps meant to provide support to survivors of violence as they seek to renegotiate the terms of their intimate relationships. Should they choose to separate, the order of protection is there to help them do so, or at least this is the ideal version. Reality is, of course, usually much messier, and the meetings that determine the terms of the orders of protection are framed in encounters of drastically unequal power that can dramatically alter the results.

In spite of this messiness, however, for those who work in the Comisarías this second era of the system, characterized by greater potential for intervention on behalf of survivors of violence, has produced results that are rather intimately felt. When I asked Marta what she saw as the major victories of the Comisaría system, she paused and looked away. When she turned back, she sighed and gave me a simple answer: it was the lives that they had saved. She went on to explain that this happened not only by directly intervening in the most violent of cases, it was also something that the Comisarías had contributed to by taking part in a broader process of cultural transformation. Even if the system that she oversaw only contributed to this project of change through its very existence, which fundamentally challenges the legitimacy and tolerability of partner violence in society, that to her was enough. Of course, the Comisarías have contributed to this through more than just their basic existence, and while many of its staff remain frustrated by its existing limitations, they rarely forget the people that they were able to help.

Sovereignty Interrupted: The "Private" Made "Public"

In some way, just about all contact with the Comisarías de Familia constitutes a form of intrusion, especially for perpetrators of violence. In the most routine instances, this is carried out through the audiences that happen within those halls. Here the work of rupturing boundaries is accomplished through the means of legal imposition, the mobilization of instruments like the orders of protection that facilitate the ability of survivors of abuse to carry state resources past previously impervious thresholds, or what were once considered to be completely "private" spaces. The means of intrusion, however, are not so limited, and perpetrators do not in fact even need to be within the walls of the Comisaría for it to occur. This is precisely the case of the home visits that social workers conduct when they track down people who have been lost to follow-up, where the knocking on doors is as literal of a means as possible of breaching social space.

Early one morning, I followed an invitation from one of the social workers to go out with her on these visits. As we climbed out of the truck at our first stop, the social worker donned her fluorescent red jacket, the back of which read "Office of the Mayor of Bogotá: Secretary for Social Integration," a barely disguised euphemism for the agency that she represented. The area of Usme we were in was farther up the mountains and one of the newer zones where communities were recently establishing themselves. The roads long ago stopped being paved and house addresses were either in flux or frequently inconsistent with our maps, so in order to find our first house we had to canvass the blocks around where our best guess was, the social worker asking anyone we passed if they could help us find our destination. Eventually, we found the help we needed and began ringing the doorbell of a two-story house. Up above us, an elderly lady poked her head out of a window and the social worker called up to her, asking her if she knew the woman we were trying to locate. She nodded, calling back down that her neighbor had left earlier in the morning and would not be back until the afternoon. In a few moments she was downstairs in front of us, on the other side of the door, and through it the social worker was asking her if she had noticed anything out of the ordinary recently, if she had heard fighting, or if she knew how this woman we were trying to find had been doing. Her answers were brief, and as we walked away the social worker explained to me that people are often reluctant to divulge the details of their neighbors' lives, either out of a sense of minding their own business or out of fear of retribution of some kind. Before we left for the next neighborhood, she wrote out a notice and taped it to the front door.

Of all the things that Marta taught me during her crash course on the Comisarías, perhaps the simplest yet most profound was that the confrontation of partner abuse is fundamentally a practice of redefining the public/private frontiers of social life.[12] One could even argue that their existence has contributed to a fundamental change in the notion of citizenship.[13] By creating public institutions whose express mandate is to enter into and help to rework intimate domestic relationships, the Comisarías have made issues and spaces that had previously been considered "private" the subject of renewed public scrutiny. While all of the work done by the Comisarías is by definition an example of this, the community rounds were perhaps the most dramatic example of it. From the conspicuous pickup truck to the social worker's bright red jacket, from asking people on the street for directions to the probing questioning of neighbors, each measure to maintain surveillance of abusive relationships carries with it its own breach of someone's intimate sovereign plan. With each knock, the carefully crafted walls of violent homes start to threaten to fall.

Even if these are not the *first* public intrusion into these spaces, they are nevertheless a new and unique kind. Unlike other intrusions such as gossip, the media, or informal networks of support for victims, the Comisarías carry with them an authority to intervene that is backed by the force of law. They are able to impose binding decisions, such as orders of protection, and they are able to mobilize state apparatuses like the police.[14] For perpetrators of violence, coming up against that authority is itself an obvious crisis, a collision of sovereign spaces, and a notice that the underlying contract of their society is again in a state of flux.[15] For survivors of violence, seeking its support is unfortunately still not an assurance of greater agency. Even for Comisaría staff, the rules, or *normas*, that endow them with that authority are no guarantee that their tools will be up to the tasks to which they set them. The Comisarías, for all of their organization and the legal structures in which they operate, are still places of great uncertainty, and that is not necessarily a mark against them. Seeing what these uncertainties mean though, and what their consequences might be, requires going back into their halls and entering their places of work.

Proof and Posturing: Coming Before the Comisarías

They walk into the office together, not speaking, not looking at one another, quiet. Both are middle-aged. Juana is Afro-Colombian and Federico, tanned, with brown nevi on his face that makes me think he works outdoors. I stand up and introduce myself, explaining who I am and what I am doing at the Comisaría, asking if they prefer that I step outside for their audience. They shake their heads and tell me not to worry, then promptly sit down and face Ana, the lawyer sitting across the desk who is attending this meeting for an order of protection. The meeting begins straightforward enough, with Ana asking basic questions like their names, cedula (national ID) numbers, contact information, and how many children they have in common, typing their responses into a template document as they talk. They both respond with slightly downcast eyes, Juana sitting a bit forward in her seat with her shoulders rolled forward and Federico leaning ever so slightly back in his chair, arms crossed. As the questions turn a bit more personal, they tell Ana that they live together but that she does not work, cannot read, and their only cellular phone is the one he owns. When she asks about their marital status, she replies "single" and he says "unmarried partners living together."

With this, Ana gets into the heart of the meeting, asking Juana first to tell her what happened on the day that led her to come make her denuncia, and telling Federico that once Juana is finished he will have his opportunity to talk. Juana sits up a bit straighter, brings her gaze up to meet Ana, and, in a voice and demeanor so calm that it surprises me, quickly tells her story. Just over a month ago, Federico grabbed her by her neck and chin, pushed her up against a wall, twisted her arm, and yelled names like "hija de puta" at her. Federico begins to bounce one knee, but just as he starts to lean forward and open his mouth, Ana lifts a hand up to him to silence him, never breaking her gaze with Juana. She continues. This was not the first time that he has been physically abusive to her, and more frequently he is verbally so, calling her names and controlling her in other ways. When she says that he does this in front of their three-year-old daughter, Federico snorts and moves to interject again. This time his intrusion brings Ana around to face him directly and scold him, telling him that waiting his turn is a matter of respect and that if he cannot show respect then this "audience" will not be possible. In just a few short minutes, Juana has finished her account and after Ana finishes typing into her document she turns to Federico for his.

Though he talks for far longer than Juana, he says very little about the incident in question and only barely confirms it when Ana repeatedly asks him if he has anything to change about Juana's story. As Juana sits back in her chair a bit, he leans forward, arms still crossed, and in an indignant tone begins with "In reality, I'm the victim here," going on to relate how she has a history of hitting him too and has even threatened him previously with a knife. Ana cuts in quickly and asks him if he made a denuncia or sought an order of protection and while he very simply says no, his expression says that he never even thought to do so. A bit dismissively, she goes on to explain that without any evidence or history of seeking help for this, it is hard to take into account for their current situation. A little fazed by this, he slowly eases himself back into his story and continues on to talk about the psychological harm that he says Juana has caused him. As she sits beside him with her eyes fixed down on her hands in her lap, he mentions suspicions that he has about her infidelity but quickly moves on and focuses on something else: gossip. For the next several minutes, getting increasingly worked up, he tells us about a "white woman" friend that Juana has made after starting to attend an Evangelical church and how she is spending more and more time with her, talking about private matters that he does not want other people to know about. Calling her a "chismosa" (a gossip), he goes on to explain how she speaks badly about him to his own family and how he has come to feel that he has no other support left in his life, even though he is not a "malgasto" (someone who wastes money) and does not spend his income on alcohol or other unnecessary things. Ultimately though, he explains, his main concern is the well-being of their daughter and that the times that he has been abusive it has been because he thinks that Juana is not taking good care of her and instead is spending long hours at her new church with her "white woman" friend.

Rather suddenly, the meeting comes to a halt. Federico looks up and fixes his eyes on Ana, and Juana slowly does the same. With a long exhale, Ana looks between the two and says quite bluntly that she is not really sure what to do. Their stories are so markedly different, "black and white" as she puts it, with each blaming the other for this situation. Also, they currently live together and so, looking at Juana, she tells her that an order of protection is more complicated but still possible. The first question it seems is corroboration, and Juana says that her friend from her church could come in to give testimony, but she does not have any proof other than what their three-year-old has seen. Somehow, slowly, over the course of the next fifteen minutes, the back and forth begins to edge further toward the idea of separation. Their romantic relationship has long "gone out," they have frequent fights in which Federico and possibly Juana become physically and verbally abusive, and, most of all, these things are happening in front of their daughter. All of a sudden, the idea gains inertia. Ana seems increasingly convinced that it is the right idea and Federico is quick to jump on board. He chimes in saying that he recognizes that this is his fault for not leaving this relationship earlier, but in part this is because his job requires him to go to Tolima sometimes and he needs help looking after their child. Suddenly, his voice breaks and he pauses as he begins to softly cry, putting his head down into his hand and covering his eyes. As Ana reaches for a tissue, Juana reaches over and slowly begins rubbing his back. Through the remaining tears, he says that his biggest worry now is making sure that he does not lose all custody of his daughter.

Now the idea of separation has taken full flight, and as I look over to Juana all I can see is panic, thinly veiled. In her lap, agitated hands with quick fingers shuffle through a stack of papers that she has brought with her. I get the unmistakable feeling that separation is not what she originally had in mind and that she is quickly losing control of where this meeting is going. With no job, little formal education, and as an Afro-Colombian immigrant to the city, her position is precarious at best. Should this meeting continue down this *road, she would be left in a very vulnerable position. Finding two papers in her pile, she brings them up onto the desk and as she passes them to Ana says something quickly about how Federico has previously threatened to kill her. Before looking down at the documents, Ana looks back incredulously and asks her why this is just coming up now. An inaudible answer escapes Juana's lips and by the time she finishes, Ana has already glanced down at the papers, folded them back up, and passed them back saying that "this doesn't tell me anything." I look on, incredulous. Ana, a person with a warm demeanor who just earlier was careful to carve out a space for Juana to tell her story, is now meeting that same person with hostility, about claims that have been made upon her life no less.*

Perhaps realizing this, Ana pulls back and starts to explain what a process of separation would entail. When she gets to the part about the "conciliation," she looks at Juana and in a much kinder voice assures her that this would be another chance for her to work through the Comisaría to dictate the conditions of support that Federico would have to provide her. This seems to calm Juana considerably and she begins to say out loud the reasons that she too would want to separate as well. When she ties it to Federico's abuse, to my surprise, Ana meets this with a rejoinder about how she needs to recognize that any separation is the fault of both parties involved. With both Juana and Federico now tentatively on board, the rest of the meeting moves along swiftly, with Ana explaining that she is convinced that separation is the best option and that she will grant the order of protection for two reasons. First, Federico has confirmed the violence under question and Juana has every right to the protection. Second, the order will provide the context to ensure that as they figure out the separation, with the help of the Comisaría, of course, that they will do so with calm heads and kind words because now the consequences are elevated should Federico return to physical violence. After a meeting of nearly two hours now, they quickly review the printed documents, sign them, and set up a follow-up appointment to determine the conditions of support. Gathering their belongings, Juana is once again as stoic as when she first entered. As they leave, she whispers encouragement to a still-distraught Federico.

Proof

The Comisarías are above all legal institutions. They exist not just because of a series of laws or because lawyers work within them but more fundamentally the work that gets done within them, and how it gets done, follows from highly legalistic logics. To actually come before them then is to have to attempt to grasp what this means in practice. Mostly it means having some additional form of proof and, considering that the decisions reached through these processes are legally binding and have legal consequences for everyone involved, this is neither surprising nor necessarily a fault in the system. What does come across in meetings with citizens though is that often this logic of proof is of singular importance, coming before all else. I learned this the very first time that I arrived at a Comisaría, when the head of the Comisaría was showing me around and introducing me to the various people who worked there, the people I would soon be getting to know. As we toured, I was allowed into an audience in progress where, as is typically the case, the two people present told dramatically different accounts of what had happened. Interrupting the cacophony in the room, the head of the Comisaría inserted herself into the controversy, maintaining a calm voice just barely above a whisper. Her first words were that the Comisaría was an agency bound by law, and that meant that each person had rights. She continued on to explain that this meant that both of them would have the chance to tell their story, as well as present the testimonies of other people or show evidence that could corroborate them. Until a history of violence could be confirmed, there was little that they at the Comisaría could do. Just as with the case of Federico and Juana, this does not mean corroborating every single point in each person's story, just a basic recognition that some sort of legally actionable event transpired. In their case, had Federico not admitted to the violence, Juana would have had to somehow produce her friend from her church, and without her support she might have been left without recourse.

There is an undeniable logic as to why supporting evidence would be required in a case of partner abuse, absent any basic consensus between those involved. In most cases this was a simple recognition of both the positional parallaxes, the "Rashomon effect" inherent to experiences of partner violence, as well as the obvious vested interests in obfuscating, diminishing, or flipping responsibility. In either case, this requirement of proof creates at least one inevitable consequence—those who come to the Comisarías to make any sort of claim about partner violence require some sort of additional proxy agent.[16] Survivors then are caught in a position where their options for future action depend both on those who work in the Comisarías, themselves proxy agents of sorts, as well as on their ability to produce some other form of support. And not all proof is created equal. Clearly the simplest and most direct form of proof is where the perpetrator of abuse can confirm to some degree the story told by the person who has survived it. Of all the other people who might possibly do so—children, family, friends, neighbors, employers—the least impeachable option is the medical exam. Indeed, on presentation to the Comisarías, many survivors are referred immediately to either a nearby emergency room or the Institute of Legal and Forensic Medicine in order to have any lesions documented by an officially sanctioned observer. In cases where both stories share no point in common and the alleged perpetrator is even able to bring in supporting testimony, having medical documentation of injuries was often the card that still trumped all. The main problem with all of this is that the experience of partner violence, in particular that which is chronic, is built on a foundation of isolation. When survivors present for help and are told that "nothing can be done" unless they can substantiate their claims, they are put into positions of further marginalization. When the mandate of the agency and the available tools are framed in such exclusively legal terms, the ability for its staff to show solidarity with those who seek their assistance becomes considerably constrained, and it leaves some survivors without even the most basic affirmation of recognizing the violence they have endured.

This logic, of course, is not just legalistic but is profoundly bureaucratic. The organization of the office, the forms, the computer system, the core instruments that functionaries have at their disposal: all fit within a bureaucratic frame of action (and sometimes inaction). In many ways then, coming before the Comisarías is another instance of living *la vida burocratica* in Colombia, complete with all of its strategies and pitfalls. I first came to appreciate the bureaucratic life when working with patients with skin cancer in Bogotá through their struggle to gain access to the health care that was supposed to be constitutionally guaranteed for them. The same plastic folders that I came to recognize then were also part and parcel of the meetings that I witnessed in the Comisarías. These folders overflowed with documents: papers from previous visits, copies of identification, assortments of proof put to paper that could not possibly be relevant to the issue at hand. Assembled and organized under the notion that almost anything might be of use at some point in time, these plastic folders were nothing short of personal archives. Their creation was part of a veritable "archive fever," an attempt not only to assemble any potentially useful information but also to reclaim some modest amount of control over a process that, at times, could seem terrifyingly out of one's hands.[17] Doing so was not always effective though, as Juana experienced when she produced papers to substantiate her claim that Federico had previously threatened her life. Proof alone is not sufficient. In order to be effective, it must be presented in a particular way. No matter how dedicated, caring, and concerned those who work in the Comisaría may be, successfully coming before those who work there requires not just proof but also careful posturing.

Posturing

Calmness, attentiveness, respect: coming before the Comisaría is a matter of strategy and also a matter of form. When I began conducting fieldwork in the Comisarías, it was impossible to not immediately take note of the literal physical postures that people adopted throughout their meetings, as well as the small signs of deference that they made. These included sitting forward, leaning back, shoulders rounded or head held high; maintaining eye contact and an even tone; and using words like *sumercé*.[18] By this I in no way mean to imply that those who come to the Comisaría generally engage in cynical acts of manipulation, disingenuous performances intended to present only a carefully crafted image to those who work there. The social poetics of self-representation more closely followed the lines of self-restraint, and we only ignore their deeper impulses at our own peril. When abusive men minimize or justify their actions, the way that they rationalize tells us something about their worldviews. When survivors and perpetrators alike burst into tears, how they hide them or show them and that they are crying at all can shock Comisaría staff out of a sense of routine. Even when abusive men lean back in their seats, cross their arms, and look away in simmering indignation, this can help us to understand better what dynamics of power and what forms of its contestation are going on behind these doors.

Almost all of these can be seen in the case of Juana and Federico in their audience with Ana and how that shaped its trajectory. From his crossed arms, indignation during the beginning of the meeting, intrusions during Juana's testimony, and attempts to regain control of the narrative, Federico did little favor to his cause. The same can be said of his attempts to justify his abuse. Just as his rationalization of his violence as attempts to protect the well-being of their daughter were common-enough claims, so too was the uninterested stance that Ana and Juana took toward them. If anything rallied sympathy toward him it was probably his demonstration of shame. When he avoided discussing his abuse of Juana, he did not just avoid the subject. He avoided eye contact with everyone in the room, his shoulders hunched forward and his body closed off from anyone around him. These kinds of postures were the kinds of bodily positions with which I became very familiar, be it sitting in audiences in the Comisarías or sitting alone in one-on-one interviews with abusive men.

If this initial part of the audience was fairly typical then, along with the understandably unsympathizing reaction of Ana to Federico's "real victim" claim, the subsequent reversal also had some precedent in its centering around the involvement of their children. Even if Federico's invocation of their daughter failed to justify to others his violence against Juana, it did drastically alter the purpose of the meeting. Satisfied that the abuse had been confirmed and that the order of protection could be granted, under Ana's direction the rest of the meeting had little to do with Juana's suffering and became fully focused on the effect that this violence had on their daughter instead. It was from this shift of purpose that the whole notion of separation came from in the first place, a trajectory that clearly had not been on Juana's agenda when the meeting began. As soon as Juana's concerns were made to take a backseat to a new set of priorities, her loss of control over the meeting was precipitous and her growing desperation a testament to it. It was also a testament to the dismal consequences we create for ourselves when we operate from hierarchies of victimhood and moral concern. In this case this meant not only the passing over of Juana's desires but also a sort of ironic recapitulation by Ana of the very paternalistic dynamics that characterized this violence in the first place. With the state now taking a sort of surrogate parental role for the child in question, an assertion I heard during any number of audiences, it was on these justified grounds that the priorities of victims could be allowed to fall, at least temporarily, by the wayside. Even if temporary, as the end of the meeting showed it to be, it underscores how these encounters are complicated, with the offices themselves contact zones between "public" and "private" authorities and their remarkably similar ideologies.

Whatever the specific consequences, through the subtleties of interaction and the intuitions of those in the room, a process emerged that no set of forms, laws, or even professional trainings could ever dictate. In the months that I spent in the Comisarías, it was in witnessing these nuances to audiences about abuse that I learned the most about partner violence in the first place. It was also where I began to more fully appreciate the accumulated expertise of the staff who worked in the Comisarías. As each audience was inevitably filled by a fluently memorized litany of laws, there was no doubt that a core competence for staff was a technical mastery over the legal tools and precedents at their disposal. What was more open to experience, and what frequently appeared to have greater bearing on a sense of efficacy, was the ability of professionals to recognize and respond to the multiple levels of simultaneous communication that were going on at all times in their offices. By being attentive to them, it was also one of the greatest opportunities for staff to break momentarily free from even the most sedimented molds of their otherwise bureaucratized response.

Toward a "Clinical" Comisaría?

Take, for instance, one of the psychologists, Julia. On a slow day when several of her appointments had not shown up, we had a chance to sit down and talk about her job in the Comisaría. She was part of the inner circle of professionals at this branch, employed directly by the government instead of being contracted on a yearly basis, and her third-story office boasted a window that looked out toward the eastern mountains. Enjoying the warmth coming in through those windows, I had a chance to finally sit down and listen as she told me about how routinized many of her "audiences" had become, how the time pressures so often robbed her of doing her job as she had originally envisioned. When the demand was high, she said, she had little time to really engage couples, the men in particular, and do her job as she felt a psychologist should. In other words, there simply was no time for any sort of therapy. Before working in the Comisaría system she had worked as a psychologist in a hospital and still maintained a small clinical practice outside of her work for the government. With a bit of a sly smile she told me how she would bring in this clinical background of hers whenever she had the opportunity to do so, and how she used it to create a space where she could get those in front of her to begin to reflect on their actions.

Unfortunately, this kind of work was simply not her mandate in a system where her job was considered to be "juridical" and not "clinical" in nature, and her priority had to be her volume of cases and not the change she could effect in any particular one. I asked her then a question that I had started asking all of the professionals in the Comisarías: what for her would be a successful day at her job? Staring out through the window, beyond the mountains behind us, she told me that her good days were the ones where she could get a sign of recognition from the perpetrators of abuse. A good day was where during her consultations she could see light bulbs go off somewhere in the back of aggressors' minds, flickers of recognition that what they were doing was not their only option. Ideally this meant getting the perpetrators of abuse to realize that "good" authority, "properly managed authority" as she put it, was not based on singular control but was based on collaboration, on the equitable sharing of power in a relationship. She added though that these days were predictably few and far between, and when any meeting began she could almost immediately tell if the person in front of her was likely to engage with her or not.

Onward

As Julia's desires start to show, any attempt to portray the professionals who work within the Comisarías simply as rational-type actors constrained to specific kinds of actions, faithful practitioners of a narrowly thought-out legal plan, would be nothing short of a bad-faith gloss. Even still, had I only ever observed and interviewed within the Comisarías, I would have barely ever glimpsed the imagination that went on in the minds behind the routines, unrealized forms of creativity that were not always articulated. Julia was simply more outspoken about hers.[19] Our real breakthrough along these lines only happened many months into my fieldwork, after I had begun working directly with perpetrators and survivors directly, and after we had begun to put together meetings at the Comisaría on a biweekly basis for a more open forum on these issues. What began initially as a way of feeding back preliminary findings of my work to the people who had most supported it quickly became a means of discussing, in a more distributed format, new possibilities for addressing partner violence in the community.

Restoring Justice

Our first such meeting was simple enough, but illuminating nonetheless. We sat there, just the four of us—the head of the Comisaría, the lawyer on staff, a social worker, and myself—in what was by far the smallest meeting that we would have over the course of these forums. As we relaxed into our chairs and couches, letting go the formality that surrounds so many conversations within those walls, we began by addressing our first topic: engaging with the accused aggressors when they present to the Comisaría. This had been a point of continued frustration, a commonly perceived barrier to the success of their work when the response by perpetrators was the arms-crossed, disinterested attitude so familiar in their audiences. I began by offering the reflection that behind such self-assured posturing were actually deeply held ambivalences over their actions and their current situations, a point that triggered some interest and discussion, a brainstorming of ways to elicit that ambivalence and foster dialogue with perpetrators, and to do so within the already insufficient amount of time allowed to them. In later meetings with more staff present, these would eventually become conversations about how to use techniques such as motivational interviewing to explore those tensions.

In that first meeting though, the real conversation did not begin until the social worker there raised something else entirely. As the interest in "ambivalence" began to stall, she took the chance to speak up about what she really wanted to discuss, the reason she had come to the meeting in the first place. She began by talking about a forum that she had attended several months back, a convocation held by a department of the city's government to talk about addressing juvenile substance abuse. What she had found most interesting, she said, and what she continued to think about all these months later was not the problem that they presented, it was a particular model of its redress: restorative justice. Partnering with an international nongovernmental organization with experience in the field, they had run through some of the major underpinnings of this alternative model of justice, points that she listed again for the benefit of our own small meeting. Immediately a lively exchange began to take place, comparing the points of "restorative" with "retributive" justice, the model of legal action that dominated the work at the Comisaría. In quick succession many of the frustrations about the limitations of their current tools emerged: why did perpetrators pay the penalties for their infractions to the state and not to the survivors? Could that money instead be used in a way to help survivors leave abusive relationships if they desired? Would a restorative approach engage survivors more actively rather than treating them as passive subjects that sat behind their office desks? Would restorative practices open up a space for perpetrators to acknowledge and openly address their own shame, making them more open to following up with other requirements like therapy? Restorative justice, it seemed, had become the perfect lightning rod for channeling the accumulated frustrations of most of the staff.

As the interest in the idea of restorative justice took flight, those present quickly came to a consensus on one basic reality: such practices could not be added on to the existing responsibilities of those who work in the Comisaría. Every year, for better or worse, there seemed to be more people coming forward to make denuncias, and even with their current caseloads they were only barely able to keep up with this demand. Either another branch opened in Usme or other options had to be sought, a realization that itself opened up a whole other avenue to explore. Not only was the idea of restorative justice different from what was normally practiced, and therefore represented a form of ideological exteriority, but now there was also interest in finding alternative physical spaces, outside the walls of the Comisarías, in which to bring those aspirations into reality. What this meant was that, even on that very first day, the group not only had begun to build an unusual space of encounter among Comisaría staff—a space in which to vent ongoing frustrations but also cooperatively imagine alternatives—but also had begun to formulate ideas about new social spaces in which to realize their work.

Searching for New Spaces

Just a few blocks down the road from that Comisaría in Usme was the public library, the same place where someone had once spray-painted on its wall "Welcome to Usmekistan" and, next to it, "Usme is Consciousness." Inside those walls, gathered together one spring morning, a public meeting was under way. Though the library had been built years ago, and had been in use ever since, that day was to be a sort of re-presentation of it to the community. The library was technically affiliated with the school system in Usme, and teachers were to become one of its key connections to the rest of the district as its new philosophy came into being. Nestled between the library's collection of books, and about a hundred educators, we listened to a series of speakers outline just what they hoped this space could become.

There were local authors and poets sharing stories they themselves had written, even a library regular who, in his dusty suit, enraptured the audience with his own personal historiography of the district. At the core of the convocation though were the library's staff, a younger group that took turns speaking in general terms about their vision for the branch to become a center for fostering peace within the community. A refuge against violence, they called it, a space in which to share, to weave, a space in which not just to read and remember but a place in which to actively construct a collective memory for Usme. A place in which to historicize it. Among them was a foreign scholar who interjected every now and then with comments about "third spaces" in society and the library as a democratic one at that. What her comments reminded me of were meetings I had previously had with the director of this library branch, the person who had organized this meeting in the first place. Sitting in his office just around the corner, we had talked about his idea for the library to be a space in which multiple kinds of knowledge could intermingle, a place where diverse and unpredictable Usminian identities could be articulated. He wanted the branch to be more than a repository of books or connection points to the internet: he wanted a space that either got people out of their seats or at the very least unsettled their assumptions.

To his credit, the programming that they had already developed spoke to these ideals. With titles like "concientizARTE," "learning laboratory," "dance to learn about your body," and "writings from Bogotá," everything that populated their weekly schedule felt like something bent in the direction of social consciousness.[20] One program in particular, a weekly meeting group for parents in which they could discuss everyday challenges, parenting, and living in Usme, became a point of connection for us. Over a series of encounters we had discussed whether or not to have multiple groups, one being a safe space for potential survivors of abuse, and how to join efforts with the Comisarías de Familia. Perhaps, we had said, staff from the Comisarías could visit some of the group meetings; perhaps the library could provide the space to explore the idea of restorative justice that had interested them. Along the way I found myself thinking back to an earlier meeting that I had had with Marta, the head of the entire Comisaría system, in which she acknowledged that most of the community connections that the Comisaría system had developed so far were focused in one direction only: gaining allies to encourage people to come make denuncias. What the unlikely setting of Usme's public library offered was something else entirely: an alternative space in which to pursue very different kinds of encounters, without having to first change the laws that underwrote the otherwise well-established Comisaría system.

Third Forces, Third Spaces, Third Places

Over the weeks following the library's convocation, we would attempt to build bridges between the library and the Comisaría staff, using the family meetings and the desire for spaces in which to advance restorative justice programs as starting points of collaboration. Unfortunately, mayoral elections and their resulting wide-sweeping changes to institutional staff, my leaving the country, and low turnout at the library's subsequent attempts at starting family meetings all conspired to frustrate those efforts. But while that particular collaboration ultimately seemed to be a failed experiment, what it motioned toward is still highly significant. While the Comisarías fill a crucial role of intrusion into intimate affairs, they are hardly the places in which more open-ended objectives might be pursued, and complex issues such as partner violence deserve complex responses, not just teleological interventions, however institutionally complicated they might be. As can be seen through the work that is done within the Comisarías today, certain compromises have been made along the way and capitulations to particular forms of social action have been necessary in order to create their existence and expand their role. If, as Marta argued though, the Comisarías have now been through two major iterations, so perhaps this eye to some kind of exteriority could mark the precipice of a third. Here again the exteriority is both ideological and spatial, and the desire among Comisaría staff to seek out new spaces in the community in which to actualize complementary forms of justice points to a desire to, in some way, break free from the constraints in which they themselves think they are bound. Rather than focus all efforts on the continuous remodeling of the criminal justice system itself, what their attempts to build new networks of action point to are the potentially liberating effects of finding points of productive tension with the juridical system as is. Doing so could eventually mean combining the imposing power of the law with the possibilities inherent to more negotiable social spaces, but doing so in a way in which one never simply subsumes the other.

What exactly these other social spaces might be is perhaps best introduced by what the visiting scholar at the library's convocation called "third spaces." Originally termed by Homi Bhabha as a means of exploring the possibilities of "hybridity" in cultural production, the term, as it was used in this encounter in Usme, also relates to the more concrete notion of "third places."[21] While "third space" indexes an emergent, and enunciative, potential space in the renegotiation between colonizer and colonized, oppressor and oppressed, "third places" has a far more literal meaning: physical spaces such as the pub, the tea house, houses of worship in civil rights movements: places of face-to-face encounter that carry the potential to develop politically subversive schemes. But encounters between whom, and subversive schemes to what ends? To these questions there is a final "third" that we might add, the idea of "third forces," a concept that was originally proposed through a particular strand of Latin American Marxist-feminism, an attempt to theorize which groups could hold together broad coalitions for social change.[22] In this theory, "third forces" were held to be groups formed under other oppressive axes of power, who through their experiences of oppression, and their suffering, could help to recognize and mobilize against another dominant system. With regard to capitalism it was thought that women might provide this third force and, without having to be beholden to any unitary notions of "womanhood," we can at least see how the process of being marginalized and exploited along multiple axes of power can foster the emergence of a more critical social consciousness. Such was clearly the case for Luz, as explored in Chapter 2, and such is one of the recognitions of more recent theories that focus on intersectionality, and such is likely the meaning behind the graffiti tags in Bogotá that read sin mujer no hay revolución (without women, there is no revolution).

What we need though is not just the consciousness, and action, of the most abused. What we need is the cultivation of consciousness for those committing that violence as well. And if the perpetration of partner violence is intricately woven into other forms of power and violence in our societies, as I sincerely hope to have shown by now, this cultivation of consciousness for perpetrators of abuse must be equally broad in reach. Just as we cannot abide by fictions that this violence is only "intimate" in scope, we cannot approach it as simply "gender-based" in any strictly delimited sense, and that means that to ask perpetrators of partner violence to rethink their notions of gendered relations we must open up spaces in which they can also rethink the other axes of power to which they relate. To set someone the task of reconfiguring a major basis on which their identity is built is no small ask, and so in order to open up spaces in which perpetrators can more critically encounter themselves we must simultaneously create spaces in which they can also more critically encounter the social worlds that they inhabit, the ones that injure them on a daily basis, the same ones in which they have come to occupy deeply conflicting positions. This means opening up new social spaces, both literal and figurative, ones in which the subaltern—survivors of violence in particular—cannot just speak but also take leadership, ones in which we not only come to encounter one another but actually have the chance to deconstruct that peculiar fiction of the "other." To reconfigure consciousness we must open up spaces for the rearticulation of social bonds.[23] As such, the cultivation of critical consciousness, for perpetrators of violence included, is not the same as the inculcation of critical theory; it is not a pedagogical process but a collective one of mutual discovery. It is also one of mobilization. To facilitate it we need to create very real, physical spaces in which that can happen, and be intentional in who has ownership of them, authority within them, so as not to recapitulate the very dynamics of power that we are attempting to address.

It is with these imperatives in mind that these notions of "thirds"— "third spaces," "third places," and "third forces"—come to combine, and it is what, at least for a moment, the public library in Usme had the potential to provide. The incorporation of restorative practices into a space of cultural production may be far from the foundation of a wide-reaching social revolution, but by facilitating a place of more open encounter it does motion toward precisely the kinds of practices that we need. By putting acts of gender-based violence at the center of those encounters, in a space whose ambitions included rewriting the history of colonial oppression, we put that which is immediately urgent into contact with the longer histories that have built up to that act.[24] The animating potential of "third forces" comes to fill the potential space that "third spaces" and "third places" try to create, and as Jairo's experience working as a nurse in a health outreach project shows, libraries are not the only places that this might happen. To varying degrees of effect we might pursue these objectives-without-end elsewhere as well, and another place, for which I would strenuously advocate, includes community health centers.[25] Wherever we pursue them, what matters is that we leave their potential open-ended, that we do not foreclose their possibilities in the same way that criminal justice institutions have limited their own, that we continue to hold these different spaces open in creative tension. Where agencies like the Comisarías enforce accountability, we need spaces in which consciousness can more openly emerge; where the Comisarías in our worlds impose penalties, we need spaces in which restitution, and transformation, can be sought. And it is being sought.

What the stories of the people who have filled this book remind us of is that not only does violence have its limits, but it can be self-limiting; not only does it have to be justified, but those justifications are fraught with unstable contradictions. Their stories point us toward the underlying dependences on which relationships of control are built, how that dependence is made to be hidden, and how that gives us an avenue into undoing the premises on which that violence is built. What their stories remind us of most of all though is that change is possible, but to achieve it we need to create the right conditions to allow it to unfold. We need to recognize that consciousness is a complex social experience that emerges from the milieus in which we are immersed. If we are to achieve these changes, we need critical spaces in which to realize this work, and if we are able to create them then we might just find, as Jairo did, that partner violence can indeed come undone. Out of the very same fields of tension from which this violence emerges we have, if thoughtful in our action, the ability to redirect those products in dramatically different directions. In that process we come to address a particularly dense nexus of power in society, and by destabilizing it we might just see these broader systems straining harder at their joints. When violence is so intricately interconnected, we can use that to our advantage; to take on this one form of it, partner abuse, is to find a point of purchase in engaging many more. This, I believe, was the underlying hope of many of the people whom I knew in Usme: that through sharing their stories, some piece of themselves, more of their world would start to make sense. In this making of sense, and the making of purpose, we bind ourselves together and, with any luck, in this binding we find at the very least some basic recognition of our selves. What they taught me, survivors and perpetrators alike, was that out of all the injury, the shame, the isolation, and the fear, we still have to believe that better is possible. To reach for it we need only make the interdependence that we deny ourselves permissible, and we need only to stake our own well-being on the betterment of others. To address partner violence, and violence more broadly, is to find new ways of finding each other and in doing so seek to escape the cages in which we have been bound. Ahí vamos.

Figure 5. Avenida El Dorado during the 2015 Marcha por la Paz, held on the anniversary of the assassination of Jorge Eliécer Gaitán. Taken April 9, 2015, by the author.

Figure 6. Graffiti along the pedestrian section of La Septima in Bogotá. Taken October 2014 by the author.

APPENDIX 1

Toward a Tengentic Approach

If the term itself "tengentics" is new, the overarching approach that it references is not, and at the end of the day it is this set of ideas, not any one particular word, that is important. The term itself is a portmanteau of the roots "tendere" and "génh," its near homophony to "tangent" only a happy accident, and it is nothing more than the most concise means that I have personally found to summarize this set of ideas.[1] At its core is the fundamental recognition that contradiction is generative, or more generally that *tensions are creative*, and while it shares some common characteristics with Hegelian dialectics, it moves beyond them in several important ways.[2]

The first of these diversions is at the core of the tensions themselves. Whereas Hegelian dialectics is largely built on binary contradictions, this approach has little interest in working through a series of diametric oppositions and their sublation, or "negation of the negation," that constitute the three classic moments of this particular approach.[3] Instead, tensions here are held to be much more polygenic, constituted at times by entire *fields* of tension, the confluence of multiple processes coming to interact with one another. Not only are these tensions polygenic though, they are pluripotent as well, and whereas Hegelian dialectics was formalized as a means of sublating oppositions to a higher set of progressively more universal truths, the products of the tensions examined through a tengentic approach are far more indeterminate in the directions that they take. Even when subsequent interpreters, such as Adorno with his "negative dialectics," introduced a modicum of diversity to the otherwise singular teleology of Hegel's initial framework, this still only began to approximate the vast indeterminacy to the products that these tensions give off.[4] Perhaps one of the primary reasons that a tengentic approach diverges here is because in Hegelian dialectics the dynamism, the generative capacity of oppositions, was thought to derive from the underlying determinations themselves, that their fundamental nature was to drive themselves into their opposites. Here no such assumption is made, and instead what tensions are found to produce, and the directions that they shoot off in, are thought to be much more related to the broader context in which that tension is held. To understand the vectors of those products thus requires a far more nuanced and situated view, one that opens up a much higher degree of possibility and, consequently, unpredictability.

Gone then is the imagination of building a hierarchy of ascending universal truths and in its place is a complex web, one whose shape is situationally dependent and often subject to change. As such there is also no one overarching architecture to a tengentic approach, and at most it scales up and down through the recognition of a common motif, a means of connecting across levels of emergence not entirely unlike a fractal.[5] Rather than the preoccupation with concepts like *entgegensetzen* and sublation then, the core questions guiding a tengentic approach are much more simple: what is in tension with what, why, and to what ends. Simple is not necessarily easy, however, and the more open format of this approach, as well as the recognition of dense nexuses of tension, makes this a difficult task to take on. Take, for example, the "what is in tension with what" question. As shown throughout the course of this book alone, those tensions might be framed in any number of ways. In the most pared-down sense they might be the inherent contradictions of control as discussed in Chapter 4, or the interpersonal dynamics that were explored in some detail in Chapters 2 and 4 through the stories of Luz, Carolina, and Diego. They might also be the sociohistorical condensations captured in ideas like "surrogate power" from Chapter 3, concepts that seek to bring together various threads that cut across scales and periods of time to create a denser understanding of the present. This is to say that tensions might be examined as existing only on a single scale of social analysis or they might be drawn across them as well; how we frame them will have significant implications for the lessons that we take away.

Understanding the products of those tensions is almost another task entirely, one in which the themes of unpredictability, indeterminacy, and multiplicity reign supreme. Because tensions in a tengentic framework are held to be so profoundly pluripotent, this means that, in order to understand the multitude of possible vectors that lead away from even a single point of origin, we must take a more contextual kind of approach. When applied to social issues such as violence, or more specifically intimate partner violence as has been examined here, recognizing that the products of these tensions can shoot off in any number of directions makes us more attendant to the particular social contexts in which they are enacted. It also makes us cognizant of the fact that the product of any one tension can very rapidly change. The example of this that I continue to find the most impactful is in the responses of survivors of violence to the abuse that they have endured. As discussed in Chapter 2, and again in Chapters 5 and 6, the availability of support to victims of violence has a major influence on the ultimate consequences of those relationships. Trapped in the shrinking space of a controlling relationship, absent any perceived exteriority to that sovereign regime, the ability of people to endure in the face of escalating violence is something that continues to amaze me every single day. With the possibility of successfully leaving that relationship, however, something that is often only true with the cooperation of others, the very dynamics of abuse that previously helped to consolidate the power of its perpetrators become themselves counterhegemonic practices, and they push those relationships closer to the breaking point. How the roles of others come to be bound up in that process, such as the role that children played for Carolina in leaving her abusive relationships, only adds another element of complexity to the mix. How they can dramatically alter the course of a life, and how they can do so in an instant, is as good a reminder as any to the considerable indeterminacy of these tensions.

We would be wise to use this indeterminacy to our advantage, as tengentics is not intended only to provide an analytical approach. It is also meant to guide our direct engagement with the world, with issues as well as the people who are at the heart of them; it is intended to trigger an iterative process whose consequences are both understanding and change.[6] Doing so requires a foundational appreciation that people exist as nexuses, often precarious ones at that, and that this can be our point of entry into even the most seemingly intractable affairs. Such was the case for me in building relationships with perpetrators of partner violence, and it was one of the primary reasons that we were able to encounter one another both critically and empathically along the way. It is also the means by which we can attempt to alter the courses of our collective fates, enter into social issues, and find alternative pathways ahead. When the existence of tension is the underlying assumption, the practice that we follow is not oriented to *resolving* tension so much as it is to redirecting the products of tensions or articulating new ones instead. Along the way we might make use of various tactics such as the application of "hinges," as mentioned at the end of Chapter 5, or in the judicious creation of particular social milieus, as discussed at the ends of Chapters 5 and 6 as well as in Appendix 2. What matters is what ultimately emerges from these tensions and, whatever the particular means, what a tengentic approach opens up for us is a wealth of possibilities into exploring their underlying dynamics, in seeing their broader connections, and in imagining new ways of putting together the two.

Therapeutic Windows and Transformative Care

One of the lessons that comes out of the stories in this book is how vital pluralistic responses are to breaking down social systems of control, and this beckons the question of how we can take this basic insight and apply it to other institutions, other spaces in our social worlds. As a student of both anthropology as well as biomedicine, for me this holds particular salience with regard to how systems of professionalized care might learn from these experiences. What might we draw from these lessons earned on the margins of Bogotá? In the most obvious sense, the connection comes from insights gained into supporting the survivors of it, providing material support as well as spaces of healing for the intense suffering and the many sequelae that can result.[1] When it comes to the question of how medicine articulates with the perpetrators of abuse, the connections are perhaps a little bit less direct, and to properly convey them I must first talk about pit vipers.

To be precise I need to talk about Brazilian pit vipers and the venom they produce, a peculiar substance that has gone from lethal poison to one of the most essential medicines that we have in our arsenal today.[2] The active element of this venom directly targets one of the most crucial axes of our physiology, and before it was ever a medicine its principal purpose was to induce a rapid and lethal drop in blood pressure for its victim. Prior to the adoption of high-salt diets, any such challenge would have been overwhelming, and living in the Brazilian Amazon, where food staples are generally potassium-rich but sodium-poor, this axis is typically turned up all the way. Any level of inhibition of it would likely be catastrophic. For most people around the world now, the challenge is, of course, the exact opposite. Having inundated our bodies with sodium, our challenge is not to retain it but to avoid the essential hypertension that can result.[3] It is for this change in circumstance that we have the occasion to actually thank pit vipers for their venom, or at least we should, considering that it was the basis for creating the class of drugs that we now know as ACE inhibitors. Today these drugs are not only some of the most effective treatments for lowering blood pressure but also some of the few medicines that have the ability to extend life expectancy in cases of heart failure, diabetes, and other common noncommunicable diseases.

What the peculiar case of ACE inhibitors illustrates above all is the notion of the "therapeutic window." In particular, it is emblematic of the central ambivalences in the practice of medicine, epitomized in the Greek notion of "pharmakos," which indicates the potential for any agent to be either a poison or a therapeutic. In the case of the therapeutic window, the way that we typically talk about it goes like this: give too little of a substance and there is no effect; give just enough and there is therapeutic benefit; give too much and the adverse effects outweigh the desired ones. This is most dramatically true in the case of ACE inhibitors, but it is also frequently illustrated with the use of older generations of cancer chemotherapies, highly toxic agents that only succeeded by killing tumor cells marginally faster than the person taking them. The case of ACE inhibitors though illustrates another aspect of the therapeutic window, one far less frequently discussed: it is not just the dosage of a substance that influences its therapeutic effect, it is the historical context in which it is taken.[4] And while this is most simplistically true for a single substance, like a drug, it also true for how we practice care more generally.

The practice of professionalized care is not a matter of putting to use supposedly universal biological "truths"; it is about facing people. It is a matter of responding to the needs and aspirations relevant to people in the particular times and spaces in which we have those encounters.[5] And while there are only so many ways in which to alter the drugs that we give—dose, duration, route of administration—we have the ability to continuously alter what *care* itself really means. It is little wonder then that the very meaning of caregiving is receiving reinvigorated attention, led by a growing number of anthropologists and social scientists.[6] By placing focus on the acts of caregiving itself, what this group of scholars is increasingly demonstrating are the multitude of ways by which caring for one another is a mutually transformative experience, one that alters not only the cared-for but also the caregiver. What all of this means is that in professional spaces of caregiving, what we require are forms of care that are mutually transformative in a more purposeful way, not just of the "patients" and "providers" themselves, but even of the very spaces in which those efforts are made.

If ever there were spaces in society for addressing violence, it is hard to imagine ones in which there is as much unmet potential as health care settings. But why health care? Health care spaces are, by many accounts, quite unique. There are remarkably few other social spaces to which there are, across many societies, concerted efforts to ensure universal access, across the life course, and whose relationships within them are so immensely privileged. This is in reference not only to the confidentiality that surrounds these encounters but also to the more expansive qualities that characterize the healer-patient relationship. These are relationships that are made face-to-face, breach the boundaries of personal space, and are intimate encounters with "the other," consistent with what Levinas described as the very first ethical act.[7] But there is not only intimacy. There is also, by promise, in every encounter supposed to also be a fundamental agonism, an acting in the interest of that "other" through an intensely empathic bond. For reasons like these we cannot afford but to make full use of these peculiar spaces: they are simply too important to miss the opportunities that they present.

There is perhaps no greater indictment of our failure to make use of them than the clinic waiting room. In that liminal space we most undeniably reveal our inclinations to promote patience and passivity, not consciousness or connection between the diverse arrays of people who every day come through the door. Speak only if spoken to, act only when asked—and though there are very real issues of privacy and confidentiality at stake, honoring them does not require the wholesale atomization of those who become "patients" somewhere along the way. What if instead we rethought that liminal space of the clinic and turned the waiting room into something else? What might happen if those who seek care stepped into these institutions and rather than quietly waiting had instead the opportunity to read the desires, hopes, and frustrations of one another as well? What if the waiting room were instead a space that patients acted *upon*, rewrote and reformulated to tell something greater about the communities that they come from, and, in doing so, seek out connections to those around them, other people who are there for the same basic reason that we are all fragile beings? Clearly, turning health care spaces into places of collective organization will require going beyond rethinking just the waiting room, but the reward awaiting us, should we do so, could be substantial. In following this line of thinking we have the potential to reformulate these places into nexuses of social engagement, indeterminate spaces that serve the interest of cultivating consciousness, new ideas and social assemblages, all of them the means by which to engage the most pressing issues of our social worlds.

It is with this kind of general concept of the clinic in mind that we can finally return again to the notion of the therapeutic window, to see what it could mean for the practice of a socially oriented transformative care. Think first about the issue of intimate partner violence. In this case the "window" represents again a space—physical, collective, mental—in which perpetrators of violence can more critically encounter the social processes that have built up to that abuse, and the means by which they have internalized them, in order to be able to more critically encounter themselves. The objective here would be to open up a therapeutic window in which perpetrators of abuse are better able to cultivate critical forms of consciousness and to open up that aperture by providing both the spaces in which to do so as well as the kinds of social encounters from which that consciousness is cultivated. By relocating the clinic as a space of collective mobilization against oppressive systems of power—political, economic, racist, or otherwise—it may be possible not only to assist perpetrators of abuse in articulating new notions of gender relations, but also to build the kinds of social relationships that support them, as can begin to be seen in the case of Jairo (see Chapter 5).

This notion of transformative care in health care spaces need not only apply to addressing intimate partner violence though; other important and related issues like substance use disorders could also benefit from such treatment. From Usme to the United States, substance use remains an issue of everyday relevance, and though these contexts have been formed through uneven histories, they both hold in common the fact that their heavily criminalizing responses have failed to adequately address the issues at hand. In the wake of those shortcomings, many have already begun to develop and advocate for alternative models of justice. One model of social change then would be what we typically see: organizing to make claims on existing state institutions, advocating to change the models of practice within the criminal justice systems themselves. Another model of change, however, would be to establish parallel systems of social redress, such as building restorative justice programs into clinics themselves. To do so would be to challenge a dominant institution like the criminal justice system by existing outside of it, establishing a competing set of practices that undermine its supposed mission of social reform, even potentially exceeding it at its own stated goals. The opportunities here are nearly endless, and for many of them there are few better places in which to explore them than within health care spaces.

Behind the privileges that already protect health care settings, we have the ability to put into play these alternative forms of social redress, taking those models and advancing them to not only be restorative but also even transcendent of the status quo. So long as there is a therapeutic promise intact, health care spaces, by being exempt from reporting on most criminalized behaviors, can be places where we subvert the logics of carceral states and replace them with ones capable of more radical action. By reassessing the kind of care that we practice, we have the potential to piece by piece remake the local worlds in which we operate, not just the personal ones of those who seek care, to mend not just the injuries from these violent systems at large but to alter the processes that continue to remake them. In short, we have both the space and the ability to foster subversive social play; we have the ability to leverage clinical spaces in the interest of broader social change.

That we have largely failed to do so is itself a shame, but by posing this challenge I do not intend to trivialize the many obstacles that continue to keep us from building a more transformative practice of care. Indeed, many of those obstacles have been thoroughly internalized into our existing systems of care, and realizing these alternatives will require rendering onto ourselves in clinical medicine nothing less than a continuous process of creative self-destruction. The payoff for doing so though could be immense, and the preceding ideas are, of course, nothing more than early motions in the directions of the many possibilities that could potentially lie ahead.

NOTES

Introduction

1. In a more recent proposal for a typology, Kelly and Johnson (2008) distinguish between four different kinds of partner violence: (1) coercive-controlling violence (sometimes referred to as "intimate terror"), (2) violent resistance, (3) situational couple violence, and (4) separation-instigated violence. The first of these types of partner violence, coercive-controlling violence, is that which is characterized by a unilateral and ongoing attempt for domination over a partner, is the form that is globally most commonly perpetrated by men, and is the form of partner violence on which this study focused.

2. Throughout the course of this book the reason for framing partner violence in terms of "sovereignty" will be continually explored, and without belaboring the point here, it does still deserve some form of introduction. There are many terms used to describe power over others and the maintenance of that power, chief among them terms like "hegemony" and "sovereignty." Whereas "hegemony" has frequently been tied more to notions of social consciousness—in particular following Gramsci's (1992) revisions of Marxist notions of false consciousness, ideas that were subsequently taken up and revised by scholars such as Althusser (1971), later Scott (1990), and, with regard to gender most notably, Connell and Messerschmidt (2005)—sovereignty, following from its own genealogy of ideas, has typically invoked a more spatialized appreciation of how power is sought and maintained. From Machiavelli ([1532] 2008) to Foucault (1977), Weber ([1919] 1965) and Schmitt ([1922] 1985) to even the more common invocations of the term, sovereignty carries with it a sense of power over others *in a particular space.* That space may have been the Italian city-state, or more recently a nation-state in a field of international relations; it could also be more broadly conceived as networks of gift relations or debt (following Mauss, [1925] 1969). No matter how diffuse the field, sovereignty as a reference to the dynamics of power has in practice been shaded by a greater sensitivity to how human relations are formulated through particular spaces, as well as how those spaces are critical to understanding the topographies of power that those relationships take. Both ideas, hegemony and sovereignty, will appear as useful concepts throughout this book, and bridges between them will be continually explored through the direct experiences of survivors and perpetrators of abuse alike.

3. The term "structural violence," originally introduced by Galtung (1969), has subsequently become a dominant paradigm of understanding the social distribution of illness and disease, particularly under the leadership of Farmer (1997, 2004). The concept of "intersectionality," termed by Crenshaw (1989), has been instrumental in bringing together any number of perspectives on how various axes of power interact in order to create more complex patterns of power and oppression in society. Originally focusing particularly on the intersec-

tion of gender and race, the concept has been continuously expanded to encompass even more hierarchies of power. Because it provides such a robust and far-reaching framework for thinking about oppression, my purpose in pushing back against this concept is not to in any way suggest its replacement with something new. What I wish to call attention to is the fact that it too is not a "theory of everything," and that with regard to questions about violence it also leaves many issues unanswered. In order to extend our understanding of why violence is committed, I believe that we need to continue to extend what it means to think about these points of intersection, emphasizing not just their unique forms of overlap but recognizing also their generative contradictions, ones that help to produce violence in the first place.

4. The word "tengentic" is to my knowledge not one in the current vocabulary, and for a brief outline of its meaning, please see Appendix 1. My primary objective here is not to introduce a neologism into an already-overcrowded lexicon though: my purpose here is merely to point toward an approach that builds on the concept of contradiction as a generative source, but goes beyond the restrictive framework of dialectics toward a more multipolar appreciation of productive tension. As will be explored in greater detail later in the book, one of the key points here is that the products of generative tensions often shoot off in directions orthogonal to the plane of their creation, and indeed that any given field of tension can have multiple, alternating, and often surprising products. Rather than framing tensions as a series of oppositions sublating to higher universals—or even progressive devolutions as Adorno's "negative dialectics" would entail—taking this more open-ended approach allows us to visualize these tensions as themselves caught within a complex web, not organized into a hierarchy, and constantly subject to re-articulation while still recognizing that each tension, at its core, is a generative force. What this means in practice, and how we can employ it toward understanding and engaging in issues such as partner violence, will be a topic of continued exploration throughout this book, and especially in Chapter 5, "Contradictions and Consciousness." And while by the end of this book I do not mean to have proposed a formalized, alternative framework to dialectics, in illustrating the application of this approach to the specific issue of partner violence, perhaps an early outline of one will begin to appear.

5. My description here is paraphrased from Geertz's (1973) "man is an animal suspended in webs of significance he himself has spun."

6. In referring to those who commit this kind of violence there are a number of options, including "aggressor," "victimizer," "batterer," and "perpetrator." I have generally chosen to use the term "perpetrator," despite its legalistic overtones, because it indexes both that violent acts have indeed been committed (unlike "aggressor") as well as avoiding the totalizing identification of the person with those acts (unlike "batterer"). For those upon whom the violence has been inflicted, I generally use the term "survivor" to indicate a recognition of the fact that to live in the face of this violence requires a very active form of survival. Not everyone survives partner violence, however, and it is for this reason that, where appropriate, I do also use the term "victim" as well. It is also worth a brief consideration of why "partner violence" is the most appropriate term to use here as opposed to others. Perhaps the simplest reason is that in Colombia *violencia de pareja* is the most common term applied to this kind of abuse. Other terms, such as *violencia intrafamiliar*, have a slightly different meaning and encompass other forms of violence, such as child abuse and neglect. It is out of deference to this local preference that I generally use the term "partner violence" instead of its English counterpart of "intimate partner violence," and it is out of recognition that this violence happens not just

within the (often implicitly heteronormative) home that the term "domestic violence" is emphatically not used throughout this book.

7. Dorinne Kondo's (1990: 224) notion of personhood as people "shot through with contradictions and creative tensions" has been particularly informative to me in understanding how to approach the complex personhoods of those whom I encountered. This perspective, that people are permeated by tensions that extend out into the social worlds in which they live, is also reflected in Deleuze's (1997) notion of "combating," which posits people as engaged in a continuous process of "becoming" by wrestling with these tensions. This emphasis on living as "becoming" puts this view of personhood, and its relationship to broader systems of power, into communication with a number of other philosophies and theories, as will be explored throughout this book.

8. In an oddly similar manner, André Maurois (Lyons, 1960: 4) likened humor to dissecting a frog: "when you take it apart, you find out what it's made of, but unfortunately the subject is killed in the process."

9. For the origin of the term "voyeuristic pornography of violence," see Scheper-Hughes and Bourgois (2004).

10. Ackelsberg (2004: 41). This notion also finds some resemblance in the words of Nelson Mandela (1994: 624) who stated that "to be free is not merely to cast off one's chains, but to live in a way that respects and enhances the freedom of others," as well as popular explorations of the negative aspects of coercive power such as the song "Ek Je Chilo Raja" from Satyajit Roy's (1969) film *Goopy Gyne Bagha Byne*.

11. This focus on positions within multiple fields of relational power, and the particular phrasing adopted here, comes from Das and Kleinman's (2000: 1) formulation of subjectivity as "the felt interior experience of the person that includes his or her positions in a field of relational power."

12. Fractals will be a repeated theme throughout this book, particularly because they serve as an apt visual metaphor for the repetitive emergence of particular motifs as we cross scales of complex systems. The analogy of the fractal is a useful one for two particular reasons. First, one of the key properties of fractals is the self-similarity in form across scales. Attention to these similarities across scales of social relations, from the personal to broadest expanses of the social, makes possible analogic forms of organizing our understandings, and it draws into focus potential tensions that might exist between these seemingly similar forms. This is a means of analysis that was formally proposed by Durkheim ([1898] 1953), and it is a topic that will be explored throughout this book. Second, fractals have the curious property of infinite perimeters enclosing finite spaces, something that we could take to analogically represent the potentially infinite frontiers of social difference and exclusion that surround social groups of finite size.

13. "The Fifth Zone" is a more popular term for Usme, sometimes seen in graffiti in the district.

14. As of 2014, the estimated population of Usme was 423,650 people (Secretaría Distrital de Planeación [SDP], 2009). Of all twenty districts of Bogotá, Usme also had the highest rate of migration to it for the 2005–2010 period, and it was estimated to continue to have the highest rate for the 2010–2015 period as well (SDP, 2015).

15. Profamilia (2011).

16. "Complicado" is a word that on one hand means "complicated" and on the other hand also carries the connotation of difficulty in the lived sense of the word, of a heavy or troubled state of affairs.

17. While Chapter 1, "La Zona Quinta," provides the most dedicated introduction to Usme, it is a topic to which I will continually return throughout the rest of the book.

18. It is also, of course, not a practice unique to residents of Usme. In much of the legal doctrine in Colombia, the family is itself recognized as the basic nucleus of society, an assertion that frequently finds its way into the legal citations of orders of protection and other related documents drafted and signed through the Comisarías de Familia. In a related but partially inverted sense, we can also see the operation of such logical motions in the adage of some feminist movements that "the personal is political."

19. The term "shifting phantasmagoria" is borrowed from the opening of Joan Didion's (1979) *The White Album*.

20. Such a notion is certainly polygeneous and has arisen from many different loci around the world. Even a Eurocentric account, however, would have to trace back to Comte (as pointed out by Sawyer, 2002) and later Durkheim ([1898] 1953). In an essay that presaged theories in neuroscience by almost a century, Durkheim argued for a distributed notion of mental representations in the field of neuroscience, a hypothesis that he generated by means of analogy from his own research on collective social representations. Such kinds of thinking have been later captured in any meta-theories of science that seek to elaborate a view of the world as a complex system, theories that often invoke analogies themselves to fractal forms in mathematics.

21. This idea of basing the authority of the state to the authority created within the heteronormative home, as discussed by both Matear (2007) and Parson (2013), is a topic that will be revisited in both Chapters 2 and 3.

22. They do form an important component to understanding them though, and as the Colombian scholar Gauta (2011) has noted, any understanding of partner abuse on the high-altitude "mesa" of Colombia must take into account both the legacy and the continuing role that colonialism plays in everyday life.

23. This notion of the "interpositional" account is best illustrated in Kleinman's *Writing at the Margin* (1997).

24. This approach is most explicitly stated by Taussig (1980) but has incidentally also been the approach of a great number of critical medical anthropologists who have worked at the most distal ends of violent systems.

25. That all the perpetrators with whom I worked were all men is reflective of the context in which we met, and while it is true that the vast majority of perpetrators of chronic, coercive partner violence around the world are men, the exclusive gender bias reflected in this work should not be confused with any presupposed heteronormative assumptions about who commits, and who is the victim of, partner violence. The predominantly heteronormative framing of partner violence here is reflective of the context in which the research was conducted, where over 90 percent of denuncia seekers were women asking for protection from male partners, consistent with broader gender imbalances in the kind of chronically controlling partner abuse that was the focus of this research.

26. The concept of "hegemonic masculinities" (Connell, 1987)—applying the Gramscian notion of hegemony directly to gender relations—has been a guiding influence in the conception of this work, as will be particularly evident in Chapter 3, "Permissible." While much of the use of the term has been made with regard to understanding how different notions of masculinity and gender compete for domination over one another, this study is oriented largely to understanding the contradictions and tensions that emerge directly through the performance of these forms of masculinity. As such, the use of this idea follows more closely

from its later update, not its original formulation, where Connell and Messerschmidt (2005) encouraged future research to engage in the examination of the "internal" contradictions of forms of masculinity, and to do so through attention to extended life histories.

27. It is worth noting that this was emphatically *not* intended to be a therapeutic process, something that at times had to be emphasized and reiterated, considering that some perpetrators of violence were legally required to seek psychological counseling, a requirement that our interviews could not fulfill.

28. It is, however, not just that existing sources of social support, say family or friends, fail victims of violence in these moments of need. It is also that one of the many consequences of intimate violence can be what Das (2007) has called "poisonous knowledge" for the survivors of abuse, knowledge that not only harms the holders of it but also continues to do damage to their social relationships, existing or potential, as well. It is a concept that bears important connections with what Dana Jack (1993) has called "silencing the self," a form of self-censure that has been documented to have significant sequelae, ranging from depression to the sense of a "divided self."

29. This general approach is best described by Butler (1993: 241) when she says that "identities and difference are constructed in and through dynamics of our engagement with each other over time, not only in the service of oppressive relations such as racism or sexism, but also in the service of the contestation of such oppression."

Chapter 1

Notes to epigraphs: Lyrics from a freestyle rap by Quinta Inicial, a group whose members are all from Usme. The song was recorded on June 3, 2015, in the Calle 40S station of the Transmilenio bus system by the author. The translation is as follows: "Excuse me if I offend / We live in a country where / There are few good memories / Bathed in blood / Immortal [political] parties / Oil exploitation / If I mention it, I cry, flora / And women trafficking / The discovery of color, has been repeated / I have indigenous roots / Indigenous malice / I represent also / The rivers, towns, paths, they / Have been forgotten, also forced / To leave their cultivations / Later peasant protests, everyone offended / Later oppressed, why? (why?) / For protesting, I tell it / hot streets, rap quinta inicial." The second epigraph is translated as "You cannot buy my life / My land is not for sale." These lyrics are from the song "Latinoamerica"— from the Calle 13 album *Entren los que quieren*—which was performed by Calle 13 and the Colombian singer Totó la Momposina in 2014 in the Plaza Bolívar in Bogotá, and then again at the conclusion of the March for Peace in Bogotá on April 9, 2015. The march in 2015 was dated to commemorate the assassination of Jorge Eliécer Gaitán, and at its concluding concert Totó la Momposina again performed the song, but this time accompanied by two rap artists from Usme. At the 2015 performance, at every repetition of the line "mi tierra no se vende," the crowd erupted in applause.

1. This kind of explicitly political graffiti is common throughout Bogotá, whose street art scene is one of the most vibrant in the world. Interestingly most of this kind of *graffiti conciencia* was relatively scarce within Usme, especially compared to the downtown area along La Septima (7th Avenue) near the city's main plaza, and along one of the main roads leading westward away from downtown, Calle 26. The kind of geographic distribution of this graffiti helps to tell a bit about who its intended audiences are.

2. For a seminal work on the silencing of histories, see Michel-Rolph Trouillot's (1997) *Silencing the Past*.

3. For examples of such scholarship with a global perspective, see Stoler (1995) and F. Cooper (2005).

4. In the Latin American context, Rodolfo Stavenhagen (1971) has most thoroughly deconstructed this myth in his *Seven Myths of Latin America*. His exegesis definitively shows that over the entire region, as has been true elsewhere in the world, cities were built out of long and vital ties to rural areas and that rural areas have not simply been left behind in the wake of urban progress as many might be led to believe.

5. Secretaría de Cultura, Recreación y Deporte (2010: 86). It is also worth noting that the introduction to this commemorative book, written by the mayor, emphasized the project for continued modernization of the city.

6. In doing so we deepen our understanding of the significance of those intersections in how they shape the *perpetration* of violence, as well as put into more dynamic motion the "geographically broad and historically deep" frameworks that proponents of structural violence such as Farmer (1997) have put forth.

7. La Violencia was a period from 1948 to 1954 when an estimated 250,000 Colombians (Safford and Palacios, 2002) were killed in a disseminated conflict fought ostensibly between the Liberal and Conservative parties.

8. "Ahí vamos" is a saying that not only literally means "there we go" but also is often used in a more general sense to convey a sense of perpetual motion, something that hopefully resembles forward progress. When talking with community organizers about issues they were confronting in their work, no matter how pessimistic or burdened with the talk of setbacks they might have been at times, our conversations often ended with these words.

9. As Pérez (2014) has shown, the razing of "El Cartucho" (meaning "the cartridge") was not a project just of beautifying an area or even making safer what was regarded as an insecure part of town. This project of displacement was intricately woven into the project for national sovereignty, made significant by its central location in the capital city.

10. The street signs are an interesting discrepancy, given that streets in the northern half of the city are not labeled as such, meaning that the north of the city is effectively the implicit referent when it comes to Bogotá's social geography. As in cases where "Caucasian" or "male" is used as the default referent in racial or gender descriptions, it is worth taking note any time that a category is made to be invisible through its implicit reference. In the case of Bogotá, the southern half of the city is frequently regarded as the poorer, more dangerous region by those who live in the northern districts, and in fact in terms of income at least it is generally true that the southern districts are significantly poorer.

11. Usme lies at an altitude between three hundred and seven hundred feet above the rest of the city.

12. For statistics on IDPs, see United Nations High Commission on Refugees (UNHCR; 2013a, 2013b). For estimates of gender disparities, see Franco et al. (2006).

13. This, however, is not primarily due to more people being displaced per se in the years immediately leading up to 2013, but is seen as responding to the changes in designation that were mandated under the 2011 Law of Victims and Restitution that officially recognized those displaced after the main paramilitaries demobilized in 2003 (UNHCR, 2013c). This change in figures indicates two issues: (1) the numbers are subject to official designations that make "accurate" cross-national comparisons difficult and (2) the numbers reflect classifications that are the results of intensely political projects of recognition.

14. UNHCR (2003).

15. Salcedo (2008).

16. In particular, Fischer, McCann, and Auyero (2014) have argued this in their edited volume *Cities from Scratch*.

17. Veena Das and Deborah Poole (2004) have promoted this kind of orientation to understanding marginality in *Anthropology in the Margins of the State*, an anthology where they seek to advance a scholarship of the *performance* of social frontiers as a means to appreciate the lived realities and experiences of exclusionary social arrangements. Doing so, as they point out, illustrates that frequently at the margins there is not an absence of the state, but rather an increased visibility of it as agents seek to make their respective apparatuses of the state be seen.

18. Secretaría Distrital de Hábitat (2011). It is also worth noting that the landfill was inaugurated in 1988 and originally slated to operate for twenty years, but in 2014 it was approved once again for another eight years (*El Tiempo*, 2014).

19. Personal communication with Dr. Andrés Salcedo (July 18, 2013), a Colombian anthropologist at the Universidad Nacional de Colombia, who has worked for an extended period of time in Usme.

20. Cuéllar and Uyabán (2011). The *Localidad Usme: Diagnostico local con participación social 2009-2010* also covers much of this history and its resulting spatial inscription within Usme (Secretaría Distrital de Salud, 2010).

21. For documentation of their historic "illegality," see Defensoría del Pueblo (2010) or Personería de Bogotá (2012).

22. In particular, Lefebvre (1970) and Harvey (2008) have argued how feverish growth of the urban built environment has been an intentional and effective pillar in the growth and ascendance of global capitalist systems, in particular due to their use in serving as sinks for surplus product.

23. For the history of Usme's annexation by Bogotá and its broader significance, see Cortés Diaz (2006).

24. Not only did the rediscovery of the burial ground indicate the central importance of the region of Usme in Muiscan religious life, but the temporary success of its use in preventing the further expansion of housing projects has contributed to what some have called the "muiscanization" of social resistance in Usme today. In other words, invoking Muiscan history and organizing around new amalgamations of indigeneity—such as through invocations of "pachamama," a term derived from Quechuan or Ayamara but with clear parallels in Muiscan history—was in the interest of contesting, or at least stalling, the further encroachment of urban expansion.

25. The history that follows here is assembled from both Fals Borda (1969) and *Usme: Historia de un territorio* (Cuéllar and Uyabán, 2011).

26. Perhaps the most dramatic example of this in Colombia is the history of what is today the largest recognized indigenous group in the country, the Wayuu of the northeastern department of Guajira (Hernandez, 1984). Prior to the Spanish invasion in 1499, there existed a number of distinct groups in the region and, though much of their history is lost today, what remains known is that all of these groups were distinct but economically connected to some degree. Upon the arrival of the Spanish, all of these groups underwent profound and rapid transformations, particularly in response to the Spanish practice of selling members of these groups into slavery in the Antilles. In order to avoid complete incorporation into the colonial system, several major adaptations happened: ethnic divisions appear to have disappeared and

a common identity known as the Wayuu was forged, a new and highly mobile lifestyle was adopted that included the incorporation of Spanish horses (today all-terrain vehicles) along with a pastoral means of subsistence, and finally the Wayuu established trade with non-Spanish counterparts. This last feature not only prevented a Spanish monopoly on trade but also facilitated access to guns for a more militant defense of autonomy. Even today, the Wayuu have been able to maintain some degree of independence from the central state.

27. Cuéllar and Uyabán (2011: 41).

28. Fals Borda (1969).

29. The gendering of the social contract is far from a novel idea, with Carole Pateman (1988) most famously having argued for the existence of a sexual contract underlying the social contract of modern states in her seminal work of the same name. In it she argues that the social contract, and indeed all of Contractarian Theory going back to Locke and Hobbes, on which most modern statehood is based, is not only predicated on the systematic exclusion of women from public life but also built on a guarantee to male citizens that they be allowed to privately subjugate women. While most of her analysis was based on Anglo countries between the years 1840 and 1970, subsequent work has helped to demonstrate important cross-cultural relevance of this work as well as its application beyond the years she studied. With regard to the Colombian context in particular, beyond these colonial indices of the gendering of sovereign power, it is worth noting that later on, written into the 1991 Colombian constitution, itself actually an attempt to redistribute power in the country, Article 42 specifically states, "The family is the basic nucleus of society. It is formed on the basis of natural or legal ties, through the free decision of a man and woman to contract matrimony or through the responsible resolve to comply with it." Similar claims can be found throughout much of the government-produced literature on partner violence in Colombia, and on this alone it is a small stretch to claim that in Colombian social and legal life the concept of an intertwined social and sexual contract bears at least some degree of relevance, even if the terms of that arrangement have been significantly contested over time, as will be later explored.

30. See Palacios (1980) and Safford and Palacios (2002). Even a brief survey of the English-language literature on Colombia reflects these internal divisions, with titles like *Colombia: Fragmented Land, Divided Society* (Safford and Palacios, 2002) or *The Making of Modern Colombia: A Nation in Spite of Itself* (Bushnell, 1993).

31. Fals Borda (1969) has written at length about this persistent split of power between the Liberal and Conservative parties, and how it resulted from an incomplete subversion of the preceding conservative colonial order. Viewing the history of Colombia under this rubric, of a progressive accretion of variably complete subversions—from the Liberal subversion to later the Socialist and even later the turn toward decentralization—helps to clarify not only what the different models of social organization today are, but how they came to exist side by side with one another.

32. For this more traditional view based on inaccessible geography, see Bushnell (1993), Kirk (2003), Safford and Palacios (2002), and Tate (2007). The political scientist James Robinson in particular has challenged this view, taking up the form of thought previously laid out by Rodolfo Stavenhagen (1981). This view was presented in a talk given at the David Rockefeller Center for Latin American Studies on October 10, 2013, in which Robinson analyzed a meeting in the northwestern region of Chocó between community members and representatives of the National Bank of Colombia. This idea of a carefully cultivated, "unregulated" periphery is still admittedly in development but is based on years of his experience in the

country and resonates the most with my own experiences in Colombia. This different analysis is based largely on a persistence of these patterns into the current era where the Colombian state has had both the capital and the technical ability to build the infrastructure necessary to connect the country, and the many cases where it has already done so. Add to this the significant role that paramilitaries later played during the political conflict of the late twentieth century, often under the covert direction of the national military, as well as the fact that many national politicians have had controlling interests in industries in these politically excluded areas, this more complicated form of governance becomes apparent. For the history of paramilitaries in the conflict and the investments by politicians in particular industries, see, for example, Hristov (2009), Kirk (2003), and Lozano and Morris (2010). For an example of the state as all-seeing entity, see James Scott's (1999) *Seeing Like a State*. For the terms "geography of imagination" and "geography of management," see Trouillot (2003).

33. See Palacios (1980) or Taussig (1980).

34. With the current coca cultivation in some regions such as Putumayo, the organization has even retaken the general form of these older latifundia hacienda systems but is now under the control of paramilitary or guerrilla groups (see Jansson, 2006).

35. In this context it is worth noting that Gaitán was not only a populist and charismatic politician on the national scale, who wanted to rethink the political economic relations that had hitherto built the country, but also someone who saw women as playing a central role in that process of reimagination. More than just an academic point, this was something frequently invoked to me by women that I knew in Usme, chief among them Luz, whose story will be a point of focus in the next chapter. Gaitán's belief that the rethinking of gendered relations had to accompany the rethinking of politics more broadly reflects the same kind of thinking behind the social/sexual contract, at the same time that it represents an immediate departure from it. It puts intimate domestic relationships at the heart of the political imagining of the nation-state at the same time that it refutes the arrangements that were put in place at that time of its founding. As such, it also represents a counterpoint to the historical experience of one of Colombia's neighbors, Chile, who later under Pinochet, as explored by Parson (2013), sought to reaffirm the notion of an authoritarian state under the logic of a strictly patriarchal nuclear family. Intrusions into this logic, as Gaitán's represents in the Colombian context, stand as some of the first major cracks in these schemes as they existed on the national scale.

36. At the Museum of Gaitán in Bogotá there is a tree planted above his grave that has been described to me as the symbolic continuation of his presence, an indication of the desire for the tree's roots to grow and eventually extend over the entire country. In this sense, Gaitán *himself* is posed as the symbolic core of the country's politics, an unfinished project that hopefully will continue to grow outward.

37. Gilhodés (1970). While cities had long been sites where political maneuvering concentrated, Gaitán's emphasis on managing a city as a means of political subversion and broader social change expanded the centrality of cities in the political life of the country. After three decades of political hegemony, the Conservative Party's control of the national government ceded to a Liberal Party takeover that would last until La Violencia.

38. See Fals Borda (1969) and Gilhodés (1970).

39. Why such killings took place around the country is discussed in a vast collection of scholarship in Colombia and is far beyond the scope of what I can address here. In order to understand it, again we must go back to how these parties split in the mid-nineteenth century

and trace not only the institutional organization of this schism but also the century of discourse that served to naturalize and justify this dichotomous split in Colombia.

40. See Fals Borda (1969), Gilhodés (1970), and Kirk (2003).

41. The urban guerrilla group M-19 would later completely disrupt such a notion, particularly when they invaded the supreme court in a hostage situation that ended in high casualties, including the deaths of several of the justices. For this notion of the "performance" of the city, see Carrasco (1999).

42. For this history of the annexation of Usme, its context, the motivations behind it, and its consequences, Cortés Díaz's (2006) *La anexión de los 6 municipios vecinos a Bogotá en 1954* is particularly instructive. For this idea of what makes a state "modern," see Herzfeld (1993: 8) where he argues that "what marks off the condition of modernity is not doctrinal impulse, but increasing centralization and scale."

43. At that juncture of the Great Depression, resident laborers on the coffee haciendas had been able to go on extended strike, living off of their own subsistence crops, and force the hacendado owners to default on their existing loans to foreign creditors who were unwilling to renegotiate debts. The history of the collapse of the hacienda system for coffee production is a significant one in the history of Colombia, especially because of the central role that coffee played in the early development of its economy. Because the crop is not a relatively capital-intensive venture, it formed the basis of the initial capital accumulation in the nineteenth century for more intensive industries created in the following century. A more complete history of this critical moment would have to include the role of the Federación Nacional de Cafeteros (FNC), the institution that since 1927 has controlled prices, promoted particular farming practices, provided loans to farmers, and positioned Colombia's coffee as a global commodity. A history must also look at the internal divisions on the haciendas, the failure of hacendados to achieve hegemonic control over their workforces, and the instrumental role of the mixed mode of production. The FNC for its part actually played a conservative role in this institutional change by perpetuating a system in which suppliers, middlemen, and exporters were all more generously rewarded than small growers (Bushnell, 1993). Also working against the overthrow of the hacienda system had been the internal divisions among workers between the permanent residents with their own plots of land, the day laborers, and the overseers: divisions that all also followed ethnic fault lines (Palacios, 1980). If the workers had been previously unorganized into effective coalitions, so too were the hacendados themselves, who, Jiménez (1995) argues, failed to organize a discourse around a nation-building project and whose often contradictory roles as estate owners, merchants, and financiers further inhibited such organization. As Kutschbach (1995) illustrates, this meant that when the global depression created drastic changes in coffee prices and brought the hacienda institution to the point of crisis through the foreign debts still owed, the owners were not able to work together whereas the workers were able to fall back on subsistence crops allowed under the system of poly-cropping and further pressure the large landowners. Only in this particular "structure of the conjuncture" (Sahlins, 1981) at this moment of crisis was a lasting institutional change possible in the core industry of the country at the time. This stands in contrast to the experience of other coffee-producing countries at the time, such as Costa Rica, that actually experienced a further entrenchment of the hacienda system following the Great Depression (Kutschbach, 1995). Following this collapse, the FNC and later foreign entities such as USAID and the World Bank promoted mono-cropping of coffee and more capital-intensive modes of cultivation that over time have actually increased the average size of farms for coffee production.

44. See Cuéllar and Uyabán (2011). Compared to the history of reaccumulation of land after the collapse of the coffee hacienda system, as related above, this means that, paradoxically, at the same time that large plots of land were being cut up and redistributed in Usme, elsewhere they were in the process of re-expanding again.

45. *El Tiempo* (November 28, 1991).

46. Rubior (1992).

47. *Semana* (December 1991).

48. Cabre (1991).

49. *El Tiempo* (March 8, 1991).

50. *El Tiempo* (February 18, 1992).

51. *El Tiempo* (May 11, 1992).

52. *El Tiempo* (July 1, 1992).

53. This heterogeneous treatment of Usme was not unique to the press either. Within the local government itself we can find a wide array of views on the district as well. In particular one could examine reports such as "New Usme: Axis of Integration to the Llanos" (Alcaldía Mayor de Bogotá, 2006) or "Inspection, Vigilance, and Control of the Development of Illegal Housing" (Secretaría Distrital del Hábitat, 2010) regarding the sometimes militant supervision of the strategic corridor that Usme represents, compared against reports on social participation by agencies such as the Departamento Administrativo de Bienestar Social (1996) and Alcaldía Mayor de Bogotá and Universidad Nacional de Colombia Facultad de Derecho (2006). Taken together, they demonstrate what scholars such as Timothy Mitchell (1999: 77) have argued: that not only are all "states" in fact profoundly heterogeneous entities, but that the dividing lines that separate them from the rest of society are equally complex. His statement that "the limits are internal to the network of institutional mechanisms through which a social and political order is maintained" indicates that the tidy frontiers that supposedly distinguish state/civil society relationships are themselves constructed illusions.

54. In the case of Colombia, this was also the basis for a major reform of the health care system that was meant to transition care from public to private provision with universal insurance coverage. Abadía-Barrero and Oviedo (2009) provide an excellent overview of this reform and its subsequent discontents. Under this proposed scheme, those with the fewest financial resources would be covered under a subsidized system that those with relatively greater resources, who would purchase insurance in the "contributory" system, would fund. More than two decades on from its implementation, the reform has struggled with the now-parallel existence of the new system with the former public system of care, which was never possible to fully dissolve, as well as endemic corruption and imposed bureaucratic barriers to care. Particularly true for those in the "subsidized" system, the reform has introduced inequalities in the access to care, and were it not for the advent of the tutela these might only be further exacerbated.

55. As Keshavjee (2014) notes in his consideration of neoliberalism and global health, neoliberalism under its construction by seminal thinkers such as Friedrich Hayek was at its core an anti-totalitarian philosophy. It served as a response to the experience of authoritarian governance in Europe in the first half of the twentieth century but its elaboration into a set of more detailed economic policies has ironically also facilitated the concentration of power in society, albeit into other hands.

56. For global perspectives, see, for example, *Dying for Growth* (Kim, Millen, Irwin, and Gershman, 2002) or *Capital Resurgent: Roots of the Neoliberal Revolution* (Duménil and Lévy,

2004). For the Latin American context, see *Understanding Contemporary Latin America* (Hillman and D'Agostino, 2011). The Colombian context statistically is a bit more complicated. The GINI coefficient for the country as a whole went from 51.3 in 1990 to a high of 60.1 in 2006 and has since trended back down to 53.5 (World Bank, 2016).

57. See Eckstein (2001), Escobar and Alvarez (1992), or Warren and Jackson (2002). In the case of Colombia, with regard to the mobilization of indigenous groups, the focus on the decentralization of power and ethnic pluralism opened up new official channels for making claims while also making acculturation and assimilation less attractive options. As these various scholars argue, while this realization does not detract from the host of negative effects that these political economic adjustments have also had, changes like these indicate that any critique of neoliberal restructuring must be sensitive to the complicated consequences of these transformations.

58. For both the history of this evolution of feminism in Latin America and its subsequent contributions to Marxist-feminism more specifically, see Chinchilla (1992).

59. The date of November 25th was chosen to commemorate the murder by Rafael Trujillo of the Mirabal sisters in the Dominican Republic in 1960.

60. As will be examined in more detail in Chapter 6, "Response," at the same time that this language was enshrined into the new constitution, other government agencies were in the process of trying to redefine the power dynamics that characterized the nuclear family. Seeking more distributive and "horizontal" topographies of interpersonal power, to suggest that the society recapitulate dynamics within a normative home, therefore, did not necessarily mean a rote recapitulation of more traditional regimes. In fact, the very advent of institutions such as the Comisarías de Familia can be seen as a basic refutation of this, as again will be explored in the final chapter.

61. As Heidi Hartmann (1981: 21) had earlier put it, "The marriage of Marxism and Feminism has been like the marriage of husband and wife depicted in English Common Law: marxism and feminism are one and that one is marxism . . . either we need a healthier marriage or we need a divorce." An extreme version of this earlier marriage between feminism and Marxism can be seen in Alexandra Kollontai's (1909) "The Woman Question" where she makes the claim that private property is essentially the sole basis of gender conflict. In resisting these bourgeois institutions then, she claims that proletariat men and women fight together as a unified front and as such undo the antagonisms that political economies created between them. While this view has obviously undergone many subsequent revisions, Chinchilla (1992) again provides a comprehensive overview of both the Latin American form of Marxist-feminism as well as its major components.

62. This argument for the necessity of women in the recognition of gender relations in resisting capitalist political economies was primarily based in the previous notion of "third forces" that would be required to glue together disparate elements of society into effective coalitional movements. Previous theorization of collective social action against capitalist systems had focused on the role of rural peasants who migrated to cities as providing crucial connections, but this new brand of Marxist-feminism recast women and the resistance to oppressive gender relations into this role (see again Chinchilla, 1992).

63. *Colombia Informa* (November 24, 2014).

64. With regard to the neoliberal reforms of this period, it is worth noting that while neoliberal economics may be fundamentally based in a distrust of concentrating power into the hands of those who run state systems of governance, within the institutions of this kind

of political economy one finds the very same concentrations and hierarchies of power. As such, it is hard to consider the neoliberal restructuring of financial institutions and government regulation in Latin America as a truly decentralizing set of reforms. More appropriately these might be viewed as reforms that sought to shift where power was concentrated and who had direct control over these institutions.

65. As previously cited, see Secretaría Distrital de Planeación (2009, 2015).

66. To borrow and invert Clausewitz's famous aphorism.

67. Across the entire Latin American region, everyday insecurities in urban environments have received a great deal of attention. Some particularly illustrative volumes on the subject include *Citizens of Fear* (Rotker, 2002), *Cities from Scratch* (Fischer, McCann, and Auyero, 2014), and *Violence at the Urban Margins* (Auyero, Bourgois, and Scheper-Hughes, 2015). For the evolving landscape of actors and their urban involvements, see Human Rights Watch (2010).

68. Though so named, "Usme Center" is near the geographic center of the district but at the very southern extreme of its densest populations, located right at the nexus between the more urban and rural zones of Usme. Its intricate social fracturing is perhaps the most literal example that I have seen of Carolyn Nordstrom's (2004: 162) assertion that "habits of war mark landscapes of peace."

69. Manjoo and McRaith (2011).

70. While not focusing directly on the perpetration of partner violence, proponents of this perspective, such as Enloe (2000) and later Belkin (2012), have been instrumental in demonstrating the intricate binds that tie processes of militarization to gendered identities more broadly. In a Latin American context, research on postconflict Guatemala has suggested that notions of machismo became further elaborated and more deeply entrenched throughout the history of the conflict (Manjoo and McRaith, 2011). Theidon (2008) has written extensively about how demobilization for combatants in Perú and Colombia requires an active process of reconstructing notions of masculinity as well.

71. Frantz Fanon (1963), in his famous *The Wretched of the Earth*, explored this issue briefly in his Case #5 of Case Series A, "A European police inspector tortures his wife and children." In a Latin American context, Theidon (1999) has called this the "domestication of violence," linking it closely to patterns of alcohol consumption after demobilization. More recently in the U.S. context this has again become an issue of public visibility, with soldiers returning from deployments and the subsequent rises in partner violence being commonly framed as connected to experiences of post-traumatic stress disorder.

72. Beyond the direct or indirect diffusion of militarized experiences, others have speculated that increases in the availability of small arms, a greater tolerance for violence in society, and the inundation of legal institutions may also play important roles in the migration of violence into more domestic spaces (see Manjoo and McRaith, 2011).

73. This notion of exceptional violence working itself into the mundane is reflective of the notion of "continuums of violence," as discussed by Scheper-Hughes and Bourgois (2004).

Chapter 2

Notes to epigraphs: In the first epigraph, translated as "To change masters is not to be free," Jose Martí, a Cuban poet and political theorist, was at the time speaking against U.S. pretensions to regional hegemony. The insight, however, applies to issues of sovereignty beyond geopolitics, as this chapter explores. The second epigraph is a quotation by Angela

Davis, a U.S. philosopher and activist, speaking at Bunker Hill Community College on March 29, 2018.

1. The same typology of partner violence referenced in the first endnote of the Introduction (M. Johnson, 2008; Kelly and Johnson, 2008) was developed largely in response to this controversy. The argument is that while some types of violence such as situational partner violence may help to understand reports of gender parity in the perpetration of violence, forms like chronic, coercive violence are still male-dominated, consistent with common experience.

2. In the Colombian context, scholars such as Jimeno, Góngora, Martínez, and Suárez (2007) have also argued against these oversimplified and misleading stereotypes. With regard to the term "coercive control" itself, it is included in the typology presented by Kelly and Johnson (2008), as well as explored in greater depth in the book *Coercive Control* by Stark (2007) and *Invisible Chains* by Fontes (2015), which is based in part on her own experiences.

3. These estimates are from a World Health Organization (WHO) (2013) review of existing data. Those regions with the highest prevalence were the African, Mediterranean, and South East Asian regions at 35 percent, with the Americas matching the global average at 30 percent. These statistics were based on a systematic review of available literature globally, but, while rigorous, there are still limitations in the potential accuracy of aggregating dissimilar studies. Of the limitations noted in the report, one of the most important is that these figures refer only to physical or sexual violence and do not include other types of abuse, such as emotional, psychological, or financial.

4. These estimates are according to the "Encuesta Nacional de Demografía y Salud" (ENDS) study by Profamilia (2010).

5. See again the discussion of this in the Introduction as to why "sovereignty" is particularly useful here. From that brief prelude, the purpose of this and subsequent chapters will be to explore what these connections to partner violence really mean, and how we might use them to gain further insights into their dynamics and broader sociohistorical roots.

6. Isolation as a means of long-term control is a widely recognized means by which perpetrators of abuse maintain domination over their partners. This view has perhaps been most popularized by the Duluth model's "Wheel of Control," a model that grew out of the insights of feminist theory.

7. The notion of "intersectionality" was formalized and brought to the center by Crenshaw (1989), but its underlying concept has been in development for some time, carried through a long genealogy that includes the work of scholars and activists such as Sojourner Truth, Anna Julia Cooper, and Angela Davis. Anna Julia Cooper ([1892] 1988) in particular presaged the assertion that those who have lived under many forms of oppression would have unusually important roles in social change, an idea later carried forward in concepts such as "third forces," which will later be explored. One particularly notable application of the intersectional approach to understanding women's experiences of partner violence can be seen in *Domestic Violence at the Margins* (Sokoloff and Pratt, 2005).

8. Luz is certainly not alone in this, and seeing vans transport groups of soldiers or national police across the city is often a daily occurrence. Another woman in Usme that I knew had fled the province of Santander after she found her brother tortured and killed for refusing to pay a *vacuna*—literally meaning a "vaccine," a bribe or tax—to a paramilitary group, which, as previously discussed, can have variable ties to the national military (see, for example Kirk, 2003). Never knowing if or to what extent the group responsible operated with the

blessing of the national army, she too found herself paralyzed on an everyday basis by the presence of national police in the city. As it was for Luz, this formed the basis of an everyday questioning of the legitimacy of those soldiers and, by extension, the government that they represented.

9. This entanglement between militarization and the construction of gender, particularly in certain forms of masculinity, was previously discussed in Chapter 1 (see Enloe, 2000; Belkin, 2012).

10. Such is the assertion of Butler ([1990] 2006), advancing an idea previously outlined by Foucault.

11. More specific than a domestic contract, see again Pateman (1988) as discussed in Chapter 1 with regard to the existence of a sexual contract that underlies the social contracts of many modern states.

12. For a more complete recounting of these historical processes, see *Linked Labor Histories* (Chomsky, 2008). In her historical reconstruction of these processes, Aviva Chomsky also draws attention to how the initial collapse of textile production was related to the insistence on overproduction by industry leaders like Draper, right up to even the major collapse of the economy in general in 1929. This kind of overproduction and global migration of capital is what geographer David Harvey (2015) has theorized in a more general sense, one of the spatial contradictions in the evolution of a global capitalist system, one driven by the tendency for surplus capital and labor to exist side by side without sufficient markets in which to sell those goods. Chomsky extends the ironies further in her historical reconstruction, describing how capitalists like Draper eventually found new avenues for profit in the production of military arms during the post–World War II era, weapons that would be in part sold back to Colombia in the later years of its own domestic counterinsurgency.

13. There are three major categories of partnership in Colombia that are most often invoked: the *union libre* (nonmarried partnership), *matrimonio civil* (civil marriage), and being married "in the Church." Considering the significant difficulty of obtaining a divorce after being married in the Catholic Church in Colombia, many people have begun to opt for one of the first two categories indefinitely.

14. "Grosero" refers to not just "rude" but also a sense of rudeness that is particularly crude or rough.

15. Similarly, Snell-Rood (2015) has explored this issue, in much greater depth, through her work with women in a New Delhi slum. In this setting, she explores the complicated networks of relationships that women cultivate, the ends to which they mobilize them, and what they signify in terms of understanding care, health, and citizenship. Unlike with Luz Elena, she explores both why many of these women stayed in family relationships that were either neglectful or overtly abusive, and the moral frameworks that supported those decisions. In this sense, what Luz's experiences are unique in demonstrating are the ways in which the cultivation of such complicated support networks can not only mediate one's survival of interpersonal abuse but also form the means of avoiding it entirely.

16. While this notion that relations of financial debt can constitute systems of sovereign relationships has taken on new meaning and interest recently, it was again Mauss ([1925] 1969) who most notably first proposed this idea. For a more contemporary interpretation of finance, debt, and sovereign relations, see Kapadia (2013). This is also where Luz's life experience stands as a strong counterpoint to the more simplistic claims advanced by microfinance enterprises, in particular with regard to their associated discourses on female empowerment.

These discussions generally appear to follow three main genres: (1) that the empowerment of women is the humanitarian crisis of the twenty-first century, (2) that the full employment of women is a linchpin for economic growth, and (3) that liberation from abusive intimate relationships can be achieved through lending credit (these three arguments are the backbone of some widely read works such as *Half the Sky* by Kristof and WuDunn [2010]). While there is undoubtedly value in micro-lending enterprises, Luz's life experience stands as a testament to several counterpoints against them. First, they are still lending schemes and to be involved in them is to be brought into a global system of power based on debt. Second, having known Luz, it never occurred to me that she had any particular desire to be a vital cog in the engine of economic growth, and to the contrary many of her life decisions were based on avoiding conformity to those exact schemes. What is worse, to posit that women like Luz are key figures in economic growth is to argue that our existing political economic relationships are not themselves unjust, only the maldistribution of their products. Third and lastly, to see someone like Luz as a subject in a humanitarian "project of empowerment" runs the risk of completely missing the point of the far more subversive insights that she gained throughout her life. Casting someone like her in this role amounts to reducing her to a subject of pity whose real function is to mobilize charitable campaigns that morally cleanse the wealthy, not recognize that the ways in which she resisted domination throughout her life can help to build a blueprint for undoing those broader systems.

17. Particularly in the context of Colombia, it is worth always noting that dispossession is frequently felt as an ever-present threat. Dispossession of land has been a main feature of the political conflict, one of the more enduring consequences that has required great attention in the ongoing process of demilitarization. This still is only one aspect of a broader and longer history of capital accumulation by dispossession, a topic that Eduardo Galeano (1971) and David Harvey (2009) have made clear on the hemispheric and global scales.

18. Attention to crucial moments within life histories, with emphasis on indeterminacy, innovation, and aspiration, has been further theorized by Jennifer Johnson-Hanks (2002) as "vital conjunctures."

19. As discussed by Davis (1998), the idea that capitalism could have erased gendered dynamics of power is rooted in the notion that such a system might have instead flattened all "labor" into one simple categorization of people, regardless of gender. This has clearly not been the case historically, but what is also interesting is that in earlier refutations of capitalism there was often the hope that struggles against it would similarly erase gendered oppression, as in Kollontai's (1909) pamphlet *The Social Basis of the Woman Question*.

20. See Davis (1998). In "Women and Capitalism: Dialectics of Oppression and Liberation," Davis argues that while sexism is not new under capitalism, a distinctive form of gendered oppression has been ushered in with it. While the capitalist mode of production held within it the potential to supersede previous sexually based divisions of labor, instead these divisions have been maintained at the same time that the very labor that they encompass for women has been progressively devalued, hence the "double inferiority." For Davis, the "*full* emancipation of women must ultimately also transcend the goal of her full and equal participation in a new and reorganized system of production" (153, original emphasis). While not usually in direct conversation with this theory, Pateman's (1988) concept of the sexual contract/social contract similarly elucidates how the promise of a more egalitarian society was once again elided in lieu of one where women were privately subjugated and publicly ex-

cluded, in this case not from economic production but from participation in the modern state.

21. This radical potential of existing "outside" a given system of power is something that has been taken up in the work of several scholars, most notably Benjamin ([1921] 1978) in his *Reflections*, and Derrida (1989) in his essay "Force de loi" (Force of law). What Luz illustrated is that "outside" is usually both literal and figurative at the same time. She did not just seek to live beyond the control of certain people, but she ruptured very physical frontiers in doing so, by walking out of offices at work and the domestic space she shared with her husband. Claiming to be "outside" of a given system is as much a matter of spatial relativity as it is symbolic.

22. As I would learn later in our interviews, that former partner, like Carolina's current one, had been intensely abusive toward her. That Carolina would later find herself before a Comisaría not for her own protection but rather to state her case for her continued custody of her children, against accusations that she was physically abusive of them, is just one example of the complicated nature of such relationships. On the one hand is the open question of whether or not Carolina actually was physically abusive toward her children, a matter that was investigated and ultimately left Carolina with custody of them. On the other hand, Carolina's experiences, position, and alleged actions speak to the complex personhoods at stake in violent relationships, where simple categories like "perpetrator" and "victim" are problematic at best. As for the implications of using hierarchies of suffering, this will be explored in greater detail in Chapter 5.

23. The issue of confidentiality was more important to Carolina than any other person with whom I worked, and this was a conversation that we would have repeatedly, not just before we began our interviews but also in asking for her permission to review her case file at the Comisaría and after the completion of the interviews in deciding how to talk about her life in any published work. To this latter issue, a bit to my surprise, her only condition in this matter was using a pseudonym (a standard practice as we had already discussed), and beyond that she felt comfortable with the dissemination of any part of her story that she had shared. Regarding the phrase "from Guatemala to Guata-peor," it is a frequently used play on words, meaning going from "Guata-bad" to "Guata-worse." It is similar to the English saying of "out of the frying pan and into the fire."

24. Seasonal work in coffee cultivation has been characteristic of it throughout its history in Colombia, given the intensive work that must be done around the time of harvest. Even after the collapse of the hacienda system in the region, smaller operations have continued to rely on migrant help.

25. Andrés Salcedo in particular has studied urban migration in Colombia through an ethnographic lens and Carolina's experience of following a meandering path to arriving in the city is a very common one that he has noted (see, for example, Salcedo, 2008).

26. Literally meaning "not to give a papaya," "no dar papaya" is a very common dictum of safety in everyday life, an adage to always be on guard within an environment that feels pervasively violent. It means not doing things that might put you at risk for trouble, such as going out alone at night, venturing into parts of the city or countryside that are not safe, or showing off valuable goods in public—such as jewelry, electronics, or your wallet. The saying also has sexualized connotations of "not being easy" or "not giving it up," and as such it combines physical danger with sexualized transgression into a hybrid of racy behavior that also helps to put some of the blame on victims of violence when something bad does happen. If someone is

assaulted, robbed, or otherwise harmed, there is usually the accompanying question of did they "dar papaya."

27. Among all of the forms through which Usme and its residents contribute to the growth of, and service to, the city of Bogotá—such as the mining of materials for construction, construction labor, agriculture and food, domestic cleaning—the work as a security guard is one of the most peculiar. Service in the military or national police is obligatory in Colombia unless you can pay for an exemption, meaning that predictably those who fill the ranks of the nation's defense come from poorer backgrounds. Those who find employment as security guards after their service essentially continue this dynamic, providing security to the nation's wealthier classes, just this time a little closer to home.

28. Though the insurance company itself is not run by the state, the health system in Colombia is a state-regulated market of insurance companies that in the early 1990s replaced what was previously a state-run system of hospitals. The system has been characterized as frequently leaving its poorest patients with years of paperwork and bureaucratic mazes to navigate in order to receive their needed care (Abadía-Barrero and Oviedo, 2009), a process that has been given the nickname of the "tour of death."

29. As discussed at the conclusion of Chapter 1, one of the theories that has been proposed for gender-based violence in postconflict settings is the general overworking of judicial systems, making legal recourse less accessible for cases of partner violence. Whether or not in Carolina's case this was the indirect result of political conflict-related cases in particular would be completely speculative, but what was clear in her experience was that the inability of the district attorney's office to keep up with its caseload had important consequences in her personal trajectory.

30. One of the overarching theories of unintended consequences is Merton's (1936) "unintended consequences of purposive social action" where he enumerates several possible reasons for unintended consequences: (1) ignorance, (2) errors in analysis or applying patterns from the past that do not apply to current situations, (3) immediate interests, (4) adherence to basic values, and (5) self-defeating prophecy. It is interesting to note a few issues that have relevance here. First, Merton's first cause, "ignorance," is an issue widely accepted across many schools of thought, and as such it speaks directly to the social positions and limited horizons that any social actor inevitably experiences, important in the very situated experiences of partner violence. Second, while Merton acknowledges a distinction between "purposive" and "rational," his theory was constructed to apply to social action that implies a greater degree of control over one's actions than many perpetrators of partner violence actually experience. Of particular interest in these cases of intimate abuse, especially Carolina's, is not so much the precise pathways by which action yields unintended consequences, it is more so how those unintended consequences have the potential to undo overarching relationships of coercive control.

31. Control over reproductive health and decision making within abusive relationships is a topic that is receiving more attention. Notably it was a topic of specific reference in the same WHO (2013) report cited earlier, and it is a topic that Elizabeth Miller has written extensively on as a specific form of partner violence (see, for example, Miller and Silverman, 2010).

32. Carolina's experience of the role of children in this regard is not uncommon, and that has been documented in the literature from Browne's (1987) *When Battered Women Kill* to *Abusive Endings* (DeKeseredy et al., 2017).

33. With regard to violent intimate-partner relationships in particular, *Abusive Endings* by DeKeseredy, Dragiewicz, and Schwartz (2017) explores how the process of leaving an abu-

sive relationship signifies the highest refutation of it, as well as consequently the most dangerous period of time for those victims of violence.

34. This form of undoing though, and the role that her children have played in it, has hardly ever been an inevitability. Note how within Carolina's life history, her children were at times her reasons for suffering through tremendous amounts of abuse—they are one of the principal reasons that she had not yet left her second partner when we met—but they were also her impetus to leave her first partner and to begin planning to leave her second one. One of the points of inflection in each of these relationships has been her partners' abuse of her children, or at least their abuse of her in front of them. When her safety and the economic well-being of her children had been held in opposition, she directed the product of that tension toward enduring the abuse directed at her, but when her children have become more directly implicated in that violence, she has directed that tension outward, toward leaving her abusive partners all together. What Carolina also shows is that children can be the motivators of seemingly antithetical results at different times, in contexts that vary only slightly and change over the course of a single person's history.

Chapter 3

Notes to epigraphs: The first epigraph is from Aleksandr Solzhenitsyn's *The Gulag Archipelago Volume 1* ([1974] 2020: 173). The remainder of the passage is also relevant here and reads, "Fortunately, it is in the nature of the human being to seek a justification for his actions. . . . Ideology—that is what gives evildoing its long-sought justification." The second epigraph is translated as "Without women there is no revolution." This phrase was written by a Bogotá graffiti artist along La Septima in 2015, a pedestrian avenue near the Plaza Bolívar, which contains Colombia's Supreme Court, National Capitol, and Bogotá's City Hall.

1. This notion that violence does not just happen, but must be justified as well, can be found anywhere from considerations of political violence (see Apter, 1997) to the very basis of the notion of ideology, at the very least when considered in relationship to violent systems, most notably here in how it applies to gendered relationships.

2. As previously discussed in the Introduction, the concept of "hegemonic masculinities" (Connell 1987) has been a guiding influence in this work, as well as particularly the later update of the idea (Connell and Messerschmidt, 2005), in which the examination of "internal" contradictions to hegemonic forms of masculinity is encouraged.

3. While the parade was technically held on the Saturday after, November 25 was a date set at the first encuentro feminista (feminist meeting) for Latin America and the Caribbean, held in Bogotá in 1981. The date was chosen to commemorate the deaths of three Dominican Republic sisters killed under the dictator Trujillo's rule.

4. Against such stultified trait models, other scholarly work, most notably Gutmann's (1996) classic work *The Meanings of Macho*, have revealed the actual performed complexity of such gendered identities.

5. In particular, what I continually ran up against was an array of implicit logics of what governance and participation really meant, most of which have been discussed in Chapter 1, "La Zona Quinta."

6. "Poetic echoes" is a term that Taussig (1980) uses to describe why examination of superstitious practices merits closer attention to the intricate symbolism of their work. As he argues, even if such practices follow the functionalist argument of providing reassurance in an uncertain world, to leave our analysis at that would be to miss the significance of what

forms these superstitions take and what that can tell us about the lifeworlds of those who employ them. Such is also the case for the justifications of partner violence. Even if these justifications are meant largely to minimize and obscure, either from shame or from an attempt to avoid legal consequences, closer examination of them helps to illuminate the ideologies of which abusive men at least try to convince themselves, as well as the broader systems of power in which they are implicated.

7. Both the inadmissibility of violence against intimate partners and the centrality of children in the lifeworlds of abusive men are also noted by Gutmann (1996) in his work on masculinity in Mexico City. Comparing his observations in the community in which he lived against the stories told by men in group sessions at the Centro de Apoyo a la Violencia Intrafamiliar (Support Center for Intrafamilial Violence), he notes that while violence against other men might sometimes be the subject of boasting in social settings, in any of these social spaces most men were very hesitant to speak openly about the violence they inflicted against their intimate partners.

8. For a brief discussion of the relationship between "sovereignty" and "hegemony," refer back to the beginning of Chapter 2, "Possible."

9. Weber ([1919] 1965).

10. Schmitt ([1922] 1985). Note that while Schmitt's notion of sovereignty as the ability to declare the state of exception has more recently been elaborated on by Agamben's (1998) resurrection of "homo sacer" and his attention to "bare life," the use of the idea here does not follow from Agamben's further theorization. The invocation of Schmitt's notion of sovereignty here is a return to his original conceptualization of it, the implications of which will be explored throughout this chapter as well as in Chapter 5, "Contradictions and Consciousness."

11. This is an important reminder that justifications must also always be understood in the spaces in which they are made. Perhaps for this reason, the justifications that I was party to differed from those made on online comment boards, such as the ones studied in Tolton (2011). That these justifications of paternal obligation were made outside these spaces as well, such as in my interviews and observation of abusive men outside of the Comisarías, also means, however, that they are not only limited spaces of legal accountability.

12. Perhaps the most comprehensive exploration of this relationship can be found in the *World Report on Violence and Health* (WHO, 2002). Despite the clear evidence of an association between substance use (in particular, alcohol) and partner violence, there remains a debate as to what extent the relationship is causal, and, if so, how exactly. Some researchers believe that alcohol makes violent acts more likely through direct disinhibition, while others believe the relationship to be culturally mediated whereby violence only happens in contexts where there are expectations that alcohol causes, or justifies, such actions. In either case, evidence presented in the report does support the notion that the *severity* of violent acts increases after the consumption of alcohol.

13. Rodriguez et al. (2012).

14. This is, of course, not to actually reinforce a false dilemma; in truth there are many other possible avenues such as contrition, reparation, transformation, and compassion, not least of all to one's self. The point here is that when one's sense of self and relating to others is tied to a very particular set of arrangements, false dilemmas like these can appear like the only options that exist.

15. Again, Gutmann (1996) has provided some of the more comprehensive illustrations that even "macho" carries with it a host of other obligations and meanings, among them parental care.

16. In a general sense of power/violence, this is precisely the relationship that Arendt (1970) proposed. For partner violence in particular, this relationship of escalating violence in chronic, coercive relationships with the threat of separation has been documented across contexts and disciplines. See Kelly and Johnson (2008) or Dobash et al. (2007) for a general overview. See Jimeno ([2004] 2011) for an ethnographic example within Colombia.

17. One could easily say that this is true only when sovereignty is not fully consolidated, that, per Weber ([1919] 1965), sovereignty is by definition the monopolization of the legitimate use of violence. Sovereignty, however, like hegemony, is never truly a fait accompli: it is always under contestation and never an ordained certainty. Legitimacy, like any form of power, must be continuously renewed and, therefore, is always subject to creative contestation.

18. The term "geography of imagination," along with its accompanying concept of "geography of management," is attributable to Trouillot (2003).

19. "Mala fama" is literally "bad fame" but more approximately "infamy."

20. In neighboring Perú, this kind of phenomenon was also made evident in a famous report written at the onset of the domestic political conflict in that country. The report was drafted by a commission led by Mario Vargas Llosa, convened to study the deaths of several journalists on a trip to the rural department of Ayacucho. What came from it was what critics called an essentialized and thoroughly inaccurate depiction of rural poverty, one that depended on the false assumption of distinctly separate indigenous or campesino societies, whose exclusion from the mainstream was cited as the fundamental reason for the violence (Theidon, 2013).

21. For a more complete history of this geography of imagination, refer to Chapter 1, "La Zona Quinta." It is also worth noting here, however, that the term "exotification" is often taken to mean the sexual fetishization of someone based on their ethnicity, race, or some other aspect of their heritage. The sexual connotations of the term map uncomfortably well onto the history of feminizing Latin America under the U.S. gaze, as well as the broader issues of both the gendering of violence and the violence of gendering.

22. Most notably, see Galeano (1971). The term "primitive accumulation" is a Marxist term referring to the initial creations of capital ownership, or the separation of control over the means of production. As Marx asserted, and Galeano illustrated in the Latin American context, "if money, according to Augier, 'comes into the world with a congenital blood-stained cheek,' capital comes dripping from head to foot, from every pore, with blood and dirt" (Marx, [1867] 1992: 925). In the Latin American context in particular, this primitive accumulation has often been tied into the construction of geographies imagined around the rubric of "cores" and "peripheries." So critical has this organization been, and so persistent the myth of their separation, that Rodolfo Stavenhagen (1981) made this the central feature of his *Between Underdevelopment and Revolution* (specifically in his chapter "Seven Fallacies About Latin America"), which detailed both the connections between these putatively separate areas of society and their continued misrecognition as such. On an even more global scale, scholars such as Frederick Cooper (2005) and Ann Stoler (1995) have advanced the view of colonial co-creation, that colonial powers themselves were shaped just as much by colonial

encounters as the colonized, a theory that fundamentally contradicts the illusion of their separation and difference from one another. For the geography of management of the hacienda systems in Colombia in particular, especially with regard to coffee cultivation, see again the historical narratives of Palacios (1980) and Bushnell (1993).

23. Fals Borda (1969).

24. Despite the general truth of this, it is worth noting that, like all sweeping generalizations, there have been critical counterexamples. Chief among them are the strands of liberation theology that radically sought to reorient the fundamental theology of the Church, in Colombia most notably through Camilo Torres Restrepo's efforts to reconcile revolutionary Marxism with Catholicism. Though not nearly as radical as Restrepo, even the priest who ran the main parish in Usme during the period of my fieldwork expressed similar sympathies.

25. To reiterate a point from Chapter 2, "Possible," this again echoes Pateman's (1988) observations about the more intimate patriarchal relations that have often undergirded the social contracts of modern liberal states. The centrality of the family in the legal imagination of the Colombian state is no exception, as is evidenced even in the country's 1991 constitution, as previously cited. Orders of protection given at the Comisarías de Familia remind citizens of this, saying that "one cannot forget that the 5th and 42nd articles of the Constitution have defined the family as the basic institution and fundamental nucleus of society." The significance of this, drawing a direct analogy between the sovereignty of the state and sovereignty within the home, in particular as mediated by perpetrators of partner violence, is a topic to which I return later in this chapter.

26. In one such encounter, I witnessed a community event, one that had been dedicated to celebrating Usme's involvement in the national peace process, devolve into a raging debate over the district mayor's lack of accountability and attempts to portray funding from the city's budget as "gifts" to the district. If sovereignty, so said Mauss ([1925] 1969), is the refusal of the gift, the community members at this meeting seemed intent to show that sovereignty is also refusing to allow someone to call an obligation a gift in the first place.

27. It is worth mentioning here that not all exercises of power have been so benevolent, unfortunately. One of the most high-profile examples has been the case of the *falsos positivos* (the "false positives"). That scandal involved members of the national military who killed residents from the poorer districts in Bogotá, clothed them in the uniforms of guerrillas, and brought their bodies to the countryside where they could be used to inflate the statistics of the number of combatants killed. In the context of an ongoing political conflict, one might argue that the actions at the heart of this scandal themselves constitute a state of exception to the normal paternalistic obligations of the state, even if the actions were initially secret from the public's knowledge. That they were committed at all indicates an exception both to the public rule of protection though, one that was concurrently fulfilled by positioning military bases on the outskirts of Usme, as well as to the norms that dictate who is allowed to be harmed when such states of exception are declared.

28. This community meeting space was far from unique, and from La Lira to Requilina, old haciendas in Usme have been preserved and converted into meeting spaces or community centers, like a state-run art space for children.

29. The páramo is a high-altitude moorland. A particularly interesting read on the history of the Páramo de Sumapaz that surrounds Usme, and its ecological significance, is *El gran misterio del Páramo de Córcega* by Luis Antonio Guzmán Celis (2003).

30. Two particularly comprehensive histories of this are Schoultz's (1998) *Beneath the United States* and Loveman's (2012) *No Higher Law.* Hunt's (1987) *Ideology and U.S. Foreign Policy* also contributes meaningfully to this understanding, including the racialized and gendered dimensions that this took.

31. Both quotes are from Schoultz (1998: 1).

32. It is little wonder in light of these kinds of attitudes that one of the leaders of the new Gran Colombia, Simon Bolívar, was exceedingly wary of the possibility of a meddling and disproportionately powerful United States. Because of those fears, he argued at the inception of the newly liberated South American states for regional cohesion in the face of such a prospect, going so far as to prophesize that "the United States seems destined by Providence to plague America with torments in the name of freedom" (quoted in Holden and Zolov, 2010: 18).

33. Perhaps there is no greater example of the United States' pretensions to sovereignty in the hemisphere than the Monroe Doctrine. The doctrine, beginning in 1823, envisioned the hemisphere not only as a political bloc vis-à-vis Europe but also as one for which the United States was the self-declared supreme protector and authority. That this has been invoked from the Monroe to Roosevelt to Reagan presidencies is evidence of the longevity of this general policy of the United States toward regional affairs. Though declared officially "dead" by John Kerry in 2013 (K. Johnson, 2013), the contours etched by nearly two centuries of its existence continued to shape regional relations, even under the Obama administration (see Weisbrot, 2011).

34. The case of the Panama Canal is, of course, by no stretch an isolated or unusual event in the history of U.S.-Latin American relations. Though not an exhaustive list by any stretch, other notable examples might include the Bidlack Treaty with Colombia (then New Granada) that in many ways preceded the intervention for construction of the canal; the Mexican War and the cessation of half of Mexico to the United States in the Treaty of Guadalupe-Hidalgo; the Bay of Pigs; Operation PBSUCCESS; Operation Condor; the Iran-Contra Affair; and Plan Colombia. With regard to the Panama Canal, it is worth also noting that the construction itself was a project of signaling U.S. superiority, particularly in the scientific expertise and industrial ability required to carry out an endeavor of such scale (Greene, 2010). Personally obsessed with rugged masculinity himself, Roosevelt was keen to take any photo opportunities that placed himself with the massive machinery used to dig the canal, and in doing so he made it evident that the project was also one of staking a masculinized view of U.S. strength in the region.

35. "The News Reaches Bogotá" was published in 1903 in the *New York Herald.* "The World's Constable" was published in *Judge* magazine in 1905.

36. Retracing the broader arcs of changes in land tenure and agricultural methods of coffee cultivation are the works of Safford and Palacios (2002) and Roseberry (1995), whereas Hough and Bair (2012) provide an overview of the role that U.S. foreign policy played in this from the 1960s onward. For further illustration of this intricate involvement, particularly illuminating moments are Kennedy's (1962) address to the Organization of American States in which he argued that the stability of coffee prices needed to become a major focus for regional development; the involvement of the U.S. Department of Agriculture (1968) in developing technical guidance for this; the eventual reflection of these changes in official publications by the FNC promoting these practices for coffee growers in Colombia (FNC, 1979); and eventu-

ally the involvement of the World Bank to leverage more durable institutional changes to promote this kind of agriculture (Thomas, 1985). Peculiarly, given this history, it is also interesting to note that, just under twenty years later, the World Bank (2003) began turning to coffee cultivation in Colombia explicitly as a model for building "peace" through political economic intervention.

37. See again the discussion of this in Chapter 1, including how the transition to monocropping, far from a mere technical distinction, is one of great importance to the vulnerability of coffee farmers during periods of global price instability.

38. Admittedly, in light of the accumulated failures of this approach, the discourse on the means to address illicit drug use has begun to change, and a wide variety of Latin American leaders and influential thinkers played central roles in that process (see, for instance, Global Commission on Drug Policy, 2011). For a more detailed history of Plan Colombia, see Kirk (2003). Subsequent evaluation of the program has revealed that regardless of any changes in the total cultivated area for coca, the program has failed to limit the production of the coca crop in any way, but it has created a number of undesirable consequences in attempting to do so (see Steiner and Vallejo, 2010). Fumigation has caused health and economic problems in affected populations; the cultivation has simply become more widely distributed, dispersed among existing crops; and the presence of U.S. agents has continued to foment anti-U.S. sentiments. Most recently this manifested in the 2013 national strikes in Colombia in which farmers in Catatumbo initially protested the killing of their crops as a part of anti-coca cultivation programs.

39. Anthropologist Lesley Gill (2004) has written most extensively on the history of the SOA, from its formation to its teaching methods and the effects that it has had on target countries. Through her analysis she has shown that the indoctrination of students at the SOA in many ways reflects what is actually mainstream U.S. policy, such as the promotion of consumer societies and the exportation of the "war on drugs." What is "aberrant" from those mainstream policies are primarily the actual military tactics that have been taught or otherwise promoted, inclusive of but not limited to torture, disappearance, and other forms of violent repression. As such, the SOA stands as an intriguing example of how the United States was able to partially transfer culpability for war crimes in the hemisphere to the domestic governments of the countries in which they were committed, and, by doing so, to partially preserve the appearance of benevolence in its continued project for regional hegemony.

40. The claim that social logics of gendered power hold across scales of society is hardly a novel one and indeed has been the subject not only of much theoretical development but also of practical invocation in the resistances against such regimes. Particularly relevant to this context is the history of authoritarianism in Chile and its relationship to gender-based partner violence, especially as explored by Matear (2007) and Parson (2013) with regard to both the justifications for authoritarian arrangements as well as the resistances against them. From dominant claims of the heteronormative family as the basic nucleus of society to counterhegemonic calls for "democracy in the country and in the home," that authoritarianism has held salience across social scales has been well established. This focus on paternalistic ideologies examines another facet of such multiscalar motifs of sovereign power, including the roles that perpetrators of partner violence play in stabilizing them through the violence that they commit.

41. Faludi (2000: 9) captures this sentiment best of all, based on her observation in batterers' groups. She comments, "There was almost something absurd about these men struggling,

week after week, to recognize themselves as dominators when they were so clearly domi-nated, done in by the world. 'That wheel is misnamed,' a laid-off engineer ruefully told the counselors. 'It should be called the powerlessness and out-of-control wheel.' The men had probably felt in control when they beat their wives, but their everyday experience was of being controlled—a feeling they had no way of expressing because to reveal it was less than mascu-line, would make each of them, in fact, 'no man at all.'" In light of this, some of the most ex-citing interventions for partner violence globally are those that directly address experiences of racism or colonialism, such as the Men as Partners program in South Africa that deals di-rectly with apartheid and the work of Sharon Spencer, a Maori woman who has built a cur-riculum in New Zealand that directly addresses colonialism and its cumulative toll (both programs are cited in Greig, 2007). This view also concords with the observations of Colom-bian scholar José Rozo Gauta (2011) in relating partner violence on the altiplano of Colombia to experiences of colonialism, as well as work conducted in the United States within Native American groups that have developed frameworks built around the concept of "historical unresolved grief" (Brave Heart and DeBruyn, 1998; see also Shkilnyk, 1985, for an ethno-graphic illustration of a similar context).

42. Of course, doing so also does not write off the imperative of accountability: that those who commit abuse against their partners are accountable to that violence and to the people upon whom they have inflicted harm.

43. As justification for this, Scott (1990) rightly offers the example of the Russian revo-lution in which early articulations of dissent against the tsar were not made on Marxist grounds, but rather that the tsar was failing in his own self-prescribed duties. Early on it was not that the premise of having a tsar was faulty, but rather that the tsar that they had at the time was bad at being one. While this is certainly a reasonable argument, it does miss the fact that at some point fundamentally different alternatives do need to be proposed, and those who lodge those early criticisms may not be the best equipped to have developed them.

44. That includes abuse toward their children. In a number of instances I witnessed the survivors of intimate abuse articulate surprisingly similar views on authority, the logics under which they were themselves victimized, with regard to the violence they had commit-ted against their children, actions that had required the attention of the Comisarías de Fa-milia for redress. It is also because of instances like these that the creation of "hierarchies of suffering" is such a potentially dangerous game to play; by doing so we run the risk of disre-garding the vulnerability and violence committed against victims of partner violence in light of the abuse that they in turn may have committed against their own children. It is a game that no one wins and one that ironically recapitulates the logics that abusive men mobilize to justify the abuse of their partners in the first place.

45. This basic insight is something that finds echoes throughout a number of theories, albeit under a different set of names. Under Gramsci's (1992) original formulation, hegemony was maintained, if not ever fully achieved, by manufacturing the "spontaneous consent" among some of the subaltern, a view that has its roots in Marx's ([1867] 1992) notion of "false consciousness." That is to say, relations of power cannot be maintained only through coercive means but also require the elaboration of a set of ideologies that people can buy into and thus support the system of relations as the natural order of things. The major contribution of Ar-endt's *On Violence* (1970) was to propose that power did not require the instrumentalized force of violence because true power was dominance that did not require "violent" mainte-nance. What Arendt was proposing though was basically the same notion as Gramsci, only

trading the term "hegemony" for "power" and therefore showing that overt violence by state systems reflected a *loss* of power and legitimacy. Later, Bourdieu (1977) would offer a similar set of insights in his theory of "symbolic violence," which referred to the many ways by which unequal relations of power were made to appear routine and even natural. The Comaroffs (1991), in their revisitation of Gramsci's original texts, made more explicit the difference between "hegemony" and "ideology." In their dissection, the former referred to ideas that were made so "natural" so as to remain uncontested, whereas the latter referred to ideas that had once again become critically examined. While each of these theories uses slightly different terminologies and leaves room open for theorizing the bases of social contestation in slightly different ways, they are all fundamentally similar ideas that are based in a notion of collective consciousness and unconsciousness where the more unconscious the logics of power remain, the more stable that system of power. Of further note is the influential theory of "hegemonic masculinities" (Connell and Messerschmidt, 2005) that directly ties this lineage of Gramscian origins to understanding power in gender relations, as referenced earlier in this chapter.

46. Across different fields of inquiry, these unifying processes have been referred to under a number of different names, most notably as "social dominance orientation" by social psychologists such as James Sidanius (Sidanius and Pratto, 1999) or as "dialectical unities" by Angela Davis (1998), who has illustrated extensively the intersections of gender, race, and capitalism. In truth it is not clear that the confluence of systems of power such as racism and male supremacy constitutes a true "dialectical unity," as Davis called it, given that, despite the tensions that can exist between these systems, they are not necessarily diametrically opposed and therefore not in direct contradiction. To call these systems a dialectical unity requires a more nuanced interpretation of Hegelian dialectics that does not necessitate the middle term—the "dialectical moment"—to be an absolute negation of the first term but merely something "set against" it, a contrary but not a contradiction (a more liberal interpretation of the *entgegensetzen*). In either case, as Davis herself points out, what is more important to recognize is that these systems serve to mutually reinforce one another *through* the very tensions that bind them. Ultimately what really matters is this mutual reinforcement, whose consequence is to privilege a particular subset of the populous, not the specific matter of whether or not these two axes of power constitute a dialectical unity in the strictest sense. It is also why the notion of "surrogate power" may prove to be useful: it can identify, through the concrete actions of the perpetrators of violence, the actual lived practices by which these systems of power come to interdigitate and mutually reinforce and, in doing so, identify the unstable nexuses of power that they are liable to create through this very process.

47. The more over-determining theories to which Scott was responding are those that either are rooted in a very orthodox Marxism based on the one-sided manufacturing of "false consciousness" or are provided by some of Marx's and Gramsci's subsequent interlocutors, such as Althusser's (1971) notion of "Ideological State Apparatuses," both of which left almost no room for conceiving of social contestation. While Scott has convincingly argued against the most extreme versions of these theories, it is worth noting that his critiques should not be understood as actual refutations of the theories of Gramsci, Arendt, Bourdieu, or others. With regard to Gramsci in particular, it appears that Scott has grossly misread his notion of the idea. Though in *Weapons of the Weak*, Scott (1987) acknowledges that his critique may be more directly applicable to later works such as Althusser's, this nuance is absent from *Domination and the Arts of Resistance* (Scott, 1990), which represents his major theoretical work. Scott appears to have misread Gramsci in two critical ways. First, Gramsci's notion of theory

was that it must always be historically located in a particular moment and must be account-able to that context alone (see Hall, 1986). In this sense, theory to Gramsci was not a search for transcendental truth but rather a means to abstract and understand particular moments in human experience. As such, his notion of hegemony was not meant to apply to slavery, feudalism, or any other political economic system other than capitalism and the struggle against it. Nevertheless, these other systems are some of the core bases of Scott's criticism. Given this misreading, it is less surprising that Scott actually unintentionally endorses a Gramscian view of hegemony when he outlines the conditions for a "paper thin hegemony." In this situation, Scott argues that hegemony could only be achieved in the extremely rare circumstances where communication between subjugated people is not possible or, more likely, in a situation where one had the ability to advance enough in the existing system so as to justify buying into it. What Scott has missed is that the myth of social advancement and opportunity is one of the foundational myths of a capitalist system, the situation in which Gramsci developed his theory. Second, Gramsci argued that hegemony was always a *struggle* and not the kind of fait accompli that would preclude contestation. This sensibility about the degree of colonizing consciousness largely renders moot Scott's questioning of how such a theory could allow for social change.

48. If this again sounds familiar to Pateman's (1988) social/sexual contract, it should. Pate-man's whole concept is that the reason why people would consent to the kind of social contract that has built many modern states is precisely because it first rests on an assumed set of gen-dered relationships that privilege the men who were originally allowed into the citizenry. The basic idea underlying the concept of "surrogate power" here is very similar—relating the rea-sons why someone would buy into a broader system of sovereignty if it meant that they could advantage themselves on a more intimate level—but extends more broadly and, importantly, highlights how this kind of surrogacy can function to bring together and bind other axes of power in society (see above). Whereas the social/sexual contract is expressly related to ques-tions of governance and the legitimacy of the sovereign state in particular, surrogate power is concerned with sovereignty in a more generalized sense, as illustrated here.

Chapter 4

Notes to epigraphs: The first epigraph is an excerpt from "Profecias" (Prophecies) by the Usme-based rap group Alma de Negro. The name of the group is intended as a double enten-dre between "black soul" (*alma de negro*) and ADN (Spanish for DNA), the inseparable threads of spirit and body. The lyrics translate as "A battle is announced / Like every day / Just hunger, wars, death / That end life / As in the search for power / Man destroys himself." The quotation by Aleksandr Solzhenitsyn is from his 1970 Nobel Lecture.

1. Drawing on a long career working as a psychiatrist in the U.S. prison system, James Gilligan (1997) has written extensively about the role that shame, and shaming social sys-tems, plays in interpersonal violence. In particular, Gilligan draws notice to the idea that shame is not just about error or fallacy as it applies to our personal character, our identity, but that shame is fundamentally about that shortcoming being seen by others. That which is shameful is that which must be hidden, from the view of others and often even from view by ourselves, and while this makes engaging people on issues of shame difficult in practice, it also imbues moments in which that visibility is allowed with an added significance.

2. As previously referenced in the Introduction, Theidon (2013) has argued convincingly on how it is impossible to maintain a "neutral" position while engaging with experiences of

violence. Speaking from her own experiences working on the legacies of the political conflicts in Perú and Colombia, she asks how it is possible to remain within a community, after the soldiers leave, if one tries to maintain a detached stance during moments of crisis. While her work relates more directly to militarized violence, her observations on neutrality remain relevant here for partner violence as well. One could similarly ask how it is possible to honestly engage survivors of abuse throughout the course of a research project if one has also engaged perpetrators of violence in an uncritical manner. This is not to imply that one must take an antagonistic stance toward perpetrators of partner violence, but if those encounters serve mostly as opportunities for self-affirmation and the continuation of justification, rather than opening a space for honest reflection, then what has really been accomplished? What has even really been learned in the process?

3. Arguing against a life-stage form of analysis, Jennifer Johnson-Hanks (2002) has argued instead for an orientation to "vital conjunctures." Highlighting the fluidity and indeterminacy of important events, she argues for a focus on aspirations rather than the events themselves as a means of interpreting how personal trajectories change at particular moments, and how this helps us to understand the interconnection of the "personal" with the "social" in nonreductionist ways. This general orientation to analysis has already been evident in the earlier consideration of Luz Elena's life in Chapter 2, focusing on particular moments, such as the Bogotazo and her quitting one of her first jobs, always with attention to how relational constructs of gender were shaped in these moments or how her desires affected her evolving sense of self throughout these crucial experiences. Here, with regard to Diego, again this approach proves useful, finding moments of great transition in his life and looking to how and why he mediated them in the ways that he did.

4. See again Salcedo (2008).

5. Once while working in the Comisaría de Familia, I was party to an audience that dealt with a particularly violent relationship. When I later expressed surprise that the survivor's daughters had played active roles in facilitating that abuse, the psychologist who had conducted the interviews explained that the survivor had been accused of infidelity and, as she believed, in Colombia infidelity is often considered a worse offense than partner violence.

6. It is worth also noting some peculiar parallels between Diego's experience, as presented here, and that of Carolina, who had survived two intensely violent relationships, whose story was discussed previously in Chapter 2, "Possible." First, both of their experiences of migrating to Bogotá were indirect ones, more protracted processes than sudden relocations to the city. Second, it was their move to Bogotá that contributed to their further social isolation. On the one hand, this meant a geographical separation from family supports that were already tenuous at best, and in both cases this was even true with particular regard to their affective relationships with their mothers. On the other hand, in moving to the city, they both found themselves in a new and frightening environment, one in which their early internalizations of the imperative to "no dar papaya" and experiences of gossiping neighbors left them unwary of others and only exacerbated their social disconnection. In Carolina's case this was all further compounded by the purposive isolation that both of her partners sought to effect, but the parallels between hers and Diego's stories are still nontrivial. What is remarkable is not just the similarities between them but the very obviously different consequences of them. In Diego's case it was an important basis of what was at stake for him in *committing* partner violence, and in Carolina's it was crucial in understanding her vulnerability to becoming a victim of it.

7. While Diego's original experiences of loss were not the result of intentional violence, for many in Colombia they have been. For the millions of Colombians who have left their homes and ended up in districts like Usme, it has not been accidental loss so much as violent dispossession. Even for those not directly affected by the political conflict, dislocation and loss too frequently are the violent consequences of human machinations. This was the case for another perpetrator of partner violence, discussed in Chapter 3, "Permissible," the person whose abusive stepfather had dispossessed him of any sense of belonging or security within his home long before he "voluntarily" left it at the age of eleven. If it is possible to see partner violence as itself a form of dispossession against those who survive it, then seeing these broader pictures can help to reframe it as one dispossession within much longer chains, ones that do not have their beginning or end within confined spaces like the "home."

8. The role of gossip in partner violence, like the role of migration and isolation, again bears a sort of mirror-image reflection to the stories told by some survivors of abuse, not the least of which was Carolina whose isolation was further maintained by her fear of gossiping neighbors and friends. Gossip as a key preoccupation and limiting feature in the lives of survivors of abuse has been reflected in other research on partner violence, for example Bhadra's (2012) examination of partner abuse, self-silencing, and depression in a Punjabi community near Vancouver, British Columbia. This preoccupation with gossip on the part of perpetrators of abuse was also a feature that became familiar to me during my time working within the Comisarías de Familia, a consistent theme that emerged in the audiences that involved abusive men. Between the stories of Carolina and Diego, in equal yet opposite ways, the isolation that they experienced—rooted in fear of others, mistrust of others for reasons such as gossip, geographic distance from family, among others—played into their respective experiences with partner violence. For Carolina it was a principal shaping of her vulnerability to it; for Diego it was a central feature in his stakes in committing it.

9. Finding transportation like this is not a totally uncommon means of getting around the city, and in my experience it was usually women and their young children whom I saw riding in the passenger seats of commercial vehicles.

10. In other contexts it has been found that strangulation is one of the highest predictors of escalation to partner homicide (Campbell et al., 2007). While Diego was not strangling Luisa in the typical sense, the general feature of asphyxiation, intentional or not, certainly would seem to indicate that his physical violence toward her had escalated considerably and to a very dangerous degree.

11. Here I mean vaginal or anal penetrative rape. Though Luisa herself did not label Diego reaching his fingers into her mouth as penetrative rape, one could certainly say that by breaching the boundaries of the body, it would qualify as such.

12. It is worth noting also that it was not just the bare fact of her leaving him, but the very visible manner in which she did so. If it was one thing for neighbors to see utilities companies post notices on his front door, it was another for the Comisaría de Familia to show up in a truck and have his neighbor inform him of what was happening. This is especially true given how careful Diego had been in trying to keep neighbors from even hearing any of their fights. As will be explored further in Chapter 6, it also has to be noted that this is a powerful indicator of the kind of presence that the Comisaría system has in intimate relationships and the kinds of new possibilities that it helps to open for survivors of abuse. Without real forms of accountability, it is unlikely that partner violence could be its own undoing, as discussed in

previous chapters, and that the Comisaría system opens up new avenues of support for survivors is a contribution that again cannot be underestimated.

13. That Luisa was able to confront Diego critically about his abuse, within their home, and in the presence of an outsider, I took to be a significant marker. Even if she did so through the means of humor, which almost always relies on a fair share of truth, I took this to signify that, at least however temporarily, the intervention of Luisa's order of protection had shifted the balance of power in their relationship.

14. While the names here are pseudonyms, their son's name was in fact a derivation of Luisa's real name, and the idea for that appeared to be Diego's. That Diego was so eager to name their son after Luisa was interesting in and of itself, something that could have spoken to any number of feelings of guilt or desire for symbolic reparation.

15. It bears noting that once again the perpetration of partner violence here, or in this case at least the imminent specter of it, is being rationalized by Diego as an undesirable but necessary means of action in the interest of a child's welfare. It harkens directly back to the consideration of paternalistic terms of justification, explored in greater detail in Chapter 3.

16. In situations like this, my tendency was to follow the lead of survivors of violence like Luisa, to take their cues on where our conversations led, whether or not we revisited topics relating to violence. My general approach was to ask questions that could be used as an invitation to revisit these topics, but could also be used to follow more banal lines of conversation. Most of all, my assumption was that survivors of abuse were the most adept at assessing the risks of raising these issues, at what times, in what company, and to follow their lead was to avoid unintentionally creating dangerous situations for them. The downside to such an approach was that, by not provoking talking about such issues more frequently, I was also implicitly contributing to the maintenance of silence regarding them.

17. One of the reasons why I tried to never arrive unannounced, beyond the more obvious issues of courtesy, was to avoid risking a scenario in which I would arrive when Diego was not home, possibly creating a scenario that would appear improper and, in doing so, could cause danger for Luisa. The only reason that I did not quickly excuse myself on this particular occasion, considering that Diego was not home at the time, was that Luisa's mother and sister were present, and as such the risk for any sort of misunderstanding seemed much lower.

18. One of the biggest ethical considerations in conducting this research was how to respond to disclosures of continued partner violence, not child abuse but violence between adult partners. As many partner violence organizations counsel, I followed the path of supportive listening and helping if desired, but I avoided at all costs pushing victims into any particular kind of action. Doing so carries the risk of recapitulating the dynamics of abuse that victims are already facing, taking control away from survivors in determining their trajectories. It also seriously risks causing direct harm by triggering an escalation in violence if the survivor is not prepared yet to leave.

19. This, of course, is hardly the only meaning of sovereignty, and the ways in which sovereignty is not just a matter of constrictive control but also a productive, generative operation of power is a topic that will be explored throughout the following chapter.

20. The pursuit of creating these boundaries is also what gives rise to the limits of the violent fiction called the "domestic," which, as is also the case at the international scale of relationships between the boundaries of sovereign nations, is not a pre-given but rather the product of what is often violent contestation.

21. Even more eloquently than James Gilligan's (1997) insights on shame, writer Milan Kundera (1999: 254) earlier claimed that "the basis of shame is not some personal mistake of ours, but the ignominy, the humiliation we feel that we must be what we are without any choice in the matter, and that this humiliation is seen by everyone."

22. This contradiction is a necessary one because, at the very least, in order to be in a position of control, one must have someone or something to control. To stake one's identity in any way on having such a position is to inherently rely on the subject that is controlled; through every exercise of control one becomes increasingly dependent on that very relationship. In other words, the position of any person or group in power is necessarily dependent on the maintenance of that relationship of domination: it is a key defining aspect of its identity. Unsurprisingly then, this basic notion is reflected throughout a number of social theories such as Marx's entire formulation of class relations and conflict, subsequent interlocutors who have advanced Marxist-feminist critiques, and Derrida's body of work that expounded on the violence of hierarchies. As the intimate experiences of partner violence make clear, gender-based violence is no exception to this pattern. Indeed much of feminist theory can, of course, also be read through this lens of dependence underlying a position of power, in the barest sense even through the recognition that any identification of "masculinity" has always required the cocreation of related constructs, not the least of which has been the notion of "femininity" and then various forms of its inferiorization.

23. With *In Search of Respect*, Bourgois (1995) has most notably written extensively about the role of respect in interpersonal violence and the gendering of masculine roles and expectations, complementing the work by Gilligan on the related notion of shame. While closely related, the notion of shame has more direct relevance to the experiences of Diego, considering how avoidant he always was of talking about the actual violence that he had committed. He rarely, unless he did not see his actions as violent, willingly talked about it. The violence he committed was not something in which he took pride, at least to the extent that he ever gave me any indication, and to the contrary his reaction to it was, if anything, shame. This was consistent with the ethnographic insights of Gutmann (1996) working in Mexico City, where he noted that men might often boast of violence against other men but would rarely boast about abusing their intimate partners. Indeed, unemployment is often noted as a risk factor for partner violence, across multiple contexts (Jewkes, 2002). Diego's shame in light of this experiences illustrates how it is predicated on a very particular notion of respect, a conditional one in which respectability is made contingent on achieving a certain kind of life. We could call this situation an experience of shame within a particular "economy of respect," a term that we can furthermore take to have two meanings. On the one hand, Diego's poverty and prior inability to save money cannot be pinned simply on wasteful spending; it was also the result of his living within a political economic system characterized by a particular "moral economy." Moral economy in this sense refers to how E. P. Thompson (1971) and others have used the term: as a question of "just price," who gets paid, how much, and why. Diego's debt and relative material insecurity in other words are inseparable from the broader political economic system in which his starkly inferior income had been justified. In another sense though, Diego's shame is related to the *economization* of respect. In this sense it is the *rationing* of self-respect and the rationalizations that justify doing so. The contingency of that self-respect then is predicated on meeting certain normative, and intensely gendered, expectations. Failing to meet them, as Diego did, meant deprivation of not just material resources

but also of moral ones of self-worth as well. Considering his shame in this manner helps to see how systems of masculine domination based on paternalistic pretenses can also be dangerous to the men wielding those justifications. When they fail to live up to their own agendas, the consequences for their own self-respect can be dire, with all of its incumbent consequences for themselves and, most of all, the intended victims of their violence.

24. For the relationship between social learning theory and aggression, see Bandura (1978). What is significant about social learning theory is that it helps to understand why someone might come to deal with psychologically threatening situations with aggression, but it does not help to understand why certain situations might be "threatening" in the first place. The purpose of exploring in detail the social origins of Diego's dependences on his partners, and why he attempted to conceal them, is to understand precisely that underlying dynamic.

25. Freud's notions of eros and aggression can be divided into two stages: early and late. Earlier in his career, aggression was thought of as resulting from the blocking of libidinal impulses—*eros*, or the drive of productive unification—essentially representing a dualism where one derived from the other. Later he proposed a second drive, the death drive (later termed *thanatos*), and within later Freudian dynamics, it is important to note that the aggression/destruction relation is not just a simple by-product of frustrated eros. In his later thought, both eros and thanatos are held to be satisfying experiences in and of themselves, and therefore they are both consistent with Freud's pleasure principle. Though this latter formulation of eros/thanatos subsequently fell out of favor, his earlier theory was further advanced outside of the field of psychodynamics by Dollard and others (1939), who theorized that virtually all aggression derived from the frustration of some impulse, or, as they framed it, the "interference of a goal response." In turn, Miller and colleagues were later countered by Bandura's (1978) social learning theory of aggression, claiming that subsequent research had shown that frustration was not necessary for aggression, frustration did not necessarily lead to aggression, and aggression was only one of many possible responses that we can learn in order to cope with psychologically threatening situations. Much later after Freud, R. W. Connell (1987) would again pick up on the psychodynamic notion of cathexis and implement it in understanding gendered power and violence in a very different manner. Including it as one of three core structures, along with "labor" and "power," cathexis became for Connell the means of characterizing the patterning of emotional investments, and as such the means by which to connect gendered structures to practice. While not invoking the particular dynamics of eros and aggression developed elsewhere, because Connell's theory deals intricately with gendered violence, this formulation marks another means of connecting these psychodynamic principles to particular forms of aggression.

26. For a broad theoretical consideration of this issue, see again Arendt (1970). Focusing more on historical patterns of changing gendered roles and identities, this is also the reasoning for partner violence that Gutmann (1996) offers in brief consideration of the issue, embedded in his broader study of masculinity in Mexico City.

27. As previously discussed in Chapter 2, *Abusive Endings* by DeKeseredy and others (2017) brings together much of the existing evidence for this phenomenon and the main theories for understanding it.

28. Nancy Fraser (2013) has referred to the notion of interdependence, along with care, as previously being one of the core tenets of earlier feminist movements. The obverse to this observation is that the denial of interdependence, such as making it an object of shame, could perhaps be seen as a core defining aspect of more toxic forms of masculinity.

29. Of course it is not just shame that interrupts the bond of a positive mutual interdependence, but it can be one of the more potent ones. We could also count a lack of trust or accountability among the other important means of promoting this kind of fragmentation. In either case, this has obvious implications outside of just partner violence. For example, take the notion of the "myth of individualism" in many capitalist societies. When scrutinized, by discouraging the acknowledgment that any achievement is a profoundly shared accomplishment, the myth of individualism appears to be nothing more than the even older mantra of "divide and conquer" carried out to its logical extreme.

Chapter 5

Note to epigraph: The epigraph is an excerpt from "Guerra Mental" ("Mental War") by Alma de Negro. The lyrics translate as "Mental revolution / Fight for authority / Control of the ability to send or execute / The power to manipulate nervous systems / The emotions of another being, and so have / The picture of any situation / This is the objective of such a revolution / Mental war, war (war, war) / Mental war, war (war, war)."

1. This focus on tensions and their creativity is reflected broadly, and what I want to highlight here is the indeterminacy of the directions of the products of those tensions, the multitude of possible vectors that can lead away from even a single origin. And while Hegelian dialectics are most often associated with the idea of creative contradiction, as will be further discussed, it is worth noting that many others have recognized this dynamic while not framing it in so rigid a manner. Dorinne Kondo (1990: 224), as noted in the Introduction, has spoken of personhood as not only "shot through with contradictions" but that those contradictions represent "*creative* tensions." Their creativity is reminiscent of Deleuze's (1997) ideas of "combating" and the process of personhood as "becoming" through the articulation of forces that cross the self. Of peculiar interest to me with regard to these contradictions and their creativity has been the notion of "han" that Korean author Pak Kyongni (1994: n.p.) described as "both sadness and hope at the same time. You can think of Han as the core of life, the pathway leading from birth to death . . . the original contradiction facing all living things, and hope comes from the will to overcome the contradiction." Though I cannot necessarily agree that all of life can be reduced to a single contradiction, the notion that life is itself a product of underlying tensions is an idea of particular relevance here.

2. Of note, framing this as a motif played out at various scales is intentionally meant to indicate an orientation to complexity and emergent systems, a perspective that automatically rules out any sort of reductionist framework.

3. Without delving into a lengthy deconstruction of the Hegelian dialectical philosophy, it is worth noting that the mode of thinking I am suggesting here finds common ground with dialectics in two important ways: (1) contradictions are held to be generative sources and not oppositions to be discarded, and (2) consistent with Hegel's intended understanding of them, the elements that comprise these oppositions are held to be in *simultaneous* tension but do not represent an A-to-B-to-C progression; the moments that connect them are more the "product-moment" variety and not points along a linear continuum of time. Diverging from dialectical modes of thought, this approach has little interest in the series of largely binary diametric oppositions and sublation, the "negation of the negation," that constitute the three classic "moments" of Hegel's dialectics in particular, or the relatively limited teleologies of the products of these tensions that even Adorno's (1973) "negative dialectics" only began to expand upon.

4. This stands in particular contrast to the limited teleologies of dialectical thought, be it the progression to higher universalisms, the progress of dialectical historical materialism, or its negation as in Adorno's (1973) negative dialectics. The notion of pluripotency here serves as a reminder that the potential products of these fields of tension are many, and each is exquisitely sensitive to the broader contexts in which they are created. To understand them therefore requires a far more nuanced and situated view, one open to a much higher degree of possibility and, consequently, unpredictability.

5. As previously stated, the specific term "tengentic" is not what is most important here, though it is the simplest term I have found to describe this approach. What matters is that we transcend the unnecessary restrictions of a formal dialectical method while maintaining the fundamental insight of dialectics that contradictions are themselves generative tensions, and what matters is what those tensions are generative of, and to what ends. What an expanded approach offers, as illustrated here, is the opportunity to view these tensions as themselves caught within a complex web, not organized into a neat hierarchy, and to recognize that the products of these tensions have the ability to shoot off in any number of directions depending on the broader social context within which they are enacted. Crucially, it also opens up opportunities to then ask how these tensions can be re-articulated, or at the very least re-directed toward producing different ends, as will be the focus in examining Jairo's life trajectory later on in this very chapter.

6. While not necessarily following directly from Arendt's formulation, and working from very different perspectives of their own, both Butler and Derrida have given similar prognoses to the issue of violence. In speaking about the violence inhering to the performative production of gender, Butler ([1990] 2006) has noted that the purpose of radically unsettling notions of the possible and the real is only to find *less* violent means of remaking them. Similarly, Derrida ([1967] 1978), in his essay "Violence and Metaphysics," noted that implicit in using language to categorize phenomena is a violence that, while we cannot eliminate it, we can at least be more "economical" in our use of it.

7. Indeed, any grand theory of "practice" (see Bourdieu, 1977) or "performativity" (see Butler, 1993) is in some way a basic recognition of this phenomenon, that power is always in a constant state of renewal.

8. The role of professionalized response systems to partner violence will be further explored in Chapter 6, but support for victims of violence extends far beyond these agencies to more informal networks as well, as was repeatedly evident in Chapter 2. A more comprehensive review of the role that informal networks of support play in addressing partner violence can be seen in Klein (2015).

9. As previously noted, Gilligan (1997) has written extensively about the role of shame in interpersonal violence, not only as an impulse for committing it in the first place but also as a consequence of those very actions.

10. This notion of identities emerging through the struggles for power, rather than preceding them, is best represented in the theories of Butler ([1990] 2006), herself following and building on Foucault as well as Thompson in his reconstruction of the formation of the English working class. As Thompson (1966: 9) famously said, "The working class did not rise like the sun at an appointed time. It was present at its own making."

11. Butler ([1990] 2006) again here, as well as Bourdieu (1977), has explored the means by which social process becomes internalized and taken for granted. It is Foucault though who has most directly examined this as it relates to the concept of sovereignty and the regulation

of social space, most notably in his essential work *Discipline and Punish* (1977). By invoking Foucault here I do not mean to suggest that we force a Foucauldian framework onto understanding partner violence though: that is not my interest. Rather I suggest that we take heed of the fundamental insight that guided a great portion of his work: that in order to understand the operations of sovereign power, we must go beyond notions of it as only repressive, coercive control. We must ultimately be able to understand it as a generative, productive set of relations as well. As such, this does not mean that we need to think of victims or perpetrators of partner violence as subjects of disciplinary power, governed by the internalized gaze of a panopticon as Foucault may have described. It does mean, however, that so long as we think of sovereignty, on the intimate and broader scales, only in terms of the ways in which social subjects are limited, restricted, we are likely to miss some of the important operations of sovereign power along the way.

12. We could therefore think of consciousness, at least on the scale of the person, as a kind of consequence of the connection between what in philosophy has been referred to as "intentionality" and what in neuroscience has been referred to as the "global workspace." For a summary of the Global Workspace Theory, see Robinson (2009). Combined with the most basic meaning of "intentionality" as directedness toward objects, this view of consciousness points in the direction of what William James ([1912] 2003) set forth as radical empiricism: a complex process that goes beyond the elemental experience of perception and includes making connections and constructing meaning. It is the way that connections are forged out of these particular intersections, the distributed mental representations that they create, and how these are intricately woven into broader social relations that is particularly relevant here.

13. That "other," of course, can also even be our own selves, a phenomenon critical to the possibility of self-consciousness, and one that finds its basis in any notion of an unconscious mind or a "stranger" within.

14. "Articulation" here refers to both senses of the term: (1) an ability to vocalize an idea or realization, and (2) the sense of forming a connection, a linkage if you will. It is also worth noting that what these encounters produce is not just "consciousness" but also "unconsciousness," a concept without which consciousness itself has little meaning. Consciousness by its very nature is an exceedingly ephemeral experience and as moments of consciousness become entrained into some kind of latent representation, be it long-term memories in the mind or institutions and spatial organizations of society, we create unconscious contours to our lived realities that continue to shape, outside of our conscious awareness, our experiences and uses of them.

15. Traditionally it has been the concept of "hegemony" and not "sovereignty" that has been placed in direct communication with any understanding of social consciousness, its formation, and its limits. By putting sovereignty into conversation with consciousness here I have no intention of suggesting a false equivalence between hegemony and sovereignty, or promoting a facile slippage between the two. Instead, what I wish to point out that is that sovereignty itself also has significant consequence in the emergence of consciousness, be it through the patterning of social encounters or the kinds of exercises of power that it allows. In other words sovereignty, or the search for it, is the process by which contours are formed in the landscape of possible connections, mental or social, the connections that form the basis for the articulations (the associations) that constitute consciousness. This focus on interaction and the amount and kinds of connection that are possible is reminiscent of Durkheim's ([1893] 1984) notion of "dynamic density" whereby the key is not just the number of people

but the intensity of interaction between them. Consciousness on the scale of the brain emerges from the *interaction*, the connection, between neurons, and consciousness on the social scales similarly emerges from the connections made between people. To pattern the kinds of connections that can be made, in the case of sovereign power by regulating the configuration of social space, is to give shape to the forms of consciousness that are ultimately able to emerge.

16. This notion of limiting the ability for social encounter and its incumbent effects on consciousness is one of the two exceptions that Scott (1990) made to his criticism of Gramscian, what Scott called "thick," hegemony, and it consequently forms another point of contact between the concepts of hegemony and sovereignty while not conflating the two. While Scott dismisses the idea on the grounds that no social isolation is ever total, even in the most extreme of circumstances, this only argues against the idea that any form of hegemony could ever be complete. The purpose of putting sovereignty into these kinds of terms is not just to swap terminology with Scott though, to echo his ideas with just a quick exchange of terms. For one, by bringing "sovereignty" into the picture, it brings a deeper sense of the spatialization of power into conversation with consciousness and our social theorizing on it. Second, as will be further discussed, bringing sovereignty into conversation here also raises the issue of how consciousness for the perpetrators of violence is also shaped, not just consciousness for the subaltern.

17. Mahmood (2001) gives an excellent illustration of why such a concept of agency is itself overly limiting.

18. The complex gendering of "social learning" and its relation to partner violence was driven home to me by a psychologist that I knew in Bogotá who practiced "logotherapy," a therapeutic approach created by Viktor Frankl (for an overview of logotherapy, see Frankl, 1967). In one conversation with her, she described to me a client of hers who was extremely possessive of his partner, obsessively inserting himself into every aspect of her life. When she asked him why he thought he did this, he related his treatment of his partner to how his mother and elder sisters had cared for him when he was young—intricately and assertively involved in all of his business. To him, "caring" meant "being on top of" another person. The purpose of noting this is neither to acknowledge this as an excuse for such possessive control nor to shift the "blame" for partner violence to the influential role of female figures in the lives of abusive men. It is instead to note how the social learning of abusive behaviors is gendered in complicated ways, and partner violence is in no way reducible to one particular "pathological" masculinity.

19. Asking him when he became an adult was quite intentional and something that I asked of all of my participants. The impetus for asking it was that adolescence in anthropology is commonly universally referred to as the period between the onset of puberty and the full assumption of adult roles (see Schlegel and Barry, 1991). Understanding when perpetrators of abuse felt they left adolescence and entered adulthood, the circumstances and relevant influences on them at the time, can potentially be just as helpful in contextualizing their worldviews and acts of violence as understanding early childhood experiences of loss or suffering.

20. As explored some in Chapter 1, militarized forms of masculinity work themselves out of those particular institutions and into the forms of masculinity represented in their broader societies, a process that has been thoroughly documented by a number of scholars (see again Enloe, 2000; Belkin, 2012). It is a process that we could perhaps see as a specific instance of a

broader one, one by which militarized practices of all sorts work themselves into the fabric of societies at large. This is what Scheper-Hughes and Bourgois (2004) referred to as "continuums of violence," what others have called "the militarization of everyday life" (seen also in Scheper-Hughes 2014), and to what Nordstrom (2004: 162) was referring when she said that "habits of war mar landscapes of peace."

21. The title of "return to center" is meant to reflect this transition for Jairo. What became a violent sort of reclamation of a "core" aspect of his legitimacy, his paternal role, was a kind of reclamation that was eerily similar to what happened on a national scale fifteen years earlier in the city of Bogotá. The motif is this: as Jairo's attention and energies continued to expand beyond the space where he based a core aspect of his identity (his home, his identity as a father), his authority within that core space continued to erode, and with it went his sovereign control over that space and the people within it. The analogous piece of history in Colombian politics was when the national government, via the national police and military, razed a large informal marketplace in the very center of Bogotá, "El Cartucho," some fifteen years earlier. The area had long ago been where the wealthiest citizens of Bogotá lived—it was located just a few blocks from the central plaza of the city where all three branches of the national government are represented—but as elites moved away from the city's center it became the focus of "urban decay" and occupation by the homeless and informal businesses. As part of a plan to "recuperate" Bogotá, El Cartucho was demolished and a park was built in its place. Other commenters (see Pérez, 2014) have noted that the reclamation of El Cartucho really was about restaking national sovereignty by regaining official control over the very core area of the capital city. As was true in a different way for the annexation of six municipalities in 1954, control for Bogotá again became a proxy for control over the country in its entirety. At the core of both Colombia's and Jairo's stories is again the question of sovereignty, and what they both illustrate is how the abandonment of a center of social life, especially one in which an aspect of one's identity has been founded, can often lead to violence through the attempts to (re)assume control over them.

22. Once again, this kind of circumstance underscores both the importance that paternal roles can play in violence between partners and also the centrality of children in the lifeworlds of abusive men.

23. That Valentina worked in the *Secretaría de Integración Social* (Secretary of Social Integration), the government department under which the Comisaría de Familia system is held, likely had a multitude of influences on both her taking prompt action and knowing how to do so effectively within a potentially complicated system.

24. Rarely have I ever heard of such a literal representation of what Wilfred Bion (1962) referred to as the "container" and the "contained," concepts that are still important today in psychodynamic therapy.

25. For the importance of motivation and psychotherapy effectiveness, see, for example, Hoglend (1999) or Ryan et al. (2011). Other factors typically considered to be important are the therapeutic relationship itself (the "therapeutic alliance") and the mode of psychotherapy employed.

26. The transformation of the meaning of paternalistic responsibility for Jairo points to the value in certain concepts as forming "hinges" in the process of change, pivot points around which new meaning can be invested without entirely discarding, at least initially, that important point of identification itself. In psychoanalytic terms this might be likened to a "transitional object," and while they could be criticized for in some way preserving some-

thing that that violence was previously based upon, in this case a particularly masculine form of identity, they nevertheless represent useful starting points in what is hopefully a more protracted process of de- and re-identification. In the end we have to start somewhere, and pivot points like these are as useful as anything else in consolidating those first steps away from the identities that make for violent relationships.

27. This primacy of the face-to-face is crucial to the philosophy of Emmanuel Levinas (1979). With regard to addressing violence in particular, while there is a long history of investigating the role that group dynamics can play in reformulating entrenched patterns of thought, one notable recent example is the work of Communities Engaging with Religion and Difference (CEDAR). Working with community and religious leaders from around the world, they have explored the vitality of the group as a means of engaging violence rooted in deep-seated prejudices, unexamined biases, and intolerance of indifference (see Seligman, Wasserfall, and Montgomery, 2016).

Chapter 6

Notes to epigraphs: The first epigraph is a graffiti message that was written along the main avenue, Avenida Caracas, just where the district of Usme began. It translates as "It's not love, it's not a crime of passion, in femicide, it's murder!" The second epigraph is an excerpt from Murray (1987: 128).

1. There is a vast body of literature examining organized and professionalized responses to partner violence, particularly within anthropology, a literature that takes on issues ranging from limitations in recognition to outright re-victimization, from the struggles to make global human rights discourses relevant in particular local contexts to the compromises made in professionalizing what were previously more grassroots movements. Some notable recent works addressing these issues include Engle-Merry (2006), Lazarus-Black (2007), Wies (2008), Wies and Haldane (2011), Parson (2013), and Beske (2016). That limitations exist through the elaboration of legal structures regarding gender-based violence and the professionalization of responses to it is a heavily explored area of interest. My purpose here is to look into the particular experience of the Comisarías de Familia in Colombia and to consider the implications of the aspirations of some of the Comisaría staff, ones that have arisen from their particular frustrations.

2. As previously cited, see Chinchilla (1992) and Parson (2013).

3. As previously noted in the Introduction, it is worth reiterating that the strong heteronormative framing of partner abuse here is reflective of the context in which over 90 percent of denuncia makers were women seeking protection from male partners.

4. Engle-Merry (2006) provides probably the furthest reaching discussion of this process of invoking global rights discourses in local politics, but with regard to Colombia in particular, Moncayo Plata (1997) provides specific evidence for how these global discourses did indeed inform national feminist movements in the setting of policy and the passage of new laws.

5. In Bogotá in particular, the system of Comisarías was first established in the following year under Accord 23 of 1990.

6. Matear (2007) and Parson (2013) discuss a similar framing in the Chilean context. It is worth mentioning again, as previously discussed in Chapter 1 and elsewhere, that this framing of the family as the fundamental nucleus of society was contemporaneous also with social movements and government programs to reframe intrafamilial dynamics of power. As such,

claiming that the family was the "nucleus of society" at this time should not be confused with a rote reproduction of "traditional" values, a return to authoritarianism, but rather, in some cases, as an echo of other Latin American movements for "democracy in the country and in the home."

7. Ruiz (2000: 11).

8. Violence as instrumentalized force is a direct borrowing from Arendt's (1970) formulation of power, violence, force, and authority.

9. The insistence on the necessity of the presence of both a maternal and paternal figure for the psychological and emotional well-being of children was a topic that came up frequently not just in the Comisarías, but in my conversations with perpetrators, survivors, and other members of the community as well. Ironically, the insistence on conciliation, intended for the "normal" development of children, sometimes played a role in perpetuating violent relationships between partners that, among many other things, negatively affected the children who were witness to them. While the insistence on the presence of a maternal and paternal figure was a consistent theme throughout my fieldwork in Usme, it should also be noted that this is hardly unique to that context and reflects a form of normative violence also found in many other places.

10. Critically, these must have happened no more than thirty days in the past. Anything beyond that is considered too dated and citizens were in my experience frequently turned away from any assistance unless they could claim more recent occurrences of violence.

11. Legally this meeting must occur within ten business days of the making of the denuncia. Given that the waiting time for other kinds of follow-up can extend to several months, this regulation is actually rather significant.

12. Indeed in the body of the text that makes up each order of protection document, there is a paragraph that is worth quoting at length: "The Constitutional Court affirms that it is the duty of the State to intervene in family relationships in order to prevent any violation of the fundamental rights of any person. This is to say that the protection by the State does not remain limited to the public field but also extends to the private space, as ordered in article 42 of the Constitution, according to which 'any form of violence in the family is considered to be destructive to its Harmony and Unity, and will be sanctioned according to the Law'" (capitalizations are from the original text).

13. This is as Moncayo Plata (1997) had previously argued, and Marta's invocation of this logic in our conversation was good evidence that this was not just some esoteric theoretical point. The contest over "public" and "private" is a vital and well-recognized purpose of what is at stake in the realization of the Comisaría system.

14. The Comisarías combine two elements of Weber's ([1922] 1968) theory: the institutional authority of technical, rationalized logics with a direct line to the legitimacy of armed actors of the state—the police—who can enforce those logics if necessary.

15. I am, of course, referring again to the notion that the social contract of many modern states is underwritten by a sexual/domestic contract as originally discussed by Pateman (1988) and previously referenced throughout this book. To have the state itself provide intrusions into the domestic sphere, ostensibly with the purpose of helping to flatten the hierarchies therein, is about as strong of a violation of this notion of a social/sexual contract as one can imagine, and again it indicates that the terms of citizenship are under a state of renegotiation, with gender at the forefront of that contest. There is also something interesting to note about the kind of "crisis" represented here. On the one hand, the initial creation of the

Comisarías—as well as their subsequent augmentations of authority such as the inception of the order of protection—represent discrete "moments" of crisis for masculine domination. The moments of their creation are crises in the historical sense, locatable as specific moments on a linear continuum of time. On the other hand, the everyday work that is done within the Comisarías represents "moments" of crisis for masculine domination in a more "product-moment" sense, a bit like a derivative on a mathematical curve. What this means is that these are "moments" that are constantly present and oriented in a particular direction, not just discrete points in time that we can easily point to. Every day, every time that someone comes into the Comisaría and makes a denuncia and seeks an order of protection, they are making a powerful refutation of a particular set of logics about power, and to the extent that people in the Comisarías can help them realize their desires, they are engaging in a slow but deliberate process of subverting both the ideologies and the structures of those systems of domination.

16. "Proxy agency" here refers to the definition as set forth by Albert Bandura (2001) vis-à-vis individual and collective forms of agency.

17. As Derrida (1995) says when he introduces the term "archive fever," the creation of the archive is not only "commencement" but also "commandment." By creating an archive we seek both to mark the beginning of a record and to stake our control over it. In the cases of these personal and mobile archives, that is often nothing less than seeking to maintain some modicum of control over one's life and options, forged in the face of what are often perceived to be the dehumanized (and dehumanizing) bureaucratic institutions.

18. "Sumercé" is a typical pronoun of respect used in the Cundinaboyacense region in Colombia, deriving from "su merced." "Merced" referred in the colonial era to one's benefactor, literally the person at whose mercy you were placed. While the term now is used more informally, it still often carries the intention of showing deference and a more formal respect to another person, over and beyond the alternative pronoun of "usted."

19. Not only did she dream of such an institution, but she also took classes in an extension course on human rights, hoping to one day be able to effect broader change by speaking through that discourse.

20. "ConcientizARTE" is a pun that has no literal translation to English because, unlike in Spanish, there is no transitive verb for "consciousness." The play on words though is the "arte" suffix, which indicates both raising consciousness for oneself (the "-te" reflexive ending) as well as "arte" meaning "art."

21. For the concept of "third spaces," see Bhabha (1994); for "third places," see Oldenburg (1989).

22. Previous theorization of social action against capitalist systems had focused on the role of rural peasants who migrated to cities as the ones who might hold together social movements, but this new brand of Marxist-feminism recast women and the resistance to oppressive gender relations into this role instead (see again Chinchilla, 1992).

23. Again, in this case "articulation" is to be taken in both senses, as both jointing and speaking or, put another way, as reconnecting and revocalizing what those connections mean.

24. For example, as previously referenced in Chapter 3, see the programs that are working with abusive men in South Africa and New Zealand that also directly take on histories of apartheid and colonialism.

25. For an expanded consideration of how health care spaces might be used, see Appendix 2.

Appendix 1

1. "Tendere" derives from Latin and means "to draw" or "stretch out." "Génh" is a Proto-Indo-European root meaning "birth" or "production." The happy accident in its similarity to "tangent," which does not derive from the same root, is because one of the points of a tangentic approach is to explore the products of those tensions, ones that often shoot off perpendicularly, literally or more often figuratively, to the vectors of their originating tensions. To limit the products of those tensions to orthogonal vectors though would itself be overly restricting, much like a more classical dialectic approach, and so while the homophony to tangent is mildly suggestive, it is ultimately an inaccurate description of this approach.

2. Without belaboring them here, the historic roots of this kind of fundamental insight are legion and are not restricted to any one continent's history. While the meaning of dialectics across the ancient world often took a more dialogic kind of meaning, from Greek to Hindu, Jain, or Buddhist traditions, an underlying theme of creative tension can nevertheless be found within them. In a more contemporary sense, Hegelian dialectics formalized this kind of approach, and the relevance of this will be explored a bit more directly here. More recently we can find the theme of creative tensions anywhere from the work of anthropologist Dorinne Kondo (1990), who uses that exact term, to Gilles Deleuze (1997), whose concept of "combating" has to do with the creation of personhood through the process of articulating tensions that cross the self. Korean author Pak Kyongni (1994), in explaining the meaning of the word "han," described it as the "original contradiction facing all living things," one which is the "pathway leading from birth to death." Even a cursory survey of many schools of thought will find echoes of this common underlying theme, and by employing it very explicitly here I make no pretense to being the first to recognize its central importance.

3. It is worth noting that not even Hegelian dialectics completely adhered to this framework, and in some of his dialectical illustrations even Hegel found himself loading oppositions with more than two elements. I point this out not so much to find fault with his analyses, but to say that even in his own work Hegel sometimes recognized that this framework was either overly simplified or unnecessarily restrictive.

4. See Adorno (1973).

5. This is one reason why analogic reasoning, and seeing commonalities across scales of social analysis, has also been a pervasive theme throughout this book.

6. In a much more general sense, this can apply far beyond social analysis, extending up and down our scales of complexity to include what we typically organize into the fields of physics, chemistry, biology, ecology, and beyond. In the interest of clarity I will forgo these kinds of considerations here, but the general point of pursuing a nonreductionist understanding and means of engagement holds true, however this basic framework is applied across these scales. Whatever the application, the intent remains the same. This should not be reserved as only a means of detached analysis: I believe it is best applied through an iterative process of engagement that helps to drive progressively more attuned understandings of the existence we inhabit.

Appendix 2

1. The plurality of mental health consequences of intimate partner violence is a reminder not just of the severity of that violence. It is a reminder that we are often best served by thinking in terms of "syndromes" rather than discrete illness categories, an approach more

comprehensively illustrated in the report *World Mental Health* (Desjarlais et al., 1996: see in particular chap. 8). The primary purpose of a "syndromic" approach is that to maintain that perspective is to maintain the sensibility that the categories that we construct in order to classify suffering, by the nature of the social processes that cause that suffering, tend to happen in constellation, and that experience transcends the ontological presuppositions that we come to make regarding them.

2. Along with a select few other classes—beta-blockers, statins, other diuretics, to name a few—the ACE inhibitors derived from this venom are on a short list of the WHO's essential medicines for noncommunicable diseases.

3. Granted, if anyone who consumed a high-sodium diet were to be directly bitten by a pit viper, their life chances would still be dismal, and it was actually because laborers on banana plantations were being killed by these snakes that the drug development connection was made in the first place (Patlak, 2003).

4. There are, of course, many other potential meanings to the concept of a therapeutic window, including but not limited to the stage in a disease course when a medicine is given, or a medicine opening up a window for another intervention to be more effective. When applied to the concept of care more broadly, and not just the application of a particular drug, the same fundamental ambivalences still hold true. However we stretch the therapeutic window it still serves as a reminder that the potential consequences of care are many, not all of them good, and what those consequences end up being is a question not just of the care itself but also the broader context in which it is enacted.

5. This is similar to Gramsci's view on social theory as Hall (1986) has reviewed it, noting that Gramsci's project of intellectual engagement was always born out of organic engagement and intended to serve political practice, not an abstract academic purpose. Recognition of this in spaces of healing would also therefore require a radical humility on the part of the medical practitioners to recognize that we ourselves, through our limited horizons and social positions, cannot really know what are those needs, what are those aspirations, and therefore a drastic devolution of control over spaces of healing is a requisite first step.

6. While interest in this field of inquiry continues to grow, chief among those leading this interest within the field of anthropology are Arthur Kleinman (2009, 2013) and Clara Han (2012).

7. Levinas (1979).

REFERENCES

Abadía-Barrero, César, and Dania Oviedo. 2009. "Bureaucratic Itineraries in Colombia: A Theoretical and Methodological Tool to Assess Managed-Care Health Systems." *Social Science and Medicine* 68: 1153–1160.

Ackelsberg, Martha. 2004. *Free Women of Spain: Anarchism and the Struggle for the Emancipation of Women.* Chico, CA: AK Press.

Adorno, Theodor. 1973. *Negative Dialectics.* New York: Continuum.

Agamben, Giorgio. 1998. *Homo Sacer: Sovereign Power and Bare Life.* Translated by Daniel Heller-Roazen. Stanford, CA: Stanford University Press.

Alcaldía Mayor de Bogotá. 2006. "Operación estratégica 'nuevo Usme—eje de integración a los llanos': Un modelo integral de gestión del suelo para el Distrito Capital y la region." Bogotá: Departamento Administrativo de Planeación Distrital.

Alcaldía Mayor de Bogotá and Universidad Nacional de Colombia Facultad de Derecho. 2006. *El control social de lo público: Un derecho y deber ciudadano.* Bogotá: Veeduría Distrital.

Althusser, Louis. 1971. "Ideology and Ideological State Apparatuses." In *Lenin and Philosophy, and Other Essays*, translated by Ben Brewster, 127–186. London: Routledge.

Apter, David. 1997. "Political Violence in Analytic Perspective." In *The Legitimization of Violence*, edited by David Apter, 1–32. New York: New York University Press.

Arendt, Hannah. 1970. *On Violence.* Boston: Mariner Books.

Auyero, Javier, Philippe Bourgois, and Nancy Scheper-Hughes. 2015. *Violence at the Urban Margins.* New York: Oxford University Press.

Bandura, Albert. 1978. "Social Learning Theory of Aggression." *Journal of Communication* 28, no. 3: 12–29.

Bandura, Albert. 2001. "Social Cognitive Theory: An Agentic Perspective." *Annual Review of Psychology* 52: 1–26.

Belkin, Aaron. 2012. *Bring Me Men: Military Masculinity and the Benign Façade of American Empire 1898–2001.* New York: Oxford University Press.

Benjamin, Walter. [1921] 1978. *Reflections: Essays, Aphorisms, Autobiographical Writings.* Translated by Edmund Jephcott. New York: Schocken Books.

Beske, Melissa. 2016. *Intimate Partner Violence and Advocate Response: Redefining Love in Western Belize.* Lanham, MD: Lexington Books.

Bhabha, Homi. 1994. *The Location of Culture.* New York: Routledge.

Bhadra, Madhura. 2012. "Self-Silencing Among Punjabi Women: The Interplay of Cultural Adaptation, Depression, and Domestic Violence." Unpublished master's thesis, Western Washington University.

Bion, Wilfred. 1962. *Learning from Experience*. London: Heinemann.

Bourdieu, Pierre. 1977. *Outline of a Theory of Practice*. Cambridge: Cambridge University Press.

Bourgois, Philippe. 1995. *In Search of Respect*. Cambridge: Cambridge University Press.

Brave Heart, Maria Yellow Horse, and Lemyra DeBruyn. 1998. "The American Indian Holocaust: Healing Historical Unresolved Grief." *American Indian and Alaska Native Mental Health Research* 8, no. 2: 56–78.

Browne, Angela. 1987. *When Battered Women Kill*. New York: Free Press.

Bushnell, David. 1993. *The Making of Modern Colombia: A Nation in Spite of Itself*. Berkeley: University of California Press.

Butler, Judith. [1990] 2006. *Gender Trouble: Feminism and the Subversion of Identity*. New York: Routledge.

Butler, Judith. 1993. *Bodies That Matter: On the Discursive Limits of Sex*. New York: Routledge.

Cabre, Gabriel. May 27, 1991. "La Zona Quinta: Una cantera de problemas." *El Tiempo*.

Campbell, Jacquelyn, Nancy Glass, Phyllis Sharps, Kathryn Laughon, and Tina Bloom. 2007. "Intimate Partner Homicide: Review and Implications of Research and Policy." *Trauma, Violence, and Abuse* 8: 246–269.

Carrasco, Davíd. 1999. *City of Sacrifice: The Aztec Empire and the Role of Violence in Civilization*. Boston: Beacon Press.

Chinchilla, Norma Stoltz. 1992. "Marxism, Feminism, and the Struggle for Democracy in Latin America." In *The Making of Social Movements in Latin America: Identity, Strategy, and Democracy*, edited by Arturo Escobar and Sonia E. Alvarez, 37–51. Boulder, CO: Westview Press.

Chomsky, Aviva. 2008. *Linked Labor Histories: New England, Colombia, and the Making of a Global Working Class*. Durham: Duke University Press.

Colombia Informa. November 24, 2014. "Por qué las mujeres de Medellín se movilizan el 25 de Noviembre?" Retrieved November 26, 2014. http://www.colombiainforma.info/mov-sociales/generos/1886-por-que-las-mujeres-de-medellin-se-movilizan-el-25-de-noviembre

Comaroff, Jean, and John Comaroff. 1991. *Of Revelation and Revolution: Christianity, Colonialism, and Consciousness in South Africa, Vol. I*. Chicago: University of Chicago Press.

Connell, R. W. 1987. *Gender and Power: Society, the Person, and Sexual Politics*. Stanford, CA: Stanford University Press.

Connell, Raewyn, and James Messerschmidt. 2005. "Hegemonic Masculinity: Rethinking the Concept." *Gender Society* 19, no. 6: 829–859.

Cooper, Anna Julia. [1892] 1988. *A Voice from the South*. New York: Oxford University Press.

Cooper, Frederick. 2005. *Colonialism in Question: Theory, Knowledge, History*. Berkeley: University of California Press.

Cortés Díaz, Marco E. 2006. *La anexión de los 6 municipios vecinos a Bogotá en 1954*. Bogotá: Universidad Nacional de Colombia.

Crenshaw, Kimberlé. 1989. "Demarginalizing the Intersection of Race and Sex: A Black Feminist Critique of Antidiscrimination Doctrine, Feminist Theory, and Antiracist Politics." *University of Chicago Legal Forum* 140: 139–167.

Cuéllar, Jimena Montaña, and Tatiana Urrea Uyabán, eds. 2011. *Usme: Historia de un territorio*. Bogotá: Alcaldía Mayor de Bogotá.

Das, Veena. 2007. *Life and Words: Violence and the Descent into the Ordinary*. Berkeley: University of California Press.

Das, Veena, and Arthur Kleinman. 2000. "Introduction." In *Violence and Subjectivity*, edited by Veena Das, Arthur Kleinman, Mamphela Ramphele, and Pamela Reynolds, 1–18. Berkeley: University of California Press.

Das, Veena, and Deborah Poole. 2004. *Anthropology in the Margins of the State*. Santa Fe, NM: School for Advanced Research Press.

Davis, Angela. 1998. "Women and Capitalism: Dialectics of Oppression and Liberation." In *The Angela Y. Davis Reader*, edited by Joy James and Angela Yvonne Davis, 161–209. Hoboken, NJ: Wiley-Blackwell.

Defensoría del Pueblo. 2010. *La minería de hecho en Colombia*. Bogotá: Imprenta Nacional de Colombia.

DeKeseredy Walter, Molly Dragiewicz, and Martin Schwartz. 2017. *Abusive Endings: Separation and Divorce Violence Against Women*. Berkeley: University of California Press.

Deleuze, Gilles. 1997. *Essays Critical and Clinical*. Minneapolis: University of Minnesota Press.

Departamento Administrativo de Bienestar Social. 1996. "Informe de labores regionales no. 6." Bogotá: Alcaldía Mayor de Bogotá.

Derrida, Jacques. [1967] 1978. *Writing and Difference*. Translated by Alan Bass. Chicago: University of Chicago Press.

Derrida, Jacques. 1989. "Force de loi: Le fondement mystique de l'autorité." *Cardozo Law Review* 11: 920–1045.

Derrida, Jacques. 1995. "Archive Fever: A Freudian Impression." *Diacritics* 25, no. 2: 9–63.

Desjarlais, Robert, Leon Eisenberg, Byron Good, and Arthur Kleinman. 1996. *World Mental Health: Problems and Priorities in Low-Income Countries*. New York: Oxford University Press.

Didion, Joan. 1979. *The White Album*. New York: Farrar, Straus, and Giroux.

Dobash, R. Emerson, Russel P. Dobash, Kate Cavanagh, and Juanjo Medina-Ariza. 2007. "Lethal and Nonlethal Violence Against an Intimate Female Partner: Comparing Male Murderers to Nonlethal Abusers." *Violence Against Women* 13, no. 4: 329–353.

Dollard, John, Neal Miller, Leonard Doob, Orval Mowrer, and Robert Sears. 1939. *Frustration and Aggression*. New Haven, CT: Yale University Press.

Duménil, Gérard, and Dominique Lévy. 2004. *Capital Resurgent: Roots of the Neoliberal Revolution*. Translated by Derek Jeffers. Cambridge, MA: Harvard University Press.

Durkheim, Émile. [1893] 1984. *The Division of Labor in Society*. New York: Free Press.

Durkheim, Émile. [1898] 1953. "Individual and Collective Representations." In *Sociology and Philosophy*, translated by D. F. Pocock, 1–34. Glencoe: Free Press.

Eckstein, Susan. 2001. *Power and Popular Protest: Latin American Social Movements*. Berkeley: University of California Press.

El Tiempo. March 8, 1991. "Freno a las invasiones."

El Tiempo. November 28, 1991. "Liderazgo y solidaridad."

El Tiempo. February 18, 1992. "A Usme todavía no llega el siglo XX."

El Tiempo. May 11, 1992. "JAL de Usme: Modelo de organización."

El Tiempo. July 1, 1992. "Una nueva historia para Bogotá."

El Tiempo. July 1, 2014. "Bogotá tiene permiso para ampliar el relleno Doña Juana."

Engle-Merry, Sally. 2006. *Human Rights and Gender Violence: Translating International Law into Local Justice*. Chicago: University of Chicago Press.

Enloe, Cynthia. 2000. *Maneuvers: The International Politics of Militarizing Women's Lives.* Berkeley: University of California Press.

Escobar, Arturo, and Sonia Alvarez. 1992. *The Making of Social Movements in Latin America: Identity, Strategy, and Democracy.* Boulder, CO: Westview Press.

Fals Borda, Orlando. 1969. *Subversion and Social Change in Colombia.* New York: Columbia University Press.

Faludi, Susan. 2000. *Stiffed: The Betrayal of the American Man.* New York: HarperCollins.

Fanon, Frantz. 1963. *The Wretched of the Earth.* New York: Grove Press.

Farmer, Paul. 1997. "On Suffering and Structural Violence: A View from Below." In *Social Suffering,* edited by Arthur Kleinman, Veena Das, and Margaret Lock, 261–284. Berkeley: University of California Press.

Farmer, Paul. 2004. *Pathologies of Power: Health, Human Rights, and the New War on the Poor.* Berkeley: University of California Press.

Federación Nacional de Cafeteros de Colombia (FNC). 1979. "Manual del Cafetero Colombiano." Bogotá, Colombia: Sección de Divulgación Científica de CENICAFE.

Fischer, Brodwyn. 2014. "Introduction." In *Cities from Scratch: Poverty and Informality in Urban Latin America,* edited by Brodwyn Fischer, Bryan McCann, and Javier Auyero. Durham, NC: Duke University Press.

Fischer, Brodwyn, Bryan McCann, and Javier Auyero, eds. *Cities from Scratch: Poverty and Informality in Urban Latin America.* Durham, NC: Duke University Press.

Fontes, Lisa. 2015. *Invisible Chains: Overcoming Coercive Control in Your Relationship.* New York: Guilford Press.

Foucault, Michel. 1977. *Discipline and Punish.* Translated by Alan Sheridan. New York: Vintage Books.

Franco, Saul, et al. 2006. "The Effects of Armed Conflict on the Life and Health in Colombia." *Ciencia e Saude Coletiva* 11: 349–361.

Frankl, Viktor. 1967. *Psychotherapy and Existentialism: Selected Papers on Logotherapy.* New York: Washington Square Press.

Fraser, Nancy. October 14, 2013. "How Feminism Became Capitalism's Handmaiden—and How to Reclaim It." *Guardian.* Retrieved October 19, 2016. https://www.theguardian.com/commentisfree/2013/oct/14/feminism-capitalist-handmaiden-neoliberal

Galeano, Eduardo. 1971. *Venas abiertas de America Latina.* Mexico: Siglo Veintiuno Editores.

Galtung, Johan. 1969. "Violence, Peace, and Peace Research." *Journal of Peace Research* 6, no. 3: 167–191.

Gauta, José Rozo. 2011. *Los golpes de amor: Colonialismo y violencia de género.* Boyacá: Secretaría de Cultura y Turismo Boyacá.

Geertz, Clifford. 1973. *The Interpretation of Cultures.* New York: Basic Books.

Gilhodés, Pierre. 1970. "Agrarian Struggles in Colombia." In *Agrarian Problems and Peasant Movements in Latin America,* edited by Rodolfo Stavenhagen, 407–452. Garden City, NY: Doubleday.

Gill, Lesley. 2004. *The School of the Americas: Military Training and Political Violence in the Americas.* Durham, NC: Duke University Press.

Gilligan, James. 1997. *Violence: Reflections on a National Epidemic.* New York: Vintage Books.

Global Commission on Drug Policy. 2011. "War on Drugs: Report of the Global Commission on Drug Policy." Geneva: Global Commission on Drug Policy.

Gramsci, Antonio. 1992. *Prison Notebooks.* Edited by Joseph Buttigieg. Translated by Joseph Buttigieg and Antonio Callari. New York: Columbia University Press.

Greene, Julie. 2010. *The Canal Builders: Making America's Empire at the Panama Canal.* New York: Penguin Books.

Greig, Alan John. 2007. "Men and Violence: Problems with Masculinity." *La Manazana* 2, no. 3. http://www.estudiosmasculinidades.buap.mx/num3/art5.htm.

Gutmann, Matthew. 1996. *The Meanings of Macho: Being a Man in Mexico City.* Berkeley: University of California Press.

Guzmán Celis, Luis Antonio. 2003. *El Gran Misterio del Páramo de Córcega.* Cali, Colombia: Proceso Gráfico.

Hall, Stuart. 1986. "Gramsci's Relevance for the Study of Race and Ethnicity." *Journal of Communication Inquiry* 10, no. 5: 5–27.

Han, Clara. 2012. *Life in Debt: Times of Care and Violence in Neoliberal Chile.* Berkeley: University of California Press.

Hartmann, Heidi. 1981. "The Unhappy Marriage of Marxism and Feminism: Towards a More Progressive Union." In *Women and Revolution,* edited by Lydia Sargent, 1–42. Boston: South End Press.

Harvey, David. 2008. "The Right to the City." *New Left Review* 53: 23–40.

Harvey, David. 2009. "The 'New' Imperialism: Accumulation by Dispossession." *Socialist Register* 40: 63–87.

Harvey, David. 2015. *Seventeen Contradictions and the End of Capitalism.* New York: Oxford University Press.

Hernandez, D. P. 1984. "Resource Development and Indigenous People: The El Cerrejón Coal Project in Guajira, Colombia." *Cultural Survival* 15: 1–52.

Herzfeld, Michael. 1993. *The Social Production of Indifference: Exploring the Symbolic Roots of Western Bureaucracy.* Chicago: University of Chicago Press.

Hillman, Richard, and Thomas D'Agostino. 2011. *Understanding Contemporary Latin America,* 4th ed. Boulder, CO: Lynne Rienner Publications.

Hoglend, Per. 1999. "Psychotherapy Research: New Findings and Implications for Training and Practice." *Journal of Psychotherapy Practice and Research* 8: 257–263.

Holden, Robert, and Eric Zolov, eds. 2010. *Latin America and the United States: A Documentary History.* New York: Oxford University Press.

Hough, Philip, and Jennifer Bair. 2012. "Dispossession, Class Formation, and Political Imaginary of Colombia's Coffee Producers over the Long Durée: Beyond the Polanyian Analytic." *Journal of World Systems Research* 18, no. 1: 30–49.

Hristov, Jasmin. 2009. *Blood and Capital: The Paramilitarization of Colombia.* Ohio University Press.

Human Rights Watch. 2010. "Paramilitaries' Heirs." New York: Human Rights Watch.

Hunt, Michael. 1987. *Ideology and U.S. Foreign Policy.* New Haven, CT: Yale University Press.

Jack, Dana. 1993. *Silencing the Self: Women and Depression.* New York: William Morrow.

James, William. [1912] 2003. *Essays in Radical Empiricism.* Mineola, NY: Dover Publications.

Jansson, Oscar. 2006. "Alternative Development in Putumayo: Example of a Complex Failure in Security Policy." Presented at Uppsala University.

Jewkes, Rachel. 2002. "Intimate Partner Violence: Causes and Prevention." *Lancet* 359: 1423–1429.

Jiménez, Michael. 1995. "At the Banquet of Civilization: The Limits of Planter Hegemony in Early-Twentieth-Century Colombia." In *Coffee, Society, and Power in Latin America*, edited by William Roseberry, Lowell Gudmundson, and Mario Samper Kutschbach, 262–294. Baltimore, MD: Johns Hopkins University Press.

Jimeno, Myriam. [2004] 2011. *Crimen pasional: Contribución a una antropología de las emociones*. Bogotá: Universidad Nacional de Colombia.

Jimeno, Myriam, Andrés Góngora, Marco Martínez, and Carlos José Suárez. 2007. "Manes, mansitos, y manazos: Una metodología de trabajo sobre violencia intrafamiliar y sexual." Bogotá: Universidad Nacional de Colombia, Centro de Estudios Sociales.

Johnson, Keith. November 18, 2013. "Kerry Makes It Official: 'Era of Monroe Doctrine Is Over.'" *Wall Street Journal*.

Johnson, Michael. 2008. *A Typology of Domestic Violence: Intimate Terrorism, Violent Resistance, and Situational Couple Violence*. Boston: Northeastern University Press.

Johnson-Hanks, Jennifer. 2002. "On the Limits of Life Stages in Ethnography: Toward a Theory of Vital Conjunctures." *American Anthropology* 104, no. 3: 865–880.

Kapadia, Anush. 2013. "Europe and the Logic of Hierarchy." *Journal of Comparative Economics* 41, no. 2: 436–446.

Kelly, Joan, and Michael Johnson. 2008. "Differentiation Among Types of Intimate Partner Violence: Research Update and Implications for Interventions." *Family Court Review* 46, no. 3: 476–499.

Kennedy, John. March 13, 1962. "The Ultimate Responsibility." Speech delivered at the White House before Latin American diplomats, members of Congress, and members of the Organization of American States.

Keshavjee, Salman. 2014. *Blind Spot: How Neoliberalism Infiltrated Global Health*. Berkeley: University of California Press.

Kim, Jim Yong, Joyce Millen, Alec Irwin, and John Gershman. 2002. *Dying for Growth: Global Inequality and the Health of the Poor*. Monroe, ME: Common Courage Press.

Kirk, Robin. 2003. *More Terrible Than Death: Massacres, Drugs, and America's War in Colombia*. New York: Public Affairs.

Klein, Renate. 2015. *Responding to Intimate Violence Against Women*. Cambridge: Cambridge University Press.

Kleinman, Arthur. 1997. *Writing at the Margin: Discourse Between Anthropology and Medicine*. Berkeley: University of California Press.

Kleinman, Arthur. 2009. "Caregiving: The Odyssey of Becoming More Human." *Lancet* 373, no. 9660: 292–293.

Kleinman, Arthur. 2013. "From Illness as Culture to Caregiving as Moral Experience." *New England Journal of Medicine* 368, no. 15: 1376–1377.

Kollontai, Alexandra. 1909. *The Social Basis of the Woman Question*. Pamphlet.

Kondo, Dorinne K. 1990. *Crafting Selves: Power, Gender, and Discourses of Identity in a Japanese Workplace*. Chicago: University of Chicago Press.

Kristof, Nicholas, and Sheryl WuDunn. 2010. *Half the Sky: Turning Oppression into Opportunity for Women Worldwide*. New York: Vintage Books.

Kundera, Milan. 1999. *Immortality*. New York: Harper Perennial Modern Classics.

Kutschbach, Mario Samper. 1995. "In Difficult Times: Colombian and Costa Rican Coffee from Prosperity to Crisis, 1920–1936." In *Coffee, Society, and Power in Latin America*, edited by William Roseberry, Lowell Gudmundson, and Mario Samper Kutschbach, 151–180. Baltimore, MD: Johns Hopkins University Press.

Lazarus-Black, Mindie. 2007. *Everyday Harm: Domestic Violence, Court Rites, and Cultures of Reconciliation*. Urbana: University of Illinois Press.

Lefebvre, Henri. [1970] 2003. *The Urban Revolution*. Translated by Robert Bononno. Minneapolis: University of Minnesota Press.

Levinas, Emmanuel. 1979. *Totality and Infinity: An Essay on Exteriority*. Leiden: Martinus Nijhoff.

Loveman, Brian. 2012. *No Higher Law: American Foreign Policy and the Western Hemisphere Since 1776*. Chapel Hill: University of North Carolina Press.

Lozano, Juan Jose, and Hollman Morris. 2010. *Impunity*. Intermezzo Films.

Lyons, Leonard. December 7, 1960. "The Lyons Den: Analyzing Humor Like Cutting a Frog—Dissect It If It's Dead." *Lawrence Daily Journal-World*.

Machiavelli, Niccolò. [1532] 2008. *The Prince*. Translated by Peter Constantine. New York: Modern Library.

Mahmood, Saba. 2001. "Feminist Theory, Embodiment, and the Docile Agent: Some Reflections on the Egyptian Islamic Revival." *Cultural Anthropology* 16, no. 2: 202–236.

Mandela, Nelson. 1994. *Long Walk to Freedom: The Autobiography of Nelson Mandela*. New York: Little, Brown.

Manjoo, Rashida, and Calleigh McRaith. 2011. "Gender-Based Violence and Justice in Conflict and Post-Conflict Areas." *Cornell International Law Journal* 44: 11–31.

Marx, Karl. [1867] 1992. *Capital*, Volume 1. Translated by Ben Fowkes. New York: Penguin Classics.

Matear, Ann. 2007. "Gender Relations, Authoritarianism, and Democratization in Chile." *Democratization* 6, no. 3: 100–117.

Mauss, Marcel. [1925] 1969. *The Gift: Forms and Functions of Exchange in Archaic Societies*. Translated by Ian Cunninson. London: Routledge.

Merton, Robert. 1936. "The Unanticipated Consequences of Purposive Action." *American Sociological Review* 1, no. 6: 894–904.

Miller, Elizabeth, and Jay Silverman. 2010. "Reproductive Coercion and Partner Violence: Implications for Clinical Assessment of Unintended Pregnancy." *Expert Review of Obstetrics and Gynecology* 5, no. 5: 511–515.

Mitchell, Timothy. 1999. "Society, Economy, and the State Effect." In *State/Culture: State-formation After the Cultural Turn*, edited by George Steinmetz, 76–97. Ithaca, NY: Cornell University Press.

Moncayo Plata, Carmen Celina. 1997. "Derechos humanos de las mujeres." Bogotá: Secretaría Distrital de Salud.

Murray, Pauli. 1987. *Song in a Weary Throat: An American Pilgrimage*. New York: HarperCollins.

Nordstrom, Carolyn. 2004. *Shadows of War: Violence, Power, and International Profiteering in the Twenty-First Century*. Berkeley: University of California Press.

Oldenburg, Ray. 1989. *The Great Good Place: Cafés, Coffee Shops, Community Centers, Beauty Parlors, General Stores, Bars, Hangouts, and How They Get You Through the Day*. New York: Paragon House.

Pak Kyongni. November 26, 1994. "The Feelings and Thoughts of Korean People in Literature." Delivered at the University of Paris.

Palacios, Marco. 1980. *Coffee in Colombia, 1850–1970: An Economic, Social, and Political History.* Cambridge: Cambridge University Press.

Parson, Nia. 2013. *Traumatic States: Gendered Violence, Suffering, and Care in Chile.* Nashville, TN: Vanderbilt University Press.

Pateman, Carole. 1988. *The Sexual Contract.* New York: Polity Press.

Patlak, Margie. 2003. "From Viper's Venom to Drug Design: Treating Hypertension." Federation of American Societies for Experimental Biology.

Pérez, Federico. 2014. "Urbanism as Warfare: Planning, Property, and Displacement in Bogotá." PhD dissertation, Harvard University.

Personería de Bogotá. November 3, 2012. "92,6% de minería en Bogotá es illegal."

Profamilia. 2010. "Encuesta nacional de demografía y salud." Bogotá: Profamilia.

Profamilia. 2011. "Encuesta distrital de demografía y salud, Bogotá 2011." Bogotá: Profamilia.

Robinson, Richard. 2009. "Exploring the 'Global Workspace' of Consciousness." *PLOS Biology* 7, no. 3: 415.

Rodriguez, M., C. Padilla, O. Valencia, and R. Oyuela-Vargas. 2012. "Pericias psicológicas y otros medios probatorios en las decisions en las comisarías de familia de Bogotá: Casos de violencia de pareja contra mujer." *Diversitas: Perspectivas en Psicología* 8, no. 1: 85–99.

Roseberry, William. 1995. "Introduction." In, *Coffee, Society, and Power in Latin America.* William Roseberry, Lowell Gudmundson, and Mario Samper Kutschbach, 1–37. Baltimore, MD: Johns Hopkins University Press.

Rotker, Susana. 2002. *Citizens of Fear: Urban Violence in Latin America.* New Brunswick, NJ: Rutgers University Press.

Roy, Satyajit. *Goopy Gyne Bagha Byne.* 1969. Purnima Pictures.

Rubior, Miller. May 11, 1992. "Cundinamarca: 30 municipios tienen presencia de la guerrilla." *El Tiempo.*

Ruiz, Esmeralda. 2000. "Conciliación y violencia intrafamiliar." Bogotá, Colombia: Imprenta Nacional de Colombia.

Ryan, Richard, Martin Lynch, Maarten Vansteenkiste, and Edward Deci. 2011. "Motivation and Autonomy in Counseling, Psychotherapy, and Behavior Change: A Look at theory and Practice." *Counseling Psychologist* 39, no. 2: 193–260.

Safford, Frank, and Marco Palacios. 2002. *Colombia: Fragmented Land, Divided Society.* New York: Oxford University Press.

Sahlins, Marshall. 1981. *Historical Metaphors and Mythical Realities: Structure in the Early History of the Sandwich Islands Kingdom.* Ann Arbor: University of Michigan Press.

Salcedo, Andrés. 2008. "Defendiendo territorios desde el exilio: Desplazamiento y reconstrucción en Colombia contemporanea." *Revista Colombiana de Antropología* 44, no. 2: 309–335.

Sawyer, R. Keith. 2002. "Durkheim's Dilemma: Toward a Sociology of Emergence." *Sociological Theory* 20, no. 2: 227–247.

Scheper-Hughes, Nancy. 2014. "The Militarization and Madness of Everyday Life." *South Atlantic Quarterly* 113, no. 3: 640–655.

Scheper-Hughes, Nancy, and Philippe Bourgois. 2004. "Introduction: Making Sense of Violence." In *Violence in War and Peace*, edited by Nancy Scheper-Hughes and Philippe Bourgois, 1–32. Malden, MA: Blackwell.

Schlegel, Alice, and Herbert Barry. 1991. *Adolescence: An Anthropological Inquiry.* New York: Free Press.

Schmitt, Carl. [1922] 1985. *Political Theology*. Translated by George Schwab. Cambridge, MA: MIT Press.

Schoultz, Lars. 1998. *Beneath the United States: A History of US Policy Toward Latin America*. Cambridge, MA: Harvard University Press.

Scott, James. 1987. *Weapons of the Weak: Everyday Forms of Peasant Resistance*. New Haven, CT: Yale University Press.

Scott, James. 1990. *Domination and the Arts of Resistance: Hidden Transcripts*. New Haven, CT: Yale University Press.

Scott, James. 1999. *Seeing Like a State: How Certain Schemes to Improve the Human Condition Have Failed*. New Haven, CT: Yale University Press.

Secretaría de Cultura, Recreación y Deporte. 2010. *Recordar, vivir y sonar a Bogotá desdes las localidades*. Bogotá: Alcaldía Mayor de Bogotá.

Secretaría Distrital del Hábitat (SDH). 2010. "Inspección, vigilancia y control de los desarrollos ilegales de vivienda: Localidad Usme." Bogotá: Secretaría Distrital del Hábitat.

Secretaría Distrital del Hábitat (SDH). 2011. "Convenio de Asociación No. 82 de 2011: Fase 4 relleno sanitario de Doña Juana." Bogotá: Alcaldía Mayor de Bogotá.

Secretaría Distrital de Planeación (SDP). July 2009. "Bogotá ciudad de estadísticas, boletín No. 9." Bogotá: Alcaldía Mayor de Bogotá.

Secretaría Distrital de Planeación (SDP). April 2015. "Bogotá ciudad de estadísticas, boletín No. 65." Bogotá: Alcaldía Mayor de Bogotá.

Secretaría Distrital de Salud (SDS). 2010. *Localidad Usme: Diagnostico local con participación social 2009–2010*. Bogotá: Alcaldía Mayor de Bogotá.

Seligman, Adam, Rahel Wasserfall, and David Montgomery. 2016. *Living with Difference: How to Build Community in a Divided World*. Berkeley: University of California Press.

Semana. December 1991. "La guerrilla cruzó la raya: La matanza de Usme muestra el grado de sevicia al que han llegado las acciones de la coordinadora guerrillera." No. 500.

Shkilnyk, Anestasia. 1985. *A Poison Stronger Than Love: The Destruction of an Ojibwa Community*. New Haven, CT: Yale University Press.

Sidanius, James, and Felicia Pratto. 1999. *Social Dominance: An Intergroup Theory of Social Hierarchy and Oppression*. Cambridge: Cambridge University Press.

Snell-Rood, Claire. 2015. *No One Will Let Her Live: Women's Struggle for Well-Being in a Delhia Slum*. Berkeley: University of California Press.

Sokoloff, Natalie, and Christina Pratt. 2005. *Domestic Violence at the Margins: Readings on Race, Class, Gender, and Culture*. New Brunswick, NJ: Rutgers University Press.

Solzhenitsyn, Aleksandr. December 10, 1970. Nobel Banquet Speech. Stockholm, Sweden.

Solzhenitsyn, Aleksandr. [1974] 2020. *The Gulag Archipelago: An Experiment in Literary Investigation, Volume 1*. Translated by Thomas P. Whitney. New York: Harper Perennial.

Stark, Evan. 2007. *Coercive Control: How Men Entrap Women in Personal Life*. Oxford: Oxford University Press.

Stavenhagen, Rodolfo. 1971. *Between Underdevelopment and Revolution: A Latin American Perspective*. New Delhi: Abhinav.

Steiner, Roberto, and Hernan Vallejo. 2010. "The Economy." In *Colombia: A Country Study*, edited by Rex Hudson, 141–212. Washington, DC: Library of Congress Federal Research Division.

Stoler, Ann. 1995. *Race and the Education of Desire: Foucault's History of Sexuality and the Colonial Order of Things*. Durham, NC: Duke University Press.

Tate, Winifred. 2007. *Counting the Dead: The Culture and Politics of Human Rights Activism in Colombia*. Berkeley: University of California Press.

Taussig, Michael. 1980. *The Devil and Commodity Fetishism in South America*. Chapel Hill: University of North Carolina Press.

Theidon, Kimberly. 1999. "Domesticando la violencia: Alcohol y las secuelas de la guerra." *Ideele: Revista del Instituto de Defensa Legal* 120: 56–63.

Theidon, Kimberly. 2008. "Reconstructing Masculinities: The Disarmament, Demobilization, and Reintegration of Former Combatants in Colombia." *Human Rights Quarterly* 31, no. 1: 1–34.

Theidon, Kimberly. 2013. *Intimate Enemies: Violence and Reconciliation in Perú*. Philadelphia: University of Pennsylvania Press.

Thomas, Vinod. 1985. "Linking Macroeconomic Agricultural Policies for Adjustment and Growth: The Colombian Experience, a World Bank Report." Published for the World Bank. Baltimore, MD: Johns Hopkins University Press.

Thompson, Edward Palmer. 1966. *The Making of the English Working Class*. New York: Vintage Books.

Thompson, Edward Palmer. 1971. "The Moral Economy of the English Working Crowd in the 18th Century." *Past and Present* 50:76–136.

Tolton, Laura. 2011. "He Beat Her So Hard She Fell Head over Heels: Normalizing Wife Abuse in Colombia." In *Living with Patriarchy: Discursive Constructions of Gendered Subjects Across Cultures*, edited by Danijela Majstorovic and Inger Lassen, 17–48. Amsterdam: John Benjamins Publishing Company.

Trouillot, Michel-Rolph. 1997. *Silencing the Past: Power and the Production of History*. Boston: Beacon Press.

Trouillot, Michel-Rolph. 2003. *Global Transformations: Anthropology and the Modern World*. London: Palgrave Macmillan.

United Nations High Commission on Refugees (UNHCR). 2003. *La población desplazada en Bogotá: Una responsabilidad de todos*. Geneva: United Nations.

United Nations High Commission on Refugees (UNHCR). 2013a. *UNHCR 2012 Global Report*. Geneva: United Nations.

United Nations High Commission on Refugees (UNHCR). 2013b. *UNHCR Mid-Year Trends 2013*. Geneva: United Nations.

United Nations High Commission on Refugees (UNHCR). 2013c. *UNHCR Global Appeal 2014–2015: Colombia*. Geneva: United Nations.

U.S. Department of Agriculture. 1968. "World Trade in Selected Agricultural Commodities 1951–1965, vol. 1 Beverage Crops—Coffee, Cocoa, Tea." Foreign Agricultural Economic Report No. 42. Washington, DC: Economic Research Service, U.S. Department of Agriculture.

Warren, Kay, and Jean Jackson. 2002. "Introduction: Studying Indigenous Activism in Latin America." In *Indigenous Movements, Self-Representation, and the State in Latin America*, edited by Kay Warren and Jean Jackson, 1–46. Austin: University of Texas Press.

Weber, Max. [1919] 1965. *Politics as Vocation*. Translated by H. H. Gerth and C. Wright Mills. Philadelphia: Fortress Press.

Weber, Max. [1922] 1968. *Economy and Society: Outline of an Interpretive Sociology*. Translated by Ephraim Fischoff. New York: Bedminster Press.

Weisbrot, Mark. 2011. "Obama's Latin America Policy: Continuity Without Change." *Latin American Perspectives* 38, no. 4: 63–72.

Wies, Jennifer. 2008. "Professionalizing Human Services: A Case of Domestic Violence Shelter Advocates." *Human Organization* 67, no. 2: 221–233.

Wies, Jennifer, and Hillary Haldane. 2011. *Anthropology at the Front Lines of Gender-Based Violence*. Nashville, TN: Vanderbilt University Press.

World Bank. 2003. "Colombia: The Economic Foundations for Peace." Edited by Marcelo Giugale, Olivier Lafourcade, and Connie Luff. Washington, DC: International Bank for Reconstruction and Development / World Bank.

World Bank. 2016. "Poverty and Equity: Colombia Dashboard." Consulted April 23, 2016. https://povertydata.worldbank.org/poverty/country/COL.

World Health Organization (WHO). 2002. *World Report on Violence and Health*. Geneva: World Health Organization.

World Health Organization (WHO). 2013. "Global and Regional Estimates of Violence Against Women: Prevalence and Health Effects of Intimate Partner Violence and Non-Partner Sexual Violence." Geneva: World Health Organization.

INDEX

ACKNOWLEDGMENTS

"Authorship" is the strangest of fictions, and the true story of any ethnography is that which we bury here. Though I am the one who tapped the keys and filled these pages, the ideas they represent have grown out from far deeper roots. Allow me to now give breath then to some of this greater truth.

This study took place in the district of Usme in Bogotá, Colombia, and it was not just by happenstance that I ended up there. Dr. Andrés Salcedo, chair of the Department of Anthropology at the Universidad Nacional de Colombia, is the one who first took me to meet his contacts in the community, a point of departure that became the initial seed out of which the rest of this research eventually grew. Dr. César Abadía Barrero, a longtime mentor of mine in Colombia, as well as a student of his, Dr. Guillermo Sanchez Vanegas, were responsible for giving me opportunities to work previously in Bogotá, as well as connect me to Dr. Salcedo in the first place. To these three I will always owe an unrepayable debt.

The very basis of this study though came from the generosity of all those who participated, in one way or another, throughout the course of my fieldwork. Their stories, their suffering, their sensibilities, hardships, concerns, aspirations, and joy form both the material and the continued inspiration for everything that follows from here. Through every conversation, every moment shared, every vulnerability that an innumerable number of people shared with me, they did far more than contribute to a study: they took me further along the path of becoming more human. I cannot call them by name here; I can only hope that along the way I have indeed begun the process of honoring the nearly unfathomable hospitality, a hospitality of the deepest sense, that I have been so privileged to receive. They include the survivors of intimate violence who shared with me some of the most painful moments of their lives, as well as imparted onto me a continued sense of hope and an urgency to turn that into reality. They include the perpetrators of violence who allowed me to see some of their greatest shame and to engage with them in a protracted process of reflection, only asking me to treat them as human in return. They include the staff and administration of the Comisarías de Familia in Usme, who became some of my closest relationships throughout my research, who relentlessly pushed me to think deeper but also helped me to take breaks and have fun, reminding me that *la alegria* is essential nourishment for the spirit. The people who formed this study even included the staff of the public library, clergy in the local parish, rap artists on public transport, street artists who have painted Bogotá in their visually provocative poetry, even fellow bus passengers who shared their limited space and, sometimes, their thoughts with me during my many commutes.

One person in particular to whom I owe special gratitude has become close enough so as to practically be family. In this book I name her as "Luz Elena" (a pseudonym), but I will always know her as one of my dearest friends. My most cherished memories of Usme will always be of our walking tours and breathless conversations (Usme is at 9,000 feet after all), the moments of speech, and the moments of silence through which we shared our love of the land. If I can manage to even approach her subtle blend of criticality and generosity throughout the pages that follow, I will have done everything that I can.

I also have my actual family in Colombia to thank, and for far more than just housing me at times throughout this process and dealing graciously with my unpredictable schedules and presence. From an early age, my grandparents, cousins, aunt, and uncle have helped me to cultivate a sense of the world that is not only larger, but also one that needn't be understood by the usual frontiers that we regularly impose upon it. If I have always been proud to be half-Colombian, it is surely because of them.

Beyond those in my family, I have also been immensely fortunate to receive tutelage along the way from the most dedicated teachers that I could find. In my very first semester of college, it was Dr. Atwood Gaines who introduced me to medical anthropology and the art of ethnography, using the books of my to-be graduate mentors, *Patients and Healers in the Context of Culture* and *AIDS and Accusation*, an introduction that would change my trajectory forever. Over the following years, Drs. Janet McGrath and Lee Hoffer grew that interest into something greater and my fellow students Kristi Ninnemann, Meghan Halley, and Aura Newlin convinced me that a PhD is in fact worth pursuing. Those vertical and horizontal mentorships continued at Harvard, and sustaining me throughout those years was the camaraderie and guidance, not to mention thoughtful feedback, from those whom I am proud to call my colleagues and my mentors, but most of all my friends: Matthew Basilico, Arjun Suri, Josh Baugh, Nworah Ayogu, Abhiram Bhashyam, Salman Bhai, Eric Lu, Vipul Kumar, Kim Sue, Amy Porter, George Karandinos, and Ethan Bagley. I am also especially grateful to Dr. Ajantha Subramanian and her proseminar course "Power" that she guided our PhD cohort through, as well as, of course, my fellow cohort mates in the Social Anthropology program who pushed me to never settle on my ideas: Darja Djordjevic, Vivien Chung, Bronwynn Isaacs, Wirun Limsawart, Max Durayappah-Harrison, Adoree Durayappah-Harrison, Meghan Rogushka, and Jon Clindaniel. Dr. Kimberly Theidon's course "Gender in Conflict" has been immensely influential in framing my research, and I am grateful both to her and those who made up our excellent seminar, including Roxanne Kristali, David Francis, Kirin Gupta, and Silvia Mejia.

Academically speaking, no one has been of greater support than Drs. Arthur Kleinman, Anne Becker, and Byron Good. Each of them had been a guide to me since long before I actually entered the PhD program, and they have remained stalwart advocates ever since. Their unique combinations of scholarly excellence and humanistic concern have always provided me with beacons to follow since the moment I entered this field. Their feedback, their uncanny intuition in pointing me where I wanted to go but did not yet realize, and their patience throughout my frequently long absences are what made all of this possible. Most of all, their encouragement and challenge provided the basic tension out of which this whole pursuit emerged. Helping me to get there was also the ever-present support of Marianne Fritz, Linda Thomas, and Amy Cohen. Together they all made certain that, when everything else failed, I was still able to get out the door and get this work under way.

This book would also never be, were it not for the generosity of spirit of several key people along the way. To Kate Marshall I owe a debt of gratitude for pushing this work to take its next major jump forward, helping to turn it into something worthy of an audience broader than a dissertation committee. To Peter Agree and Walter Biggins at the University of Pennsylvania Press, I will never fully understand why you chose to take the leap and support an unproven upstart like myself, but I appreciate it nonetheless. Anyone who chooses to pick up this book and peruse its pages has you to thank, and you will always have my most heartfelt gratitude. To the anonymous reviewers who read through an unpolished manuscript and offered such thoughtful and incisive feedback, I can only hope to have honored your generosity of time in my revisions.

As I come to the end, I find myself where it all began. My parents, Fabiola and John; my sister Lara; my aunt Judith; and my late grandparents, Jane and Jack: each has played roles that no number of pages could ever contain. The words for them hardly exist. I suppose that all I can say is thank you for putting up with me all of these years, especially the last few, and making certain that I always remember that, in the end, it comes down to love. And that is enough.

The dedication for this work is to my partner, Nia. Everything that my family has taught me, you have deepened. Whenever I have needed guidance, a vision of what it means to be more fully human, you have been there for me. I can imagine no greater blessing.